THE
TWENTYSOMETHING
TREATMENT

A Revolutionary Remedy
for an Uncertain Age

MEG JAY, PhD

SIMON & SCHUSTER

New York   London   Toronto   Sydney   New Delhi

1230 Avenue of the Americas
New York, NY 10020

Some of the material in "How to Think" on pages 59 to 71 has been adapted from an article that was previously published in *Harvard Business Review*, "What to Do When Your Mind (Always) Dwells on the Worst-Case Scenario" by Meg Jay, posted on September 15, 2020, https://hbr.org/2020/09/what-to-do-when-your-mind-always-dwells-on-the-worst-case-scenario.

First Simon & Schuster hardcover edition April 2024

SIMON & SCHUSTER and colophon are registered trademarks of Simon & Schuster, LLC

Simon & Schuster: Celebrating 100 Years of Publishing in 2024

For information about special discounts for bulk purchases,
please contact Simon & Schuster Special Sales
at 1-866-506-1949 or business@simonandschuster.com.

The Simon & Schuster Speakers Bureau can bring authors to your live event.
For more information or to book an event,
contact the Simon & Schuster Speakers Bureau
at 1-866-248-3049 or visit our website at www.simonspeakers.com.

Interior design by Ruth Lee-Mui

Manufactured in the United States of America

1   3   5   7   9   10   8   6   4   2

Library of Congress Cataloging-in-Publication Data has been applied for.

ISBN 978-1-6680-1229-1
ISBN 978-1-6680-1231-4 (ebook)

For Jay and Hazel—

and for twentysomethings everywhere.

Author's Note

This book is about my work as a clinical psychologist and educator who specializes in twentysomethings. In the pages ahead, I tell the personal, and sometimes poignant, stories of clients and students and readers who have taught me about the twentysomething years. To protect their privacy, I have changed the names and the details of their lives. In some cases, I have created composites from those with similar experiences and with whom I had similar conversations. I hope every twentysomething who reads this book sees themselves in the vignettes I include, but a resemblance to any particular twentysomething is coincidental.

Contents

PART III: WHAT NEXT?

THE TWENTYSOMETHING TREATMENT

The best way to deal with everyday problems of living is to solve them directly or to wait them out, not to medicalize them with a diagnosis or treat them with a pill. Overcoming problems on your own normalizes the situation, teaches new skills, and brings you closer to the people who were helpful. Taking a pill labels you as different and sick, even if you really aren't.

—Allen Frances, *Saving Normal*

When Josie sat down in my office for the first time, she told me she was feeling better. She had called my office for an appointment a few weeks earlier, so I thought perhaps the problem had passed or improved. That happens a lot. Rather, Josie told me, she had gone to see a general practitioner, who prescribed an antidepressant and two types of antianxiety medication. That happens a lot, too.

Before the medication, Josie was tossing and turning at night, she said. She was worrying all the time and crying too much. The worst of it was when she had what she called "an anxiety attack."

"An anxiety attack," I said, using her words and not presuming to know what she meant.

"Yeah," she said, closing her eyes and shaking her head like she didn't want to think about it. "My heart started racing, and my skin was tingling, and the room went white. I thought I was going to pass out."

"What brought that on, I wonder," I said, searching for context.

"Nothing . . . I don't know . . ." Josie shrugged, shaking her head again. "I was sitting in a training session in this conference room at work, and a call popped up on my phone from an unknown number. And something about that . . . another unknown."

"Another unknown," I echoed.

"Yeah, I have a new job," Josie explained. "When I first started, I'd get so anxious about going to a meeting, I'd be late for it. Or, I was so worried about getting some task right, I wouldn't finish it on time. Every time I saw my boss or opened my email, I thought I was going to get fired."

Josie reached for a tissue and folded it into a small square.

"You probably think I'm a snowflake or something," she continued, sniffling a bit and dabbing her eyes with the square, "that there's all this awful stuff going on in the world, and I'm having an anxiety attack about my phone."

"That isn't what I was thinking," I said. "I was thinking that your situation sounds stressful—and quite common."

"It *is* stressful," Josie emphasized, picking up on the first part of what I'd said.

Since she started taking medication, Josie told me, she wasn't feeling so anxious anymore. She was, however, sleeping a lot, including nodding off in a meeting. When she wasn't sleeping, she felt too sluggish to get much done, which was only creating new problems at work.

"*All* my problems started when I got this job," Josie said, now through tears. "Well, that and my boyfriend and I broke up. It's lonely because I just moved here last year, and I hardly even know anybody. Plus, I'm freaking out because the doctor I saw diagnosed me with panic disorder. *And I didn't even know I had that!* Now I'll probably need this medication for the rest of my life."

"I wouldn't be so sure," I said.

• • •

Medication is sometimes, but not always, the best medicine. Yet, more and more, young adults are in danger of being overmedicated and over-diagnosed. That's because all too often, when a physician sits with a young adult like Josie and hears them speak of sleepless nights or crying jags or a pounding heart, too little consideration is given to what might be going on in that person's life. And, for your average twentysomething, what might be going on is a lot.

There are 75 million adults between the ages of 18 and 35 in the United States, most of whom are living through the most uncertain years they will ever know. When they wake up in the morning, they don't know where they will work or where they will live in five years. When they go into the office—if they go into an office—they don't know how they are doing or whether their jobs will last. When they go out in the evening, they don't know where they stand with their friends, if they even have friends, or whether they will always go home alone. When they try to fall asleep at night, they don't know if their lives will work out, if they'll ever be happy, or when they'll be able to pay their bills.

To get away from it all, many twentysomethings turn to their devices for a distraction, only to run headlong into headlines about whether their government or their planet will survive. Round-the-clock notifications warn of climate change, inflation, recession, bank failures, layoffs, pandemics, natural disasters, and the threat of nuclear war. Polemics about politics and polarization leave them feeling whipsawed by the left and the right. On screens and couches everywhere, streaming takes the place of more fulfilling hobbies, and porn is more available than love. Yet, on social media, everyone has a partner, it seems, as advertisements for egg-freezing suggest that time is running out. Even when young adults aren't looking at their phones, calls from unknown numbers disrupt their meetings and their lives.

In 1927, H. P. Lovecraft said, "The oldest and strongest emotion of mankind is fear, and the oldest and strongest kind of fear is fear of the unknown." Indeed, in recent years, twentysomethings have caught a fair bit of flak for being risk-averse when what they are averse to, really, is uncertainty—and so is pretty much everyone else.

A 2020 study by the American Psychological Association found adults of all ages to be more distressed than ever before, owing to persistent and unprecedented uncertainties all around. A hefty 65 percent of men and women of all ages said that unknowns related to the pandemic, politics, and the planet were causing them stress, and 60 percent felt downright overwhelmed. Yet, our youngest adults reported being the most stressed and least happy of all, with 67 percent feeling unable to plan for a future they cannot envision or one they worry they may never see. In bold terms, the report warned of "a national mental health crisis that could yield serious social and health consequences for years to come."

In many ways, our national—and global—mental health crisis begins with those like Josie. Seventy-five percent of all mental health disorders emerge by the age of 25, which is why, for twenty-five years, I've worked as a developmental clinical psychologist who specializes in twentysomethings: because that's where the action is. The pandemic may have finally brought it into the headlines, but young adults have long been more likely than older adults to struggle with their mental health—about 40 percent of twentysomethings report problems with anxiety, about 30 percent complain of depression, and about 50 percent have symptoms of one or both—at least since large-scale measurement began around the time I saw my first twentysomething client in 1999.

Our twenties are the time when many mental health symptoms first tend to show up, and they're also the years when people first tend to show up in doctors' offices—or try to show up in doctors' offices—looking for help. Unfortunately, good help can be difficult to find. Compared to older adults, young adults are twice as likely to have a mental health diagnosis, yet they're less likely to be receiving treatment. The stigma attached to seeking help may be waning, but it does remain, especially in communities of color, and the children of immigrants often feel that compared to their parents they have little reason to complain. For twentysomethings who do decide to look for a mental health professional, navigating the healthcare system in the United States, frustrating for those of any age, is downright daunting to those who are just starting out.

For the insured and uninsured alike, affordability is a problem across race, class, and gender, and around the country, accessibility is a problem, too. About half of U.S. counties have not a single mental health provider—never mind those who might actually specialize in young adults—and the providers who do exist are often prohibitively expensive or booked for months. As a result, a disproportionate number of youths lean on hotlines, telehealth, or digital apps for support, and they visit emergency departments or general practitioners for medications. Above all else, they look online for information or they go on social media, where young adults seem to be either enjoying their best lives or suffering from a mental health disorder when, likely, the reality is something in between.

On all corners of the internet, public figures and everyday twenty-somethings are speaking out about what clinical psychologists, and those like Josie, already know: that, perhaps contrary to popular belief, young adults are far from problem free. Testimonies about anxiety, depression, and countless other mental health concerns have exploded on social media, and many such posts have millions and even billions of views. This may sound like progress—and, in a way, it is—but the results are mixed. Some young people go online and find out that they're not as alone or as troubled as they thought they were. Others, however, mistakenly diagnose themselves with, or build their identities around, disorders they don't have or problems that might not last for long. Still others fall deep into content holes about anxiety, depression, eating disorders, or suicide, sometimes with tragic outcomes.

Part of the young adult mental health crisis, then, is that there simply aren't enough resources for all who want and need them. This is why I write books: because education is an intervention and because, let's face it, the 50-minute hour does not scale.

We can't staff our way out of a mental health crisis, and maybe we shouldn't be trying to. Help doesn't have to come in the form of one-on-one therapy sessions held behind closed doors and, in fact, it's better if it doesn't. Bringing twentysomething struggles and solutions out into the open makes them more available and more, well, normal—something that everyone can learn from and that anyone can do. Besides, most twentysomethings don't have disorders that need to be treated; they have problems that need to be solved. Although medication is sometimes useful or necessary, twentysomethings need skills—not just pills—and that's what this book is all about.

There is a young adult mental health crisis in America, and it is a crisis of proportion and perception. So many twentysomethings are struggling, yet as a culture we're not sure what to think or do. Perhaps, it is said, young adults are snowflakes who melt when life turns up the heat. Or maybe, some argue, they're triggered for no reason at all. Yet, even as we trivialize their struggles, we're quick to pathologize them and to hand out diagnoses and medications to twentysomethings whose brains and lives are still on the move.

The Twentysomething Treatment is an age-specific approach to young adult mental health—one that places it in the context of personal, national, and global uncertainty. It is a proven prescription that reveals what twenty-five years of listening to twentysomethings—and the latest research—have taught me about what works with this group. It is a revolutionary remedy that upends the medicalization of young adult life and advocates instead for skills over pills.

In the chapters ahead, you'll learn about three key routes to better mental health for twentysomethings: education, experience, and expectations.

In Part I: Why Now?, we find out why our twenties are so difficult, as well as what uncertainty has to do with mental health. We learn about the nocebo effect, or why diagnoses—whether from physicians or the internet—can sometimes make us worse. We find out why medication isn't always the best medicine, and how young adults can be more informed consumers. We find out why our mental health is most likely to improve outside of a doctor's office—through skill building—and why, for the young adult brain in particular, the time for skill building is now.

In Part II: Now What?, we take a wide-ranging look at the skills twentysomethings need—or what you need to be practicing or doing—to be happier and healthier. How to think less about "What if" and more about "What is." How to feel uncertain without feeling unsafe. How to work on your mental health—at work—and why jobs may offer your best chance for change. How to be social when social media functions as an evolutionary trap. How to befriend someone during what are, surprisingly, the loneliest years of life. How to love someone even though they might break your heart—and why heartbreak means you are healthy, not sick.

How to have sex when porn seems easier and safer—even though it isn't. How to move more and how physical activity can be as effective as therapy or meds. How to cook your way toward confidence and calm. How to change a "dosage problem" or what you put in your body and your brain. How to make life's most defining decisions when so much about life is still undecided—and how the paradox of purpose makes this easier over time.

In Part III: What Next?, we find out what twentysomethings have to look forward to in their thirties and beyond. We find out why mental health gets better as we get older, and how we can all have hope for happiness ahead. We learn about the power of positive expectations and of imagining that life might go well. And, in the end, we find out why embracing uncertainty—and each other—may be the most life-changing skill of all.

Mental health has never been more in the zeitgeist, as today's youth are the most willing in history to talk openly about it and to seek help. Yet, what kind of help they find and what those conversations are *matters*, not just for the twentysomethings of today but for the thirtysomethings and fortysomethings and fiftysomethings they may become. It's time to change the topic from criticism to context. It's time to talk less about diagnosis and more about development. It's time to take young adult mental health seriously, not because twentysomethings like Josie can't get better but because they *can*.

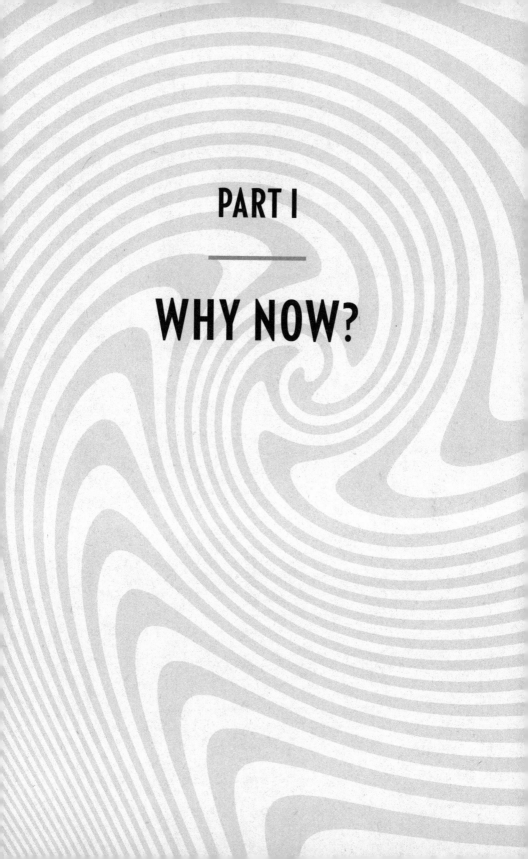

PART I

WHY NOW?

ONE

AN UNCERTAIN AGE

There is a remarkable human capacity to adapt to both prosperity and adversity. One thing people do have a hard time adapting to is uncertainty.

—Carol Graham, *The Economist*

"My psychiatrist told me to talk to you," Irene began, already breathless. "He thinks I have, like, social anxiety or I don't know what. I told him I haven't been wanting to see people as much as I used to, like before the pandemic. I have to make myself text people—I hate it when they don't text me right back; I worry they're thinking something bad—and I have to make myself go out. Then when I get there, I have an okay time, but when I get home, I can't sleep. I already take sleep meds sometimes, so my doctor thinks maybe I need some other anxiety meds, too. It's just that I'm having all these irrational thoughts. *Crazy* thoughts. Like when I'm supposed to be sleeping. It's 2:00 a.m. and my brain just keeps seeing what it can come up with to worry about or feel sad about. Like, what am I going to do if my parents pass away? I'm worried because they're getting older, and I moved across the country for this new job, and I don't know when I'll settle back on the West Coast again. What if I didn't do the right thing coming here? And I dragged my partner along! I mean, I'm about to turn thirty, and time is passing. Things are getting *real*. My number one goal in life is to have a routine, so maybe this job will give me that. There has just been so much limbo. I don't have a lot of *knowns* in my life. There aren't a lot of *facts*.

"Sometimes on the weekend, I feel so overwhelmed by everything that still has to happen somehow that I'll spend all day in bed or all day watching TV, like I'm depressed or something. Then at night, there's so much, I don't know, *uncertainty*. I just toss and turn and worry about whether my job is going to work out . . . whether my relationship is going to work . . . whether I should be freezing my eggs or something. Then, I get worried about not sleeping, and I pace around, and I wonder if have some sleep disorder and, like, if I'll ever be able to sleep again. That's when I decide to finally take my chill pills—you know, my sleep meds—so I can finally chill out and go to sleep."

In 1789, Benjamin Franklin famously said that nothing is certain except for death and taxes. While most people take this as a comment on, well, death and taxes, Franklin was pointing out that uncertainty has always been and will always be a big part of life.

Franklin wrote these words to scientist and friend Jean-Baptiste Le Roy, who was enduring the throes of the French Revolution. "It is now more than a year since I have heard from you. What can be the reason? Are you still living? Or have the mob of Paris mistaken the head of a monopolizer of knowledge, for a monopolizer of corn, and paraded it about the streets on a pole," Franklin inquires in his letter before suggesting that his fledgling country, the United States, was also no sure thing. "Our new Constitution is now established, and has an appearance that promises permanency; but in this world, nothing can be said to be certain, except death and taxes."

So, in the history of civilization, uncertainty isn't new, but it is new for twentysomethings. Year after year, generation after generation, a new crop of young adults—those whose lives were once scheduled and structured by school—graduate into their twenties and into the great unknown. Before that, there were syllabi that told them exactly what to do and when to do it. There were grades that quantified where they stood and how they stacked up against their peers. There were yearly advancements that signified clear progress and an upward trend. Then, sometime around age 20, young adults trade a lifetime of school for the new world of work—or they try to—and they see nothing but uncertainty all around them.

Today's young workers will have, on average, nine different jobs by the age of 35. That's right: *nine*. Along the way, about half of young adults receive financial help from their parents, and about a fifth have bills that are unpaid and overdue. About a quarter of twentysomethings move each year, often to follow a job or to look for a better one. Meanwhile, about a third of workers now work from home, which for many twentysomethings is an overcrowded apartment with paper-thin walls. Sure, a fortunate few young adults may be globe-trotting digital nomads but for most, working remotely means migrating from coffee shop to coffee shop, with laptops and chargers in tow.

As coffee shops and jobs and cities and apartments come and go, friendships and relationships do, too. That's why, although we may think of our twenties as an incredibly social time, they are in fact the loneliest years of all. About two-thirds of twentysomethings say they have no close friends; about half of twentysomething men and a third of twentysomething women are single, although about half of the unattached say they want more in friendship or love.

The percentage of young adults who will eventually marry is on its way down, however, and for those who choose to tie the knot, the average age to say "I do" is on its way up. Thirty is now the mean-average age to walk down the aisle or to stop by the courthouse, and it's also the median-average age to have one's first child. As families and careers and salaries are likely not established until one's thirties, the average age of a first-time home buyer is at an all-time high of 36 years old. Still, because housing inventory is low and prices are high, owning a place of one's own can feel more like a fantasy than a part of the American Dream.

Twentieth-century twentysomethings were likely to wake up to a spouse, a career, a baby, and maybe even a home and a purpose. These days, such sources of stability are more likely to be realized in one's thirties and beyond—if at all. For many reasons, twenty-first-century young adults, like Irene, settle down later than earlier generations used to, which means that they're likely to spend the first decade or so of adulthood *feeling* unsettled. And it's not just young adult lives that are unsettled; the *era* in which they live is unsettling, too.

Today's twentysomethings grew up in the shadow of 9/11 and the threat of terror raining down on a sunny day. They went to classes amid more than 375 school shootings—and counting—since the year 2000. Hundreds of thousands of them have been exposed to gun violence, and nearly all of them know what it is like to crouch under their desks in an active-shooter drill. From there, they've moved on to the workplace, which may feel no safer. Work is the most common site for mass shootings, as well as where roughly 50 percent of women and 25 percent of men may one day say "Me, Too."

Walking down the street amid cries that "Black Lives Matter," some feel overwhelmed by the racial, social, and economic inequality they see on every corner. Going out in the evening after a reversal of *Roe v. Wade*, others feel they have lost control of their bodies and their choices. Watching politicians attack each other in the news, still others feel like children in a home with warring parents as they brace themselves for a national divorce. Coming of age during a pandemic, nearly all wonder if some of their best years and greatest opportunities were lost to lockdowns. And trying to envision a future under the cloud of climate change, many question whether they should bother at all to think ahead.

Every decade of life is difficult, but for twentysomethings, uncertainty is the most difficult part of all. According to Google, the word *uncertainty* was used in the English language at a rather steady rate until about the year 1950. From then on, it crept upward to a peak at around the year 2000, where it has remained ever since. Indeed, twenty-first-century twentysomethings, like Irene, are living with peak uncertainty in almost every way, and this has an indisputable, but vastly underrecognized, impact on their bodies and their brains.

• • •

The brain interprets uncertainty as danger. That's because, from an evolutionary perspective, it feels dangerous not to know what's around the corner or what's happening next. Thousands of years ago, young adults might have been wandering the tundra, unsure of whether they might meet a bear or a mammoth, whether they would find food that day, or whether they might become separated from their group. Today, our uncertainties are about whether we can pay our bills, whether we are making the right decisions, why someone isn't texting us back, or whether we even are part of a group. Today's uncertainties are about, as Irene put it, not having a lot of "knowns" and not having a lot of "facts."

The brain reacts to uncertainties both ancient and modern by firing up the amygdala, or the fear center. The amygdala is "where the trigger stimuli do their triggering," as neuroscientist Joseph LeDoux explained, long before there was such a thing as a trigger warning. When confronted with uncertainty, the amygdala triggers the release of stress hormones as it prepares our bodies for fight or flight. Our hearts race. Our minds race. Our breathing quickens and shallows. We feel tense and stressed. Our skin sweats, and we get goosebumps. We feel a sense of dread and maybe a nervous stomach. In various ways, we are thrown into a state of readiness for whatever may come.

The amygdala is often likened to a smoke detector, and uncertainties are like smoke. When uncertainty sets off the smoke alarm, we try to figure out whether the problem is burnt toast or a house fire, so we can respond quickly and appropriately. But because many modern uncertainties—like work and love and family planning and finances and climate change—may not be resolved quickly, many twentysomethings live with smoke alarms that blare both day and night, for weeks or months or years on end.

If that sounds distracting or unpleasant, it is. Uncertainty is generally considered to be an aversive experience—even *more* aversive than actual negative events. In a classic 1964 study, many subjects who were expecting an electrical shock opted to receive a larger shock sooner rather than wait some undetermined amount of time for a smaller one. Indeed, most people describe "hating waiting" for unknowns, and when they're made to wait, they have trouble functioning at their best. In a study published in 2020, students who were told they *might* have to give a speech in the future made more mistakes on puzzles and tasks, or gave up altogether while they waited, even when compared to students who *knew* they would have to give a speech.

Evolutionarily speaking—and statistically speaking, too—it is normal to have trouble living with unknowns. How humans feel about uncertainty is "normally distributed" in the population, meaning that, on a graph, it looks like a bell curve. At one end of the curve are the fortunate few who easily embrace uncertainty or hardly seem to notice it. At the other end are those who are extremely intolerant of anything unsure. Most of us, however, are somewhere in the middle. Our brains and bodies feel unsettled by uncertainty, and we struggle with what to think or do.

From this perspective, uncertainty is seen as an individual variable, in that some people have an easier time handling it than do others. Decades of working with twentysomethings, however, has taught me that uncertainty is a developmental variable, too. Some *times* of life are more uncertain than others, and young adulthood is the most uncertain time of all. Our twenties are the years when the number of unknowns peak, and they're also the years when we have the least experience dealing with them. What that means is that the average young adult is likely overloaded with uncertainty every day. Twentysomethings like Irene can be in the middle of that bell curve yet still feel buried under a mountain of unknowns.

In the past few years, there has been an explosion of interest among researchers about how uncertainty affects our mental health—and the answer is "a lot." Uncertainty is what's called a *transdiagnostic stressor*, which means that it is a source of stress that puts us at risk for a wide variety of mental health concerns. First and foremost, uncertainty is associated with anxiety. Think back to the bodily changes that often accompany the brain's registering of unknowns in our lives. Racing thoughts. A pounding heart. A nervous stomach. Sweaty skin. A sense of dread. Difficulty breathing. These are all indicators of anxiety.

Uncertainty and anxiety are inextricably linked in our bodies and in our brains, and in our language, too. The very definition of *anxiety*—a feeling of stress, worry, nervousness, or unease about a future event or an uncertain outcome—describes what it feels like to face the unknown. Not surprisingly, then, young adults who are living the most uncertain years of their lives are going to feel anxious. They're going to talk about being anxious. They're going to describe themselves as anxious: "My resting state is anxious," Irene said. They're going to think they have anxiety disorders and maybe even meet the criteria for those disorders.

Because uncertainty is a transdiagnostic stressor, it can also manifest as other sorts of mental health problems: depression, substance abuse, problems with eating or sleeping, suicidality, and more. Some people become avoidant when they feel uncertain, meaning they shut down and stay at home or even remain in bed. Others toss and turn, and pace their bedrooms, instead of sleeping. Others use food or other substances to calm themselves, or they reach for their devices for distraction. And others become what psychologists call *reassurance junkies* as, again and again, they go to parents or bosses or therapists for comfort and relief. Still others don't know how to make their lives better, so they think about not going on living at all. And many, like Irene, do a combination of these things, and more.

Fortunately, the relationship between uncertainty and mental health struggles is not a given, and the extent to which uncertainty functions as a transdiagnostic stressor has a lot to do with how we think and feel about those unknowns. Think about whether you agree or disagree with the following statements:

I feel anxious or angry when life is not settled.

Unforeseen events make me upset.

I feel frustrated when I don't have all the information I want.

I dislike not knowing where I stand with people.

I would rather avoid uncertain situations.

When life is uncertain, I cannot function well.

I dislike being uncertain about the future.

When I'm uncertain, I need other people to reassure me.

I have trouble making plans for the future.

I like to know the right answer or that I'm doing the right thing.

I want to be able to organize and control things.

When faced with choices, I doubt my decisions and myself.

If you answered yes to one or more of these statements, then you are human. Our smoke-detector brains are going to agree with at least some of these statements at least some of the time. Yet, uncertainty functions as a transdiagnostic stressor, especially when we see uncertainty as almost always awful. So, the more you agree with more of these statements more of the time, the more likely you are to feel anxious and sad, as well as all kinds of bad.

"Young Adults in California Experience Alarming Rates of Anxiety and Depression" read a 2022 headline in the *Los Angeles Times*. According to a recent survey commissioned by the California Endowment, the story went on to report, more than three-quarters of youth felt anxious and overwhelmed in the past year, more than half felt depressed, and about one-third had thoughts of suicide. When asked how they felt about their futures, the leading response was "uncertain," for 57 percent of the group, followed by "worried" for 43 percent. In alerting the media to their findings, the director of communications connected with the poll had this to say: "You never think of young people as being worriers. That's usually left to all of us who are turning gray."

I actually *do* think of young people as being worriers because, every day, twentysomethings like Irene bring their worries to my office. And I think that way because I know the research. On average, younger adults worry *more* than older adults, and there are many good reasons why this is so. As we've seen, young adults live with more unknowns than older adults because they have less control over their work and school, and friends and love, and rent and healthcare, and really, most aspects of their lives. Uncertainty makes our emotions—both good and bad ones—feel more intense, and twentysomethings have less experience managing those intense emotions. They have had less practice controlling their thoughts, so they are more likely to habitually think negatively. And they have more of life still ahead of them—and more decisions that are still undecided—so they worry more about what's to come.

Given all this, it is interesting to reflect on the fact that, as a culture, we view it as backward that young people worry. We like to imagine that all those millions of free-floating young adults are carefree: "What do they have to worry about?" we may ask. But that's not how it is. Young adults everywhere are struggling, and for good reasons, yet panicking and pathologizing do not help them. Telling young adults that it is alarming they have problems, or that it is wrong they're not happy, only adds to their mountain of concerns.

Instead of playing whack-a-mole with Irene's various mental health symptoms (as we will see, that's how twentysomethings wind up with multiple diagnoses and medications), I instead offered up the unifying lens of uncertainty. There were so many unknowns in Irene's life—her job, her town, her friends, her relationship, her parents' mortality, her own aging, her fertility—that I let her know it was normal to feel so unsettled.

Irene had characterized her worries about her parents dying as "crazy" or "irrational" when, in fact, her worries were quite rational. Her parents *were* getting older—and so was she—and maybe her concern that she may not see them enough was something to heed as she decided how to set up her life in the years ahead. Maybe she would prioritize living closer to her family. Or, maybe she would make sure to spend vacations or holidays with her loved ones. Or, maybe being so far away from her parents was just new to her and something she'd get used to. The fact that there was no single right way to set up her life was another uncertainty she had to face.

Likewise, Irene's worries about seeing and texting people were unsurprising. Maybe making new friends in a new place felt uncomfortably unfamiliar. Or, maybe starting all over again socially, at almost age 30, rightly seemed daunting. Meanwhile, she was beginning to think more about how and when to be a partner and a parent, and all that seemed daunting, too. In different ways, her brain was signaling that, no matter what her age, it was important to have people around her whom she could rely on—friends, family, partners, kids—and that, at the moment, she wasn't sure she did.

One year later, Irene had settled down in more ways than one. She and her now-fiancé had decided to move back to the West Coast to put down roots near family and friends. She had a new job she was excited about, with a company she thought she might like to stay with for a while. She still didn't know what she wanted to do about family planning, but now that other areas of her life felt more in focus, whether and when to have kids was something she felt she had time to figure out. Not coincidentally, she almost never took her "chill pills" anymore.

"So, you don't think I have anxiety?" Irene asked me somewhere along the way.

"I think you have the kind of anxiety you find in the dictionary," I said. "But worrying about the unknowns in your life is different from having a mental health disorder."

"Does that difference matter?" Irene wanted to know.

"Yes," I said, with the nocebo effect in mind. "It does."

TWO

THE NOCEBO EFFECT

It's not clinical. The doctor says it's situational depression. It's just that I keep on having new . . . situations.

—Matt Haig, *The Midnight Library*

In the summer of 2022, in a development that shocked the mental health world—and made international headlines—the *DSM* became a surprise bestseller. "There's a new Bible on the bestseller list: It's the *DSM-5* and that's not necessarily great," read one headline. "The *Diagnostic and Statistical Manual of Mental Disorders* is suddenly a bestseller on Amazon—this is not good for anyone's mental health," read another.

The *DSM* is the shorthand title for the *Diagnostic and Statistical Manual of Mental Disorders*, now in its fifth edition. Often called the "Bible" of psychiatry, this nearly 1,000-page volume is more like an encyclopedia that dryly describes disorders ranging from autism to zoophobia, primarily by listing the symptoms for each. Since 1952, some version of this reference book has sat on the shelf of nearly every mental health professional. Outside of their offices, however, you'd be hard pressed to find a copy. Then suddenly, seventy years after the first edition was published, the *DSM* went mainstream.

Without a doubt, the reason for the *DSM*'s surge in popularity was the parallel surge in mental health symptoms, and conversations about them, during and after the pandemic. People everywhere were struggling with sadness and sleeplessness, and worry and irritability, and substance use, and more, and they wanted to understand what was wrong with them or what they "had."

When life feels confusing, one way we find clarity is by joining up with various identities: religious, political, fraternal, and even diagnostic. So, it can be tempting to find order by identifying with a mental health *dis*order. Suddenly, there's a name for what we're feeling or thinking or doing. In an instant, there are people out there—on the internet, in support groups, in the world somewhere—who understand us and what we're going through. In an uncertain age, diagnoses can feel like rare certainties; they can feel like answers and, ideally, can be a step toward healing and health.

Because of the nocebo effect, however, that's not always the way it goes.

Around the time the *DSM* was flying off the shelves, a college student named Henry flung himself and his backpack onto the couch in my office. There, he slouched deep in the corner with his elbow on the armrest and his face in his hand, as if his head couldn't support itself otherwise. I wondered where Henry would begin.

A 2022 study of young adults from around the United States shows that, over the past ten years, the leading problems of those seeking therapy are, in descending order: anxiety, depression, relationships, stress, trauma, work or school, suicidality, and substance use. Yet a neat breakdown like this fails to convey that, typically, young adult clients come in with several, or even all, of these concerns at once.

Indeed, before our first session, Henry had completed this checklist of mental health concerns:

- ✓ Anxiety / Worry
- ✓ Concentration / Attention
- ✓ Depression

Eating / Body Concerns

Family Issues

Grief

Mood Swings

Panic Attacks

✓ Relationship Problems

✓ Sex / Physical Intimacy

Sexual Assault / Unwanted Sexual Contact

Sexual / Gender Identity

✓ Sleep Problems

✓ Social Problems

✓ Stress

Substance Use

Suicidal Thoughts

Trauma

✓ Work / School Problems

Other

Despite his varied and overlapping problems, Henry began by telling me that he had "major depression." When I asked what he meant by that or how he knew, he told me he'd read about it not in the *DSM* but online: "I went on Reddit to try to figure out my problem, and it's pretty obvious that I'm depressed."

"Last semester," Henry explained, "I stopped getting out of bed or going to class. I stopped taking care of myself and turning in my work. Some of my professors emailed me about it, but I didn't even respond, which is really bad. I ended up failing two classes, which was pretty catastrophic. I've hardly ever even gotten a B before."

I kept listening.

"I'm here because I'm scared all that is going to happen again. I've missed a few assignments already this semester—actually, for a class taught by one of the same professors who failed me before. Now I'm avoiding going to class because I think he's disappointed in me. I've always been the smart one in my family and with my friends. I've never stumbled before, so all this has really made me question who I am," Henry explained. "I read that people who get depressed like this once get depressed over and over again, and now I'm worried that maybe that's going to be me. I was supposed to have so much promise, but now I don't know. I think maybe I'm going to wind up being a failure."

The nocebo effect is the opposite of the placebo effect.

When most people think of the placebo effect, they think of sugar pills. That is because the early studies of the placebo effect tested active medications against inactive ones, such as sugar pills, called *placebos*. These studies found that many patients who received sham medications that they were told would work showed as much improvement as those who were given the real thing. This surprising result led the author of the first-known study of the placebo effect to conclude, in 1799, that "an important lesson is here to be learnt, the powerful influence of the mind upon the state and disorder of the body."

Now, more than two hundred years later, doctors and researchers have recently begun to recognize that the placebo effect has implications far beyond the sugar pill. Broadly speaking, whether medication is even involved, patients who have a positive view of the prognosis or treatment of an illness are more likely to get better over time. Various forms of the placebo effect have been shown to favorably influence up to 90 percent of physical and mental health conditions, including pain, anxiety, depression, hypertension, Parkinson's disease, recovery from surgery, and aging. Neurobiological research shows that the expectation of healing activates the areas of the brain that regulate our cardiovascular, endocrine, respiratory, nervous, and immune systems. That is, the body prepares for what the brain believes is coming.

If the placebo effect is the power of positive expectations, then the *nocebo* effect is the power of negative expectations. Put simply, we are less likely to feel good, or feel better, when we think we can't or won't. Here are a few examples. We know that telling patients a procedure will hurt increases their experience of pain. We know that focusing on troubling symptoms, such as by tracking sleep problems, can make them more likely to occur. We know that alerting patients to the side effects of medications makes them more likely to experience those side effects (which raises a conundrum about informed consent). We know that believing stress is debilitating, rather than enhancing, raises the levels of our stress hormones. We know that believing anxiety won't improve predicts future anxiety.

We even know that educating people about their genetic risk for health problems can exacerbate their risk. This is because when we tell someone they are apt to suffer from a particular ailment, this distressing information not only alters their physiology but also can make them feel less in control of the outcome and thus less motivated to take preventive measures.

There is a nocebo effect that can go along with having—or believing one has—a mental health disorder, too. Depending on the information they receive, young adults like Henry may see themselves as different, or damaged, or doomed. Henry had concluded from Reddit posts that he was depressed and, perhaps more important, he was under the impression that his problems could not or would not improve. From what he'd read, Henry understood depression to be a recurring problem that would keep coming back all his life. While Henry once saw himself as "smart" and as someone "with promise," he now described himself as "a depressed person" and "a failure."

To be clear, receiving a diagnosis doesn't always result in the nocebo effect. Ideally, a good diagnosis can help people move forward with the right treatment. For example, here is a message I received from a young man who came to my office because he was struggling (and had always struggled) in school: "I was feeling pretty hopeless academically and I had lost the desire to learn new things before we determined I have ADHD. Now that I know how to succeed even with ADHD, I'm very eager to learn and do my best in the rest of my academic career. I feel a new motivation that I honestly haven't felt in years."

But sometimes diagnoses can hold us back and even get in the way of the help we need most. Consider this very different message from a man who wrote to me: "I have been lost wandering from therapist to therapist for a while, stuck in this need for a diagnosis. This has led me nowhere, as I have ended up receiving a number of diagnoses and little understanding of who I really am. Underneath all this, I think, fundamentally, I am struggling to adapt to adult life, struggling with my own mind, thoughts, fears, and goals."

Although some curious or confused young adults "wander from therapist to therapist" in search of a diagnosis, perhaps even more concerning is that, increasingly, young adults are self-diagnosing via the internet. Decades ago, we called this medical student syndrome, or what happened when med students learned about the symptoms of various physical and mental disorders and called their parents to say, "That's me!" Now, for better and for worse, information that once could be found only in boring, obscure reference books is readily available in short, interesting snippets online. Even more than they pore over the *DSM*, young people turn to the internet with their mental health questions. And too often, a form of cyberchondria ensues; because of what they read on the internet, twentysomethings wind up thinking they're sicker than they are.

Social media in particular has become a venue where tears and fears abound. The numbers are continually changing, and generally exploding, such that, in one 2022 study, TikTok videos associated with the hashtag #mentalhealth collectively had more than *25 billion* views. Researchers who analyzed one hundred of the #mentalhealth videos found that more than half had comments that were validating, making TikTok a potential source of social support and social awareness. Validation and support sound good but, sometimes, the conclusions young adults have drawn about themselves—and about their mental health—need to be questioned.

Also, there's a fine line between social awareness and social contagion. That is, the more young adults learn about various mental health problems, the more they may believe they have those problems, and even act as if they do. Video platforms like YouTube or TikTok have been found to be especially fertile ground for social contagion because emotions and behaviors can be expressed so vividly and imitated so closely.

Here's an example.

In 2020, in what was called a "pandemic within a pandemic," both TikTok and neurology clinics saw a spike in young people with tics, or seemingly involuntary behaviors such as repeatedly blinking, shrugging, or saying a particular word. In an effort to understand the connection, researchers analyzed twenty-eight videos from twenty-eight influencers that, together, were watched more than 33 million times. On the whole, tics shown in the videos were more severe, more frequent, and more debilitating than what's typically found in the general population. Two-thirds of the influencers said they'd developed at least one new tic from watching other videos, and over half displayed the same vocal tic: saying the word *beans* with a British accent. Soon, teenagers and young adults around the world began showing up in doctors' offices saying "beans" in a British accent, too, leading researchers to dub this a "TikTok tic."

As harmless or as silly as that may sound, there can be real consequences for stumbling onto information and misinformation online. Young adults who are curious or confused about their mental health may turn to the internet for answers, only to be exposed to posts or videos that, depending on a site's algorithm, can very quickly become less accurate and more repetitive. This is how twentysomethings move from curious or confused to convinced in an unnervingly short time.

A 2021 *Wall Street Journal* article explained how this happens on TikTok for viewers, or for the bots used in their investigation:

> The TikTok experience starts the same way for everyone, with a variety of videos, many with millions of views. The app takes note of subtle cues, such as how long you linger on a video, to zero in on what users really want to watch. Over time, the video choices become less mainstream, less vetted by moderators and sometimes more disturbing. Some [bots] ended up lost in rabbit holes of similar content,

including one that just watched videos about depression. Others were served videos that encouraged eating disorders and discussed suicide.

The nocebo effect results from rabbit holes, or content holes, that exist not only on the internet but also in our own minds. As with Henry, once we decide or are told we have a disorder, we can become trapped in a certain way of thinking about ourselves and of talking about ourselves and of seeing ourselves. For young adults, it's especially bad timing, in that they may latch onto a diagnosis right when their identities are taking shape. More and more, I see clients in my office who start their sentences with, "Because of my anxiety, I . . ." or "Because of my personality disorder, I . . ." or "Because of my insecure attachment, I . . ." A diagnosis they often mistakenly think they have becomes their only way of understanding how they think and feel and act.

From there, a diagnosis can be self-reinforcing, as it impacts the choices we make: what we watch, what we read, what we talk about and listen to. It can affect who we hang out with and even how we introduce ourselves to each other. One Twitter user put it this way: "Gen Z dating profiles are, like, 'Here are my current mental illnesses. I like to sleep a lot; don't message me.'" It's a twenty-first-century version of assortative mating, huddling up and cuddling up with those who have similar mental health complaints. This is how, on and off social media, we can dig ourselves deeper and deeper into our supposed disorders, sometimes without truly understanding what having a diagnosis does, and doesn't, mean.

As straightforward as it may sound to take one's issues to the *DSM* and to find them neatly laid out on the page, the *DSM* has some issues of its own. One of its many shortcomings is that it doesn't take adult development into account—at all. So, while some of the symptoms that are key features of disorders—such as unstable relationships that mark borderline personality disorder or the mood swings associated with bipolar disorder—might be concerning in 45-year-olds, they're quite common among 25-year-olds at least some of the time. As a result, many diagnoses pathologize everyday young adult struggles, leaving those like Henry feeling broken and sick.

Let's look at three disorders for which twentysomethings often meet the *DSM*'s criteria.

First, there's major depressive disorder, or what Henry called "major depression." To receive a diagnosis of major depressive disorder, at least five of the following symptoms must be present: low mood, diminished interest or pleasure in activities, indecisiveness or loss of concentration, fatigue or loss of energy, sleeping too little or too much, appetite changes, feeling worthless or guilty, thoughts of suicide or death. Moreover, these symptoms must be present for at least two weeks. *Two weeks?!* While living out the most uncertain years of their lives, a time when jobs and relationships and apartments and friendships routinely come and go, what young person doesn't have something to feel depressed about for two weeks or more?

Then, there's generalized anxiety disorder. This is worry—about love or work or the future or anything else—that leads to some combination of irritability, fatigue, restlessness, difficulty concentrating, muscle tension, or sleep problems. According to the *DSM*, these symptoms must cause problems for at least six months to warrant a diagnosis, but in my experience, many young adults spend months, if not years, worrying about how their lives are going and what will happen next. It's also my experience that, if you walk into a doctor's office and rattle off symptoms of anxiety, you will likely walk out with a diagnosis, and maybe even some medication, that very day, no matter how long the problems have—or have not—been going on.

And, last but not least, social anxiety disorder is the fear of situations in which one may be scrutinized by others. Examples of such situations might include starting a conversation, meeting new people, going to a party, throwing a Frisbee, having a job interview, giving a presentation, or really any other experience in which one might feel evaluated or judged. These situations are extremely common, and so are diagnoses of social anxiety. More than half of twentysomethings are estimated to have at least moderate social anxiety that will usually get better with age and experience.

Young adults often think they're more troubled than they are, and sometimes part of my job is to keep them from jumping to diagnostic conclusions. Statistically speaking, most twentysomethings, even those who seek help, are not sick. Yes, they are struggling and, yes, their problems are real, but that does not mean they are disordered. This is an important—but sometimes difficult—distinction to make.

"Medicine is a science of uncertainty and an art of probability," wrote Sir William Osler, the father of modern medicine. What he meant is that medicine doesn't always, or even often, provide clear answers. This is especially true when it comes to diagnosing mental health disorders, for which there are no blood tests or EEGs that might offer definitive data. Psychologists, like many other doctors, must rely on their judgment instead. Often, that means considering whether symptoms are severe (enough), or distressing (enough), or problematic (enough), or long-lasting (enough)—whatever enough is—to warrant a diagnosis.

Yet, young adults almost always seek help because their symptoms feel problematic, and often, as for Henry, their distress can be severe, at least for a while. Even the notion of duration is a tricky one. Sometimes, symptoms that come on suddenly, such as manic highs, immediately suggest a diagnosis (and likely some medication) are needed. Other times, chronic symptoms can be indicative of chronic stressors, such as childhood trauma or poverty, that need to be addressed.

So, here are some questions I often ask myself when I'm weighing whether to diagnose a young adult with a mental health disorder: Do I need to give this person a diagnosis in order to help them? How might a diagnosis move this person forward, and how might it hold them back? And, most important, might a person's symptoms be better explained by something *other* than a mental health disorder and would it be more helpful for us to focus on *that*?

One of the diagnostic criteria for most *DSM* disorders is that they cannot be the result of a physical condition. For example, psychologists shouldn't diagnose a client with major depression if that person has a thyroid condition that would account for those symptoms. Yet, puzzlingly, there are no such criteria suggesting someone like Henry should not be diagnosed with major depression if their symptoms can be attributed to an event or circumstance like the loss of a loved one or a job.

This is too bad, because medicine *is* the art of probability and, for most young adults who are struggling, it's more likely that their problem is not a mental health problem but, rather, a life problem. That's why, even though the *DSM* does not recommend it, the most important question I ask myself and my clients—and the question anyone else can ask themselves when they're struggling—is some version of "Why now?" For example, Has something about life changed or become more difficult? Or, What's different about this month or this year compared to the last? Or, Has an old problem started to cause new problems? Or, Has some aspect of life become unbearable or overwhelming? Or, Why am I looking for help with this *now*?

"I had my first big breakup a few months ago," Henry told me when I asked him these questions. "It was crushing because . . . well . . . I'm gay and this was the first person I've ever been with who made me happy about it. I really struggled with being gay when I was growing up, not wanting it to be true, thinking I couldn't have all the good things other people were going to get to have, like relationships or a family. Then with this person, I thought I saw what a happy future could be like, even being gay. I mean, someone was texting me and loving me, and it was this great feeling like all my friends get to have. But then, the guy dumped me— ghosted me, actually—and I couldn't get out of bed or do anything. Then, when I stopped being fun to be around, my friends ghosted me, too. I just can't stop trying to figure out what happened. Why I got dumped by my boyfriend *and* my friends. Why I got depressed. That's why I was reading up on it on Reddit."

Henry was describing what psychologists call a *situational stressor*. These are situations or problems that feel difficult or even overwhelming to handle. Some such situations are concrete, like preparing for the bar exam or going through a painful breakup, while others are more diffuse and long-lasting, like growing up with an alcoholic parent or living with climate change. For more than fifty years, multiple studies have found negative life events to be the strongest predictors of the emergence of depression. Thus, when it comes to mental health problems, especially in young adults, the simplest—and most likely—explanation is a situational one.

In response to situational stressors, adults of all ages commonly show symptoms of, and even meet diagnostic criteria for, depression and anxiety. This is what psychologists informally refer to as *situational depression* or *situational anxiety*, meaning depression or anxiety that is brought on not by a problem in one's brain but by a problem in one's life. Then, as would be expected, as the situation passes or improves—or as we get better at handling it—the symptoms pass or improve, too.

Perhaps the biggest downside of diagnoses—and part of the reason they may contribute to the nocebo effect—is that, implicitly or explicitly, they locate the problem inside the person rather than inside their situation. So much of what I do with clients like Henry is widen the lens so that their view includes not just the person in the foreground but also the situation in the background.

"What if we look at it this way?" I suggested to Henry. "What if you lost an important relationship, felt really sad about it, and had trouble going about life as usual? Then, when you did poorly in school, it shook your sense of self as a smart person with a bright future, and that got you feeling even more depressed. But none of this makes you a depressed *person*. Just because you meet criteria for depression now, it doesn't mean you'll always be depressed."

"But on Reddit there are all these people who've been depressed over and over," Henry countered.

"Who *isn't* on Reddit," I pointed out, "are the people out there who *aren't* depressed over and over. About half of people who are depressed at some point *don't* go on to be depressed again and again. But we never talk about them on social media or even in the research."

Henry started to look interested.

"And for people who are depressed more than once, we have to remember that depression can recur because situations recur. There will be more heartbreaks and stumbles for you, and some will probably be bigger than the ones you're dealing with now. But I wouldn't assume it's always going to go the same way. Last semester, you couldn't get out of bed, and you wound up with Fs. This semester, you came in here and asked for help. So, you're already getting better at figuring out how to handle tough times."

"So what do I do now?" Henry asked.

"We need to improve your situation. We need to get you into some better friendships and relationships. But the first thing we need to do is get you to class. You've got to talk to your professor about the missing work. Failing out of school is not going to help you feel better."

After a few false starts—including one time when Henry almost went to class, placing his hand on the doorknob to the lecture hall only to turn and walk away—he summoned the courage to walk through the door.

"So, I talked to my professor this morning and he was more than accommodating," Henry said one afternoon, looking relieved and energized, and sitting straight up in the center of the couch. "He's letting me make up the stuff I've missed. He said failing one class doesn't make me a failure."

"Of course, it doesn't," I said. "One F doesn't make you a failure, just like one depressive episode doesn't make you a depressed person."

"He even said he thinks I have promise," Henry added with a tearful smile. "He said that his college years were also filled with a bunch of personal crises, and he said that his professors' willingness to work with him was the only thing that got him through. Can you believe that?"

Indeed, I could.

When I was in college, I struggled with my own situational depression, and my situations were not small. A financial-aid kid, I had food stress and school stress, and other than good grades and a few good friends, there wasn't a lot of good in my life. There were problems back home I'd gone to college to get away from, but being a happy-go-lucky co-ed wasn't so easy. I dropped in and out of school more than once. Finally, twenty-something that I was, what really got me down was when a boyfriend who I'd lived with for more than two years dumped me and broke my heart.

When that relationship fell apart, I fell apart, too. I became convinced that not only had the past been a depressing and desperate slog but that the future, should I stick around to see it, would probably turn out about the same. For months and months, I cried too much, I ate too little, and I had a tough time being around other people who all seemed just fine. Day after day, as I crossed the railroad tracks on my walk to campus, I thought about maybe stepping in front of a train.

Unsure of where to go for help—affordability and accessibility were problems back then, too—I went to the office hours of a favorite psychology professor and asked if I could shut the door. Then, I broke down in tears and told him I could hardly get through the day. Sometimes the nights were so tough, I confessed with hands shaking as I wiped my face, that I thought about calling a hospital and trying to check myself in.

"Don't do that," my professor said. "Call me instead. I'm in the phone book." (It was the nineties, after all.)

That statement—that intervention—might have saved my life and certainly altered its course. What my professor said changed the way I thought about myself, my problems, and people my age. He was telling me that even though I might have been scaring myself, he wasn't scared of me at all. In fact, he spent the next hour, and many more in the months to come, getting to know me and my situation, helping me verbalize my own "Why now?"

If I were to walk into a doctor's office today with the same complaints, things might go a bit differently. I might likely wind up with a diagnosis, and maybe even some medication, in no time because, unfortunately, when it comes to offering prescription drugs to twentysomethings, the prevailing thinking seems to be "Why not?"

There are, in fact, many reasons why not.

THREE

WHY MEDICATION IS NOT ALWAYS THE BEST MEDICINE

With psychiatric medications, you solve one problem for a period of time, but the next thing you know you end up with two problems. The treatment turns a period of crisis into a chronic mental illness.
—Amy Upham, in Robert Whitaker's *Anatomy of an Epidemic*

Anh came to my office about a year after quitting the antidepressants she had taken for a decade. "I started medication at twenty-five, when I started law school," Anh explained. "I was so anxious I thought I was going to have to drop out. Failing was all I could think about, and I was miserable, so my family doctor put me on antidepressants. The pills made all those thoughts go away, so I didn't think much else about it. Ten years later, I was out of law school. I was married. I had two kids. My life was totally different than it was before, so I wasn't sure I needed medication anymore."

The way Anh described it, she had stopped antidepressants "just because," but when I asked for more detail, she also said that life on medication had always felt kind of "meh": "I felt less anxious, but I felt less *everything*. My lows weren't low, but my highs weren't high. I was even-keeled, everything was always fine, but I was also sort of checked out.

I never really felt *happy* about anything. I didn't care about having sex, which hasn't been great for my marriage. I thought I'd see how life was without meds."

Going off antidepressants, she recounted, had been much more difficult than she expected. She felt dizzy and nauseated for weeks. She also experienced what are called brain zaps or brain shivers, which are distressingly strange shock-like sensations in the head. "I went off medication slowly, like my doctor told me to. I was cutting pills in half or trying to get them even smaller, trying to make it bearable, but nothing made it bearable. I worked so hard to get off antidepressants, and it was awful, absolutely awful," Anh said. "*No one* told me I'd have to go through that when I decided to go on the pills."

Before long, Anh started to feel her feelings again, which was good for a while, but as soon as life became difficult, she felt even more overwhelmed by anxiety. This time, rather than her starting law school, the stressor was her 5-year-old twins beginning kindergarten. The emptiness of the house swallowed Anh whole, and some days she cried every hour they were away. She felt sick and could not eat. Her mind raced, and she couldn't sleep. Anxious thoughts flew at her—and stuck to her—she said, "like bugs smashed on the windshield of a car going fifty miles an hour."

"I wish I'd never gone *on* the meds, or I wish I'd never gone *off* the meds," Anh cried. "Either way, this is not a place I want to be."

It bears repeating: When it comes to mental health, medication is sometimes but not always the best medicine. Yet, as of 2022, about one in four young adults were taking a prescription psychoactive medication—one that affects how we think, or feel, or act. Antidepressants are the most commonly used psychoactive medications in the United States. They're also the single most commonly used prescription drug *of any kind* among adults ages 20 to 59. This has not always been the case.

In 1987, the FDA approved the first selective serotonin reuptake inhibitor, or SSRI, for the treatment of depression. This first SSRI-type antidepressant was Prozac, and its launch led to what historian Edward

Shorter called "a media psychocircus of suggestion." The green-and-white capsule appeared on magazine covers; it was hailed in newspaper headlines and news programs as a wonder drug. Suddenly, there was a "breakthrough drug" that could make a person "better than well."

Antidepressants had existed before Prozac, but the SSRIs were unique—and uniquely exciting—because they seemed to specifically and safely target the neurotransmitter serotonin. Depression, it was now hypothesized, was the result of low serotonin levels in the brain, and SSRIs boosted those levels. Not only were SSRIs purportedly more tolerable as medications but also this "chemical imbalance" theory of depression was more tolerable. It meant that depression wasn't a character flaw or a weakness. It was a medical problem: a disorder of the brain.

In a presidential proclamation, George H. W. Bush declared the 1990s the "Decade of the Brain," and funding began to flow toward mental health research and "brain disease." Meanwhile, psychologists and psychiatrists were eager to be seen as "real doctors" and, in line with an increasing reliance on the *DSM*, many adopted the same medical model that had long been applied to physical disorders: identify symptoms; make a diagnosis; treat with medication; reduce symptoms, and presumably restore health.

But when it comes to mental health, two assumptions of the medical model—that an illness has a clear biological cause and that the medications work—are sometimes wrong. Although antidepressants have long been touted as straightforward antidotes to depression, much like aspirin that reduces pain or antibiotics that fight infections, the evidence is not as straightforward as laypeople, and even physicians, have been led to believe.

The meteoric rise in the use and popularity of antidepressants can be attributed, at least in part, to the fact that an estimated 80 percent of people think that depression is caused by a chemical imbalance in the brain. And despite the fact that data have been mounting for years that this is not the case, many doctors, especially those who aren't psychiatrists, also subscribe to the low-serotonin theory. Yet in 2022, a headline-making study

evaluated years of available research on whether depression is indeed associated with low levels of serotonin: "Our comprehensive review of the major
strands of research on serotonin shows there is no convincing evidence that
depression is associated with, or caused by, lower serotonin concentrations
or activity," the researchers concluded. "It is time to acknowledge that the
serotonin theory of depression is not empirically substantiated."

Put simply, the serotonin theory of depression is just a theory: the
data do not back it up. Maybe this is why, all along, SSRIs haven't been
the magic bullet they were supposed to be. Consider this 2008 study published in the *New England Journal of Medicine*. To get the best answer on
just how effective SSRIs are (or aren't), researchers obtained data submitted to the FDA between 1987 and 2004. Out of seventy-four clinical trials, antidepressants performed better than a placebo in only thirty-eight
of these trials. In the other thirty-six trials, patients on a placebo either
did better than those on antidepressants or the results were questionable.
What this means is that antidepressant drugs outperform placebos only
about half the time. This is something that, perhaps owing to marketing
materials and publication bias, too many laypeople—and even doctors—
just don't know.

This same 2008 study also examined what happened to the findings
from those seventy-four clinical trials. Of the thirty-eight studies in which
antidepressants performed better than placebos, thirty-six were published
in research journals accessible by physicians. Of the thirty-six studies that
showed negative or questionable results, however, only three went on to
be published as they were; the other thirty-three either were not published
or were published in a way that suggested that the antidepressants had
been beneficial.

This bias toward publishing positive results—also known as the "file
drawer problem," in which studies with no effects or negative effects are
filed away—is so strong that when one surveys the available literature, 94
percent of antidepressant trials appear to be positive when, in fact, only
about 51 percent of trials are. Physicians, and then the public, are primarily hearing about studies in which antidepressants work.

Some argue that SSRIs seem to work about as well as placebos because of the placebo effect; that is, people feel better because they think (or are told) that they will feel better. It's more likely, though, that antidepressants perform about as well as placebos because of regression to the mean—the fact that elevated symptoms of depression and anxiety are often temporary and so commonly decrease on their own. Because many mental health concerns are situationally driven rather than biologically driven, they tend to pass or improve as situations pass or improve, no matter what kind of pill you are or aren't taking.

To be clear, antidepressants do have effects, because all psychoactive drugs act on the brain in one way or another. In my practice, users commonly report lows that don't dip quite so low, and for those like Anh, anxious thoughts may fly past rather than "stick" in their minds. For some, antidepressants can make a lifesaving or life-altering difference, and those who benefit most tend to be those whose symptoms are severe and intractable. For those with mild or moderate symptoms of depression, however—which is most people—the effects of antidepressants seem to be minimal or of questionable clinical significance. For these patients, the upsides may not outweigh the downsides.

Unfortunately, the most thorough discussions of the downsides of antidepressants happen more often online than in a doctor's office, yet the adverse effects of SSRIs are not as negligible as early research had suggested. In studies from around the world, even those who feel they are benefiting from antidepressants are concerned about their emotional side effects: numbness, a restricted range of feeling, feeling foggy or detached, feeling less like oneself, being less able to feel good feelings and caring less about others. Physical side effects are common, too, including drowsiness, weight gain, and sexual problems such as decreased interest, arousal, and orgasm. In a small minority of users, some antidepressants may trigger manic episodes, and their widespread use has been implicated in the rise of bipolar disorder among youth.

All of this means that laypeople and professionals alike may be overestimating the benefits of antidepressants and underestimating their risks.

Meanwhile, SSRIs are only increasing their reach. They've been approved by the FDA not just for use with depression but also for other disorders, such as social anxiety disorder. In addition, they're often prescribed for a variety of off-label conditions—problems for which they have not been FDA approved—from hives to premature ejaculation.

Off-label prescribing is not necessarily inappropriate, and some of it is supported by strong empirical research. Yet, one ten-year study of more than 125,000 medical and pharmacy claims found that more than half of all antidepressant prescriptions for young adults were written for off-label purposes, for which there was little or no evidence to support their use. What all this means is that today's young adults are likely to receive a prescription for antidepressants for an ever-broadening array of physical or emotional concerns. It's been called the "rise of all-purpose antidepressants"—but this trend is not limited to antidepressants.

The use of benzodiazepines has more than doubled since 2000. A popular type of antianxiety medication, "benzos" are fast acting, but not long-lasting, sedatives. Like the word *antidepressant*, the term *antianxiety* is a misnomer, in that it doesn't quite capture the full scope of their use. Benzos are commonly prescribed for any condition or situation in which someone might benefit from, quickly and temporarily, being more relaxed: insomnia, muscle spasms, seizures, dental procedures, public speaking, stress, a tough day, and more. Although benzos are meant to be used for only about eight to ten weeks or less, long-term prescribing is on the rise. This is a problem because these drugs are habit-forming, so our brains and bodies can become dependent on them and need more and more over time.

"I've taken benzos every day for years," one 31-year-old told me. "Usually when I try to go without, I get awful panic attacks, sweats, headaches right away, so I take some more. I would do anything to get off them." Not long after this disclosure, the man went to detox, a process that was sobering in more ways than one. "I had no idea I wasn't supposed to take so many benzos or for so long. I was just doing what my doctor told me to do!" he said, exasperated. "My doctor said they were working, so I should keep taking them."

Stories like this are why psychiatrist and former *DSM* task force chair Allen Frances says that "general practitioners should stop prescribing them, period. Doctors and patients should be much more aware that the gain from benzos is vanishingly short term but the pain is often lifelong."

Besides being addictive, as if that weren't reason enough to proceed with caution, benzos are second only to opioids in prescription drug overdoses. The group most likely to wind up in a hospital emergency department? Young adults. About half of women, and a third of men, who present with benzodiazepine poisoning report having suicidal intent. The rest misuse their medication by taking too many pills or by combining them with other substances, like alcohol, or antidepressants, or stimulants.

Stimulants—medications such as Ritalin or Adderall commonly used to treat attention deficit hyperactivity disorder (ADHD)—are on the rise as well, and not just among those with bona fide attention problems. The use of these medications has more than tripled since 2000, even skyrocketing during the pandemic. More and more, these so-called smart drugs have become drugs of choice for those who want to get things done. But please take note: A 2023 study found that stimulant use in neurotypical young adults is counterproductive. When young adults without ADHD were given stimulants, they worked longer and harder on tasks than without the drugs, but their work was of lower quality. They made more errors and were less efficient with their time such that those who performed above average without stimulants performed below average on the drugs. The findings led the researchers to conclude that, for neurotypical youth, taking "smart" drugs to perform better at work or in school is perhaps not so smart.

Yet, as of 2015, about one in five college students (many of whom likely need better study or time-management skills) misused stimulants, and most gained access to the pills from peers who have prescriptions. Increasingly, young adults are getting prescriptions of their own, often off-label and without a formal evaluation for ADHD. According to a 2019 study by the Centers for Disease Control (CDC) that examined dispensing estimates from almost 50,000 pharmacies in the United States, stimulant prescriptions for adults now outnumber those for children. And according to a 2023 study—in what was called "a prescribing cascade"—about half of adult stimulant users were also prescribed one other psychoactive medication, such as an antidepressant or an antianxiety medication, and about a fourth had prescriptions for two or more such meds, all despite little evidence that would help us understand their combined benefits and risks.

Quietly but quite seriously, off-label prescriptions for antipsychotics are increasing, too. Once reserved primarily for adults with schizophrenia or bipolar disorder, antipsychotics are now used for a wide range of ages and difficulties, from young children with behavioral problems to elderly folks with dementia. In the words of one researcher, "antipsychotics are becoming antidepressants, antianxiety drugs, mood stabilizers, cognitive enhancers, antiaggressive, anti-impulsive, antisuicidal and hypnotic medications." Indeed, when antidepressants or antianxiety drugs fail to alleviate every symptom a patient presents with (as medications often do), antipsychotics are now frequently layered on top as a form of polypharmacy, the apparent goal being to cumulatively medicate away every complaint a person has. Most concerning, but rarely mentioned to patients, is that—among the psychoactives—the side effects and dangers of antipsychotics can be the most severe of all.

Last, but certainly not least in terms of popular and scientific interest, are psychedelics. To be sure, hallucinogens such as LSD, psilocybin, ketamine, and MDMA (Ecstasy) show promise as game-changing treatments for severe depression, anxiety, and post-traumatic stress disorder. Most exciting is that they seem to provide relief not by reducing symptoms but, rather, by creating new connections in the brain. It's still the early days, however, and it's unclear how to best put that promise into practice. Some young adults scour the internet for dosages and directions, while others resort to doctors who may not provide quality care. "She doesn't meet with anyone at the ketamine clinic," one mother explained to me about her daughter who was deeply depressed. "She fills out a questionnaire, she gets the infusion, and she leaves." Apparently, no one at the clinic was concerned—or even knew—this woman's daughter was rarely showering or leaving her room.

In the words of journalist Robert Whitaker, "the psychopharmacology revolution was born from one part science and two parts wishful thinking." In my experience, those two parts are that the fix will be quick and the fix will be easy. Yet, years of listening to clients—and to the data—tell me that the only thing truly quick and easy about psychoactive medications is getting a hold of them. Prescriptions for psychoactive drugs are shockingly easy to come by, and rarely even require a trip to a mental health specialist. A stunning 80 percent of first-time prescriptions for antidepressants are written by primary care professionals such as pediatricians, general practitioners, or nurse practitioners. So it goes for 90 percent of antianxiety prescriptions, 65 percent of stimulant prescriptions, and 50 percent of antipsychotic prescriptions. Fewer than one-third of those who receive such prescriptions also visit a mental health professional, such as a psychologist.

Also concerning is that, since the rules about in-person visits with physicians were relaxed during the pandemic, prescriptions for psychoactive medications are now provided by way of telehealth companies, many of which advertise on social media platforms. Although most such companies say they aim to make therapy and medication more accessible— a worthwhile endeavor, especially for young adults whose budgets are stretched and for those in rural areas where mental health services may be hard to come by—there are serious questions about whether these companies are actually improving the mental health of underserved populations or simply profiting by tossing pills their way. According to a 2021 article, workers at a large mental telehealth start-up describe their company as a sort of Uber for prescriptions, whereby subscribers receive diagnoses and medications on demand. When callers don't get the drugs they ask for— typically after a single 30-minute session—the company often receives bad reviews online (and no company wants bad reviews).

Psychoactive drugs are some of our most complex, least understood medications, and they're acting on the most complex, least understood organ: the brain. Yet, the doctors and nurses who most commonly prescribe these drugs—either in person, or on the phone, or online—are often the ones who know the least about them. These professionals may be well meaning, but they're also likely to have received promotional materials about psychoactive drugs from pharmaceutical companies rather than specialized training in the drugs' use and misuse. The result is that an ever-increasing number of patients of *all* ages are taking medications that they, and even their prescribers, may not fully understand. In my experience, few young adults know—or have been told—what they may be getting into when they start taking medications or what they may be in for when they try to stop.

Within a week of her children starting kindergarten, Anh was in crisis. Every day and during many nights, her heart raced, and her mind did, too: What if something happens to the twins while they're away from home? What if they're scared and don't know how to ask for help? What if there's a school shooting? What if other kids are mean to them in middle school? What if they fall into drugs in high school? And what if they move across the country when they are in their twenties, and I only get to see them once or twice a year?

As Anh rattled off her list of what-ifs, she seemed unaware of how pointless it was to worry about events so far into the future. "I feel like I'm trying to learn all these things I probably should have learned when I was younger, like how to face the future and the possibility that things could go wrong," Anh said. "And, obviously, I need to face the fact that I never did anything with my law degree, and maybe it would be better for me, and for my kids, to have something in my life besides them."

I wish I could say that, within a few sessions, I was quickly and easily able to help Anh do all that. But that's not exactly how it went. Anh had some good hours, and even some good days, but her anxiety kept roaring back. "I have never felt this bad before, not even in law school," she told me. "I'm so scared I'll never stop feeling like this. My heart is pounding. My skin is tingling. I feel like I'm going to die. This is downright traumatic."

When I reminded Anh that a medication consult was always an option, she refused at first: "Getting off of antidepressants," she said, "*that* was even more traumatic." But before long, Anh reluctantly decided to see a psychiatrist, and not long after that, she reluctantly went back on antidepressants, too.

Anh's story is not unusual. Rather, it is a poignant example of how, for some people, psychoactive drugs have brought us the twenty-first-century version of mental health's "revolving door." In the twentieth century, the revolving door referred to severely ill patients being released from psychiatric hospitals without adequate support in the community, only to become rehospitalized soon afterward. Today, that revolving door is more likely to be at your local pharmacy.

Here's how it works.

People of all ages—but especially young adults—experience symptoms of anxiety or depression, often in response to a situational stressor, such as the end of a relationship or the beginning of law school. They want relief and, understandably, they want it sooner rather than later. Pills are prescribed. Depending on the medication, symptoms abate within hours, or days, or weeks, so the patients go back for more. Months or years later, when they try to quit the drugs, their symptoms can re-emerge, often worse than before, as the brain balks at being deprived of a substance it has grown accustomed to—which only seems like proof that they still need medication.

When this happens, at least part of what may be going on is discontinuation syndrome, which is the polite term for drug withdrawal. Dizziness, nausea, lethargy, agitation, and the brain zaps that Anh mentioned are common, as are worsening symptoms of depression and anxiety. A 2019 review of studies of antidepressant withdrawal found that about half of users were negatively affected by stopping the drug, with about a quarter rating their symptoms as severe. Too often, those who would like to discontinue antidepressants simply find it too difficult to stop. So, they go back to the pharmacy, and back on their medication, and round and round it goes.

Although many young people go on drugs like antidepressants for short-term relief during a difficult time in their lives—"I thought maybe I'd take them for six months or a year," Anh recalled—about 50 percent of users will remain on them for more than five years and about 25 percent will stay on them for a decade or more, or have plans to do so forever. All this, despite the fact that what we know about the effectiveness and safety of antidepressants is drawn from studies that followed patients for only about two to three years.

This brings us to what is the least discussed potential negative side effect of all: While psychoactive drugs may provide relief in the short run, and while some patients may fare well on them in the long run, research suggests they may *worsen* long-term outcomes for most others. Good longitudinal data are difficult to come by, but studies published in 2021 and 2022 suggest that relapse rates are higher—and long-run quality of life is lower—for those who take medications than for those who do not.

One reason for this is that medications don't teach us anything. Maybe they take the edge off or turn the volume down on unwanted thoughts and feelings, but they don't help us learn how to handle unwanted thoughts or feelings, or prevent them in the first place. Then, once the medication is removed, our ability to cope or to manage our lives may be no better than it was before.

Perhaps even more concerning is that some experts have begun to wonder whether psychoactive medications are perturbing the still-developing brains of teens and young adults in ways that will hinder their mental health down the line. By flooding the brain with levels of psychoactive agents not found in nature, medication may actually *introduce* the very sort of chemical imbalance they are popularly thought to correct. Because of this, some researchers and psychiatrists, including those who specialize in young adults, have concluded that, for many, psychoactive drugs like antidepressants may "do more harm than good."

I don't know if Anh will ever be able to live life without antidepressants, nor do I know if she needs to. In this chapter, I am not suggesting that psychoactive medications are never helpful or warranted, nor am I suggesting that I never recommend them to my clients. What I am suggesting—and what the most recent research suggests—is that, as consumers, we ought to proceed thoughtfully and cautiously when considering psychoactive medications, especially for young adults. There are very few mental health disorders for which medications ought to be the first step in treatment—and there are *no* mental health disorders that are best treated with pills alone.

As psychologist Kay Jamison wrote in *An Unquiet Mind*, her bestselling memoir of living with bipolar disorder, "No pill can help me deal with the problem of not wanting to take pills; likewise, no amount of psychotherapy alone can prevent my manias and depressions. I need both." To be sure, skills combined with pills is the most effective, most ethical treatment for chronic, brain-based mental health disorders such as bipolar disorder and obsessive-compulsive disorder (OCD), as well as ADHD.

At the same time, however, this formula of skills plus pills has been too broadly applied to nearly every mental health concern, even those that are more situational than they are neurological. Yes, sometimes young adults need pills, at least for a while, to be able to learn new skills. And sometimes, as Jamison says, they need skills to agree to take the pills. But in mental health treatment, more isn't always more, and both isn't necessarily better. That is because, side effects aside, when we tell twentysomethings they have a brain problem and we hand them a medication to fix it, pills often *take the place* of skills. And when that happens, pills may reduce symptoms and maybe even help someone feel better—at least for a while—but they do not solve problems and they do not help anyone grow.

Besides, most twentysomethings I know who are using pills to support their mental health don't want to be on medication forever. They want to be able to rely more on skills and less on pills over time. So, here's the thing: As a twentysomething, because of the way the brain works and because of the way life works, whether you're on medication or not, the time to build your skills is now.

FOUR

WHY THE TIME FOR HOW IS NOW

Life itself still remains a very effective therapist.

—Karen Horney, psychoanalyst

"I am a twenty-five-year-old living in Houston," a man named Owen wrote to me. "I have spent the last two years working remotely from my apartment, and I feel as though I have fallen into really bad habits. For the past six months, I've been severely anxious and depressed as I went through the process of applying to business schools. I was so angry that my job was remote and that I was stuck by myself in an apartment that I didn't take the time to really lean in to the work I was supposed to be doing. I feel like I spent so many days not speaking to people and doing the bare minimum.

"Now I am getting acceptances, and I feel like a complete fraud if I go. I feel like the only reason I was able to get in was because I ignored everything and everyone else in my life and in my job to write my essays and study for the GMAT. I have wanted to go to business school since I was eighteen but have lost complete faith in myself and my ability to be successful. I keep thinking I have wasted the last two years of my life stressing my parents and my friends out for a career option I might not even be capable of handling. There is no way I can imagine running a company or trying to be a manager of any kind.

"I am worried I have permanently fucked up my brain and my

relationships with my friends and family over the last two years. I am now on antidepressant medication, and I feel like a complete failure all of the time. I've never even dated because I've been so focused on getting into business school and never really took the time to put down roots where I am. I am worried I've messed up my life and I don't know how to pull myself out of this. I feel like I am going to spend the rest of my life being jealous of people who go on to succeed when I can't.

"I have a month to decide whether or not to go to business school, and I feel paralyzed by the thought of making a decision. I graduated at the top of my class, with so much potential, and have completely wasted it. I just don't know how to fix it. In the past couple of years, I formed no connections, I learned no skills, I saved no money, and I didn't even have fun, and somehow I became addicted to Adderall and antidepressants. I am so jealous of everyone else's lives right now, and I never used to be. I don't know where to turn or what I'm supposed to do. Can you help?"

I include Owen's rather long message here because he—and all the Owens out there—are why I write books. Young adults everywhere, not just the ones with therapists, deserve to know they—and their brains—are not "permanently fucked." Your twenties may be a mental health low point, but more often than not, they're a turning point, too. Longitudinal research shows that, across the life span, mental health often follows a J-shaped curve: It takes a dip from childhood to young adulthood and then rises steadily in the decades after that. These are the years when, after trending downward, how we think, and feel, and act starts to take an upward turn.

A meta-analysis of almost one hundred different studies shows that, by around age 35, most young adults report feeling less depressed, less anxious, less angry, less moody, and less reactive—and they also report experiencing more of the good stuff. By your mid-thirties, you're likely to feel more confident, more responsible, more decisive, more positive, more intentional, more ambitious, more persistent, more socially competent, and more future-directed.

Education *is* an intervention, but as a client of mine said to me once, education is not execution. So, even if I were able to tell Owen all this, just my saying so would go only so far. What Owen was struggling with is perhaps the most terrifying uncertainty of all, and that's all the things he did not know how to do . . . yet.

According to Owen's email, he didn't know how to work. He didn't know how to decide about business school. He didn't know how to make friends or how to date. He didn't know how to have good habits. He didn't know how to handle stress. He didn't know how to save money or maybe even how to have fun. And because of all this, he'd lost faith in himself and in his ability to succeed. To feel better, Owen thought he needed a therapist, but what he really needed was skills.

Skills are our abilities. They're our know-how, or what we know how to do well—usually because of experience. Know-how comes not just from asking someone how to do something but also from getting out there and doing that thing many times. Just as it takes practice to become skilled at snowboarding, or robotics, or writing, or teaching, it takes practice to get better at working, or loving, or deciding, or *life*. As Shinichi Suzuki, founder of the famed music education program, put it, "Knowledge is not skill. Knowledge plus 10,000 times is skill."

Uncertainty functions as a transdiagnostic stressor *especially* when we lack confidence in our own abilities. We may never be able to make the world a perfectly predictable place, but one sure way to reduce unknowns is to increase what we know how to do. And, because of the way the twentysomething brain develops, the time to develop that know-how is now.

We have long had growth charts that show average height and weight as we age, but only recently have scientists been able to piece together what brain development looks like across the life span. In 2022, a team of researchers published data from brain scans from more than one hundred studies with more than 100,000 participants, ages 0 to 100 years old. These scans show that, of all the growth that the brain goes through in life—most of which happens in the first three decades—white matter development occurs last.

Although we often talk about the brain in terms of gray matter, white matter makes up half the brain's volume. White matter is the pale-colored nerve fibers that constitute the wiring within and across the different parts of the brain. White matter *matters* because it's how the different parts of the brain talk to each other—and because white matter is what changes when we acquire new skills.

From birth through young adulthood, white matter develops from bottom to top and from back to front. Just behind the forehead lies the prefrontal cortex, which is the last area of the brain to be wired up in each individual, as well as the last area of the brain to have evolved in humans. Not surprisingly, then, the prefrontal cortex is where we carry out our most evolved brain functions, including dealing with uncertainty.

The prefrontal cortex is also where we manage and coordinate the three key components of mental health: thoughts, feelings, and actions. It is where we balance difficult emotions—like fear and anger—with rational thinking. It is where we solve complex problems and make decisions, especially those that don't have right-or-wrong answers. It is where we control short-term impulses and consider long-term consequences. It's where we set anxiety aside and gather up the courage to do something, or to try something, or to meet someone new. It is where we work hard and persevere even when times are tough. It's where we plan our days and our years and where we take responsibility for how our lives are going to go.

The prefrontal cortex is where we "adult," yet white-matter growth in this area reaches its peak around the age of 29, while meaningful declines don't begin until about age 50. This trajectory might sound slow but, really, it's right on time. The prefrontal cortex wires up *in* young adulthood because it's wiring up *for* adulthood. The brain learns from experience and so it has to *have* adult experiences to properly prepare for what's ahead.

In a process called *smart wiring*, how exactly *your* brain wires up depends on what you see, and hear, and do every day. In early childhood, for example, if you spend your first five years of life in Germany, you'll speak German, and if you grow up in Morocco, you'll be fluent in Arabic. But that's not all. A 2023 study found that the brains of those who speak German look different from the brains of Arabic speakers. Similarly, children who regularly practice a musical instrument before the age of 7 have different white-matter pathways from those who do not. Smart wiring is how the experiences you have on the outside change who you are on the inside.

Similarly, in young adulthood, all those twentysomething firsts—first decisions, first jobs, first loves, first breakups, first successes, first tough conversations, first apartments, first mistakes, first failures, first problems, first friendships—wire the brain for what's to come. They tell us something about the specific skills we will need for the lives we will lead—and they give us an opportunity to build them. From this perspective, our young adult struggles are not just normal, they are purposeful: they train the brain for what's ahead.

So, whether you're 18 or 25—or 35, for that matter—now is always the time to get out there and acquire some new skills. Things will go wrong, and when they do, you'll likely feel stressed, or depressed, or anxious for a while. But that doesn't necessarily mean there's something wrong with you. Maybe it means that your life isn't settled yet, or that there are still some things you need to work on. You'll feel better when life gets better, and it takes practice to get better at life.

Here's my favorite fact from a pie chart about how people change in therapy: The largest slice of client improvement—a whopping 40 percent—comes from what happens *outside of sessions* rather than from what happens in the room. Compare this to the 15 percent of improvement that comes from what you learn in treatment or the 15 percent that comes from the placebo effect. In other words, although education and expectations matter, your mental health is most likely to be improved by what's happening—and by what you're doing—at work, at home, in school, around your town, in your country, and in your relationships.

As a therapist, then, I'm a pusher rather than a puller. I'd rather push people out into their lives than pull them in closer to me. The therapy relationship can be important, but as I tell my clients, if I'm the most important person in your life, then I'm not doing my job. Change might happen in your therapy session, but there are 167 other hours in your week that are much more likely to impact who and how you are.

Remember those teens with TikTok tics that sprang up during the pandemic? They're better now. A 2023 follow-up story revealed that, although some took medication to reduce their symptoms, the overwhelming advice from professionals was to get off their screens and back into the world.

I didn't have the answers to Owen's life, but if he were to come to my office, I would likely suggest he give business school a try. Because *that's* where he would learn some of the things he didn't know, such as how to be a worker, or a leader, or a friend. That's how he'd find out what happens to his depression and anxiety when he is out of his apartment and off Zoom. That's how he might start making connections—in his brain and in his life—and maybe even start dating and having some fun. Besides, business school is something Owen had dreamed of and worked hard for, and so I'm not sure how it would be helpful for him to decide he was too screwed up to go. What would be helpful would be for Owen to believe that he could still change.

When I work with young adults, I expect growth and change in a positive direction. In no way do I presume that the 25-year-old I work with today will look much like the 35-year-old I may one day meet on the street. In fact, I assume they won't. Work is changing. Love is changing. Life is changing. And, because all this is happening as the *brain* is changing, our mental health is changing, too.

Being a twentysomething is like being an airplane soaring up into the sky just after takeoff. It's a time when a small change in course can make an enormous difference in terms of where you land with work, and love, and life. The same goes for mental health. The twenties are an up-in-the-air, turbulent time, but the best way to navigate that uncertainty and wind up somewhere better is to learn how to fly your plane. The skills you gain in your twenties accompany you wherever you go—across jobs, and cities, and relationships, and decades—and unlike health insurance, they never run out.

Part II that follows is about twentysomethings who come to my office or to my classroom because, maybe like Owen, they hope I can help them with their twenties—and in some ways, I can. I can tell them what I know about why young adulthood is so difficult and what exactly twentysomethings can do now to feel better.

Most of all, though, the stories that follow are about twentysomethings who build their skills not by looking to me for certainties but instead by daring to live their uncertainties. When they don't know how to work, they start working. When they don't know how to love, they start loving. When they don't know how to have sex, they start kissing. When they don't know how to cook, they start cooking. When they don't know how to live, they start living. *Life* is the best therapist of all, and it is affordable, and accessible, and right outside your door.

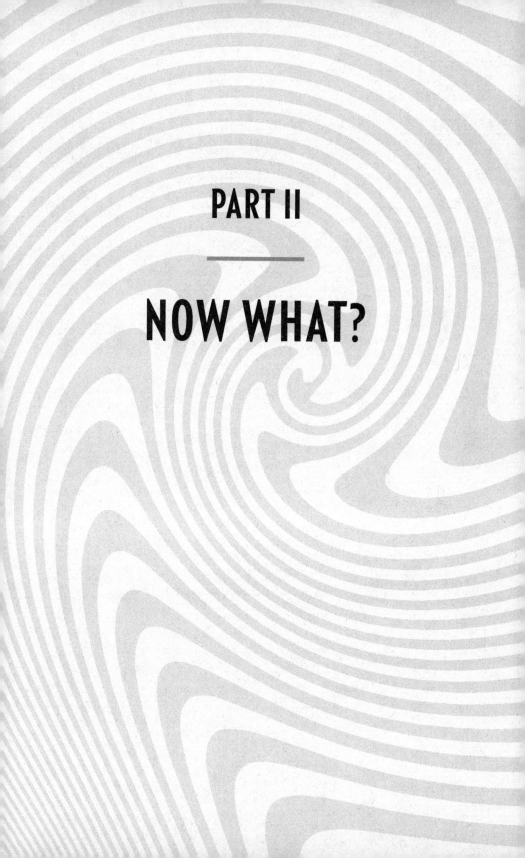

PART II

NOW WHAT?

FIVE

HOW TO THINK

You can't keep the birds of worry from circling your head, but you can prevent them from building nests in your hair.

—Proverb of unknown origin

Paul walked into my shift in the emergency department. There, we were jammed together in an office the size of a large broom closet, our two chairs—and our two sets of knees—just inches apart. Lurching forward, and in shouts and tears, Paul told me his life was ruined. A medical student who'd grown up in Taiwan, he was sure he'd failed an exam taken a few hours before, and he was sure he'd fail the next one happening that night. As Paul brought me up to speed, he yelled so loud that I wondered whether (and maybe hoped that) someone might come in and intervene.

"I can't take my exam tonight!" Paul shrieked, more at himself than at me. "I'm going to fail out of med school! I don't deserve to be a doctor! I'll never be able to face my parents! This is a complete catastrophe!"

As I soon found out, Paul had spent the last few hours pacing back and forth in his apartment, his thoughts racing around in his default-mode network.

The *default-mode network* refers to the areas of the brain that are busy when we don't seem to be. An interconnected group of structures, the default-mode network was discovered mostly by accident as scientists studied subjects who engaged with mental tasks. Using PET (positron emission tomography) scans, researchers noticed that some areas of the brain became active when subjects locked onto activities that required concentration, such as memorizing lists of words or counting dots on a screen. Collectively, these areas were called the *task-positive network*. Surprisingly, however, other areas of the brain seemed to be doing something even when subjects were in a resting or passive state. Those areas were dubbed the *default-mode network*.

Before long, studies using both PET and MRI (magnetic resonance imaging) technology revealed that the default-mode network is not truly passive, in that these areas of the brain become active not only during so-called rest but also during certain kinds of mental work, such as when we think about ourselves and other people, and the future and the past. When not otherwise engaged, then, our brains revert to puzzling over our deepest uncertainties about our lives. In default mode, the brain acts as a prediction machine of sorts, continually running mental simulations of what might happen or what might be true.

The problem is, when we run mental simulations, it's human nature to imagine that what might happen or what might be true is almost always bad. It's called *negativity bias*, which is the tendency to generate more bad possibilities than good ones and to give those imagined disasters more attention and weight. "Bad is stronger than good," researchers say. We do this because our brains are wired to keep us alive, not happy. When it comes to survival, the cost of *under*estimating danger is higher than that of *over*estimating it. So, our brains take a better-safe-than-sorry approach to unknowns. When uncertainty triggers the smoke detectors in our brains, we assume it's a house fire and not burnt toast, and we imagine that everything we own is going to burn up.

Unfortunately, younger adults spend more time than older adults in default mode, and they have a harder time switching out of it. Maybe that's why one of the most common complaints I hear from young adult clients goes something like this: "I feel bad when I'm alone or I'm bored or I don't have anything to do." Many describe their downtime as a time when their thoughts and their feelings are at their worst. They say life is better when work keeps them focused on something or when they have projects that need to get done. Some might see this as proof that "kids today" need constant stimulation or that their parents kept them too busy for too long. Maybe. But maybe it's also true that default mode is simply a tough place to be, especially for twentysomethings.

"My life has been filled with many tragedies," Mark Twain said, "most of which never occurred." Those imaginary tragedies that Twain was referring to come from what psychologists call *catastrophic thinking* or *catastrophizing*.

The most extreme form of negativity bias, catastrophizing is worst-case-scenario thinking, in which we conjure up our greatest fears, often in the form of worries and what-ifs. What if I get fired? What if my life doesn't work out? What if I made the wrong decision? What if this relationship doesn't last? What if I make a mistake? What if something awful happens to my parent or partner or child? What if I fail? Because these what-ifs often will take place in the future, catastrophizing is sometimes called "future tripping" or "time traveling," as we panic about what might happen in the hours or days or months ahead.

Catastrophic thinking endures because, evolutionarily speaking, it has survival value; it helps us anticipate what might go wrong. Yet, technically speaking, it is considered to be a thinking error, too. That's because catastrophizing is based on fears, not facts, and as a result, it is neither rational nor linear. Anticipatory what-if anxiety increases when the likelihood of a negative event shifts from 0 to 1 percent—but not when the chances of the event go from 34 to 35 percent, or even from 50 to 51 percent. Thus, when we are catastrophizing, we are often mistaking what is *possible* for what is *probable*.

What's more, when we catastrophize, we tend to overestimate not only the likelihood of a negative event but also its possible consequences. A single worry leads to another and another, each more dire than the one that came before. Around and around we go, spiraling down until we hit bottom either by exhausting all negative possibilities or by wearing ourselves out. Not surprisingly, then, catastrophizing is associated with a variety of mental and physical health concerns, including anxiety, depression, and chronic pain. If we think life is probably going to be awful, then it is difficult not to feel worried, and sick, and sad.

Because our catastrophic thinking can sometimes seem reasonable, to gain some perspective it helps to look at the downward spirals of others. Consider this telling study in which researchers asked young adult worriers about what might happen if they did poorly in school. Importantly, worriers in this study were not people with anxiety disorders; they were just people who tended to worry a lot. Here is a catastrophizing sequence from one such worrier who was asked what might come after a bad grade:

1. I won't live up to my expectations.
2. I'd be disappointed in myself.
3. I'd lose my self-confidence.
4. My loss of self-confidence would spread to other areas of my life.
5. I wouldn't have as much control as I'd like.
6. I'd be afraid of facing the unknown.
7. I'd become very anxious.
8. Anxiety would lead to further loss of self-confidence.
9. I wouldn't get my confidence back.
10. I'd feel like I wouldn't have any control over my life.
11. I'd be susceptible to things that normally wouldn't bother me.
12. I'd become more and more anxious.
13. I'd have no control at all, and I'd become mentally ill.
14. I'd become dependent on drugs and therapy.
15. I'd always remain dependent on drugs.
16. They'd deteriorate my body.
17. I'd be in pain.
18. I'd die.
19. I'd end up in hell.

As is typical, each negative possibility is more disastrous than the one that came before it and often is estimated to be even more likely to happen. In this list, for example, the worrier said that the chance of winding up in hell—you know, facing eternal damnation—was 80 percent.

Of course, one issue with this study is that young people who tend to worry might have worried about their grades many times before, and this could have affected the lists they came up with. To correct for this, researchers also asked subjects to ponder a hypothetical situation they almost certainly had never considered previously: What if they were the Statue of Liberty and they weren't happy about it? What might their concerns be? As you read this worrier's list, note that this research was done *before* 9/11:

1. That I wouldn't be able to move.
2. That I would be attacked.
3. That I would not be able to fight back.
4. That I would not be able to control what other people did to me.
5. That I would feel inadequate.
6. That other people would begin to think I was inadequate.
7. That I would not be respected.
8. That I would not have any influence over others.
9. That other people would not listen to me.
10. That it would cause a loss of self-esteem.
11. That this loss of self-esteem would have a negative effect on my relationships.
12. That I would lose friends.
13. That I would be alone.
14. That I would have no one to talk to.
15. That I would not be able to share any thoughts or problems with other people.
16. That I would not get advice from others.
17. That none of my problems would be adequately sorted out.
18. That [my problems] would remain and get worse.

19. That eventually I would not be able to cope with them.
20. That my problems would have more control over me than I had over them.
21. That my problems would prevent me from doing other things.
22. That I would be unable to meet new people and make friends.
23. That I would be lonely.

Although, in this study, each catastrophizing spiral was different, researchers noticed a theme of personal inadequacy that ran through the worriers' lists. It wasn't getting a bad grade or being stuck as a statue that was a problem; the real problem was that worriers felt unable to take action or to turn things around. For them, the *real* uncertainty was not their situation as much as their perceived inability to do something about it. Their own sense of incompetence left them feeling unsettled and unsure.

Here's a related theme the researchers did not note, but I did: the concern that one's personal inadequacy would lead to lifelong mental health problems. This is something I see often in my office: a tendency to catastrophize mental health struggles and to believe there is nothing one can do to feel better over time. Young adults like Paul see symptoms of anxiety and depression as indictors of impending insanity, or rejection, or doom. Paul was sure something bad was about to happen: He might fail his exam, or med school, or his parents—or maybe even need to kill himself.

And, for a brief moment, he had me thinking it, too.

Walk-in slots in the emergency department are thirty minutes long, which is one reason I like them: I've got half an hour to make a difference or a decision. That decision sometimes involves whether someone is well enough to walk back out the door or if I need to suggest, or require, an in-patient stay. Even so, it's unusual for me to have the feeling, as I did with Paul, that maybe I'm not safe with a client.

I took this as a signal to ask Paul if *he* was feeling unsafe. But, to get a real answer, I needed to shift Paul from his default-mode network to his task-positive network. I needed him to stop future tripping and time traveling and come into the present and the room with me.

"Let's count backward from five," I said to Paul, "but, as we go, I want you to do something for me."

Paul took a deep breath, seeming relieved to have a task.

"Look around the room and tell me five things you can see," I said.

"I see a defibrillator. A fluorescent light. I see you sitting there. There's a metal cabinet. And an eye chart."

"Okay. Now tell me four things you can feel in your body."

"I have a slight headache," he said, closing his eyes for a moment. "I feel kind of sick to my stomach. I feel tension in my shoulders. The muscles in my legs feel tired."

"Now, what about three things you can hear."

"I hear you talking to me," he said, opening his eyes and looking around again. "And I hear machines beeping somewhere. And voices out in the hallway."

"Now, what about two things you can smell?"

"I smell that hospital smell. It's tough to describe, but you know what it is," he said, slowing down to concentrate. "And now that I think about it, I smell my deodorant and that's probably good since that means it's working, and we're in this tiny room."

I smiled at his joke, and with the relief that he was settling down.

"One more, Paul," I said. "What's one thing you can taste?"

"Coffee," he said right away. "That's an easy one. That's about all I've had to eat or drink all day."

I pulled a protein bar out of the metal cabinet Paul had mentioned, and as I handed it to him, I noticed how much better he seemed already. Some might call the exercise we did together a distraction, but when we tell young adults to distract themselves, we are giving them only half the instructions. To *distract* means to get your mind off something, yet the only real way to do this is to put your mind *on* something else. You give yourself a task to focus on whether it is watching a movie, or playing basketball, or diving into a project, or reading a book, or counting objects in a room.

Now that Paul had settled down, I asked if he was thinking about hurting himself or someone else.

"Sometimes I wish I wasn't here," he sighed, "like I just want everything to go away."

"Like how?" I asked.

"Like by taking a bottle of pills," he said vaguely. "That makes me sound crazy, I know."

Suicidal thoughts are more common in young adults than we'd like to believe. According to a 2022 study of college students nationwide, an estimated one-third thought about killing themselves during the previous two weeks. Although suicide is sometimes described as a permanent solution to a temporary problem, many young adults aren't so sure their problems are temporary. Often, thoughts of hurting themselves come from thinking that there is no other way out of the difficulties they face.

"Most people don't know this," I told Paul, "but thinking about suicide isn't a symptom of mental illness. It usually has more to do with being in crisis, with feeling like your problems can't be solved, like you don't know what else to do."

"Yeah, no," he said, shaking his head. "I want my *problems* to go away, but I don't want to go away. Or, maybe I just couldn't do it. It would be too shameful for my family. My sister would be really sad. But I still worry about sticking around and being an embarrassment to them. You know, like what if I fail my exams and I fail out of med school? What if everything I've worked for doesn't work out?"

"You're catastrophizing, Paul, and catastrophizing is about fears, not facts," I answered. "Let's try to focus on some facts."

"But there *aren't* any facts," Paul lamented, sounding a lot like Irene from a few chapters earlier, and in a way, of course, he was right.

Paul was struggling because so much was still uncertain in life, particularly whether he would succeed in med school and go on to become a doctor. So, I led with a few facts of my own. As he slowly ate the protein bar, I told him about the default-mode network and the task-positive one. "You're a med student," I said, "so you can understand this. You need to practice moving out of the emotional parts of the brain, like the amygdala, and into the problem-solving ones, like the prefrontal cortex."

"How do I do that?"

"By thinking less about what *if* and more about what *is*."

"Okay . . ." he said skeptically.

"But you'll have to educate me. I need you to help me get clear on some facts," I said as he again looked relieved to have a task. "Have you ever failed an exam in medical school?"

"No . . ."

"Okay, good. What happens if you do?"

"I guess I take it again," he explained. "Med students can take their exams more than once."

"Oh, *excellent!*" I said, suddenly feeling better myself. "So, maybe you won't fail your exam tonight. And if you do, the worst case is you'll have to retake it."

"No," Paul countered. "Worst case is that it keeps happening, and I fail out completely."

"Let's say that happens," I said to Paul's surprise. "Let's play that out."

This is where laypeople—and professionals—often fall short when dealing with catastrophic thoughts. They stop at trying to talk themselves or others out of their worst fears, and they forget the step of *solving* for them. Solving for worst-case scenarios is a bit like exposure therapy, in that we confront rather than avoid our most terrifying ideas.

"What would you do if you failed out?" I went on. "Where would you go?"

"Where would I *go*?" he asked. He shook his head like he was shaking up his thinking to imagine new things. "I'd stay here, I guess. I like it here. I'd go into research probably, which isn't what I planned."

Paul thought some more.

"But sometimes I think I like science more than the pressure and the patients."

"Oh!" I said, again pleasantly surprised. "So, even if your worst-case scenario does come true, your life could go on. Maybe even in a better way."

"Maybe," Paul said.

"So, maybe your worst-case scenario isn't even a worst case. It's just a case."

Catastrophizing isn't the only sort of thinking that gets us into trouble sometimes. Here are five more thinking errors that are common, especially among twentysomethings:

Overgeneralizing: assuming that one problem means a lifetime of problems. "This relationship didn't work out, so none of my relationships will work out." Or, "I'm depressed now, so I'll always be depressed."

Personalizing: assuming that everything bad that happens is about you. "My boss yelled at me; he hates me." Or, "My friend didn't text me back so they don't want to hang out with me."

Magnifying: focusing on and enlarging mistakes, or flaws, or negatives often by talking too much or thinking too much about them. "I keep thinking about this mistake I made." Or, "I can't stop talking about how much my partner makes me mad."

Black-and-white thinking: seeing life in perfectionistic, all-or-nothing terms. "If I don't have everything figured out by the time I'm thirty, then I'm a failure." Or, "My boyfriend and I had a fight; he's not going to want to be with me anymore."

Filtering: ignoring the positive and noticing only the negative. "They were just being nice when they gave me that compliment." Or, "All I can think about is the one dumb thing I said in that meeting."

Paul was engaging in each of these ways of thinking—and so does everyone—because they're all related. They all spring from negativity bias, that better-safe-than-sorry thinking our brains do when we're faced with unknowns. Understanding this is important because too many twenty-somethings pathologize themselves for making thinking errors, and in doing so, they make thinking errors *about* their thinking errors: "What if I keep having these thoughts forever?!" Or, "What's wrong with me that I can't think rationally about this?!" Or, "I need to fix the way I think so I never do this again!" Or, "Why can't I just decide to be happy?"

That's not quite how the brain works.

Thinking errors are automatic, first-and-fast ways of thinking, so trying to think differently—more rationally, more positively—can feel second-and-slow. Still, the more often you practice it, the easier and more automatic it becomes.

One way to start is to do on paper (or on your phone) what I was doing in the moment with Paul: Write down your fear-based statements, then name the thinking error at work; then, replace those fears with some facts by asking yourself "What is?," as in "What are the facts?"

Or, train your brain to consider alternate ways of viewing things by asking yourself "What else?" "Nothing is as dangerous as an idea when it is the only one you have," said French philosopher Émile Chartier. So, ask yourself, "What else could be going on?" Or, "What else could I be saying to myself about this?"

All this comes more easily to some people, and in some situations, than to others, and occasionally medication is needed to help people do it at all. But, regardless, this process almost never feels natural or automatic to a twentysomething. Yet, the more practice we all have replacing fears with facts—or with alternate possibilities—the more we train our brains to do it on demand. And remember: Repetition is especially important for twentysomethings whose white matter is still wiring up. Each time we place the various parts of the brain in communication with one another, we make those lines of communication stronger.

Still, if dragging your mind, again and again, from fears to facts sounds like, well, a drag, consider it as a means, not an end. Putting your mind on something besides your worst-case scenarios or your worst interpretations doesn't just help you survive the moment. It also helps you get out of your head and into the world. That's where you collect more data points and more facts. That's where you learn more about what *is*.

Paul and I were running out of time.

"We need to decide what to do, Paul," I said with an eye on wrapping things up. "You walked in today because you felt out of control, like maybe you weren't okay or like you couldn't take your exam tonight. I can keep you here, if that's what you need to feel safe."

"I'm feeling better now," he interjected.

"Great," I said. "Still, you can skip your exam and get a note showing you were in the emergency department, if you feel like that's necessary . . ."

"No," he interrupted, "I think it would be good for me to take it."

"Agreed," I said. "The real cure for catastrophizing is competence. Every exam you get through will make you more confident about the next one. It's normal to feel really anxious before a big challenge. In those moments, it helps if you can remind yourself of tests or challenges that have gone well. Like you said, you need more facts. You need to know more about what *is*."

Paul and I made a plan to keep him out of his apartment and out of his default-mode network. He would go to the cafeteria to study and have dinner. If he started to catastrophize along the way, he would write down his fears and replace them with facts. Then, he would take his evening exam, after which he would go home, shower, and go to bed. We scheduled a follow-up appointment for the next morning, and I gave him the after-hours emergency number, just in case.

Of course, it occurred to me that Paul might fail his next exam— or imagine that he had—and perhaps do something to harm himself or someone else, as a result. That was my own catastrophizing, my own better-safe-than-sorry thinking. But based on our conversation, and on my own data points from years of working with young adults, I felt confident that he would make it through.

The next morning I was relieved, but not surprised, to see Paul in the waiting room. What did surprise me, however, was how different he looked with a smile on his face. As we walked down the hallway, he told me somewhat sheepishly that he had not, in fact, failed either of his exams and "all that catastrophizing was for nothing."

Maybe it wasn't for nothing, I suggested as we sat down together again. Maybe he'd learned something that would help him next time.

"Yeah," he said, still smiling. "Fears aren't facts."

Paul had three follow-up sessions. Every individual has their own default-mode way of thinking so, in those sessions, we talked a bit about where his particular what-ifs had come from.

In Paul's culture, he explained, being a doctor was the only route to "making it," and top scores were the only way to stay on that path. "Where I grew up," he said, "students were pitted against each other, and every test score was posted for everyone to see. Only a few people at the top were going to make it to medical school. It was very stressful, very scary. Nothing was ever enough. All I did in high school was work, and no one was a friend."

What Paul described sounded a lot like the way he was living now. Currently, Paul informed me, he studied nightly until three in the morning. Rather than attending lectures, he watched them from his apartment on Lecture Capture software at two times the normal speed. He spent hours preparing for tests that were graded pass/fail. He had not allowed himself to make a single friend in medical school: "We are all just competing for the same thing," he explained.

Paul's way of thinking (and living) might have made sense in high school or in Taiwan, I tried to explain, but perhaps—in medical school, in the United States, in adulthood—it no longer fit the situation. Now that he was at a top university, it was no longer true that only a few students would "make it"; most everyone could likely go on to enjoy success of some kind. I wondered aloud if worrying about As was still so necessary, as many classes were graded pass/fail. I pointed out that watching lectures at home might be faster, but it was interfering with his ability to connect with students and with professors who could help.

"I feel like my brain hasn't caught up to my situation," Paul said. "Like it just can't believe that what you're saying is true."

"You don't have to believe me," I said. "You're a scientist, so you can test out what I'm saying. Talk to other med students—talk to your professors—and see what *they* have to say."

"My mother called me last night," Paul said later, during our last session. "I finally told her I've been having a hard time and that I'd even seen a therapist about it. I expected her to be angry or just not get it. You know, she doesn't want to talk about mental health. But she told me that she really had a hard time in med school, too. She said she applied to med school more than once before she got in—*and* that she didn't get the residency she really wanted."

Paul paused to wipe his tears. "In all the years she's been talking to me about becoming a doctor, she's never told me that before," he reflected, his voice cracking a bit, "but that was the most helpful thing she's ever said."

SIX

HOW TO FEEL

Focus attention on the feeling inside you. Accept that it is there. Don't think about it. Don't make an identity for yourself out of it. Then see what happens.

—Eckhart Tolle, *The Power of Now*

"I had a screaming match on the sidewalk with my boyfriend," Katy began as a way of introducing herself to me. "Well, with a guy I thought was my boyfriend. But according to him, he's not. So, I got upset and made an ass of myself. In my defense, though not really, I'd had way too much to drink. Then I went home and cut a bit, which isn't great because that's something I haven't done in a while. That makes me nervous because things were better, but now they're not."

"Now they're not . . ." I repeated.

"I used to cut in high school," Katy went on. "I hadn't done it in a while, but now I'm waiting for a new job in D.C. to start, and I think maybe that's why I started this thing with this guy. Sometimes I think maybe I can't stand the waiting around, and I want the distraction and the drama. That's what the internet says. I was diagnosed with borderline personality disorder back when I was cutting. I didn't really know what it meant back then, but lately I've been seeing more about it online. I identify with it so much—all the videos about how, you know, you have no idea about how you're going to feel every day. If my skin looks good, then I feel good. Or if this guy texts me, then I feel good. But if this guy *doesn't* text me, then I feel bad. That's what people say borderline is."

The word *borderline* has a rather long and convoluted history in psychology, as does the diagnosis of borderline personality disorder. Nevertheless, *borderline personality disorder* generally refers to someone with unstable emotions, unstable relationships, and an unstable sense of self. Maybe, like Katy, she is quick to anger or tears (or both) but slow to calm down. Her relationships can be stormy, and she is sensitive to rejection. Her moods may shift with the weather, or her acne, or how she looks in the mirror, yet more often than she would like, she feels depressed, or anxious, or irritable, or bored. To keep things interesting, maybe she drinks too much or finds other risky things to do. When she gets really upset, maybe she even cuts herself.

I use the pronoun *she* because about 75 percent of those who are diagnosed with borderline personality disorder are female. (And, yes, there's a wealth of literature about the rather sexist nature of the diagnostic criteria.) Even so, it's estimated that true borderline personality disorder affects less than 1 percent of the population, which makes it quite rare. What isn't rare, however, are the young adults who present with borderline-like mental health complaints. Shifting identity? Changing relationships? Rollercoaster emotions? Poor coping skills? That pretty much sums up what it's like to be a teenager or a young adult who's just starting out in life.

"It's tough to feel settled on the inside when life isn't settled on the outside," I suggested to Katy, "but let's not get too hung up on diagnoses today."

Katy had been diagnosed with borderline personality disorder several years earlier, during a brief and frustrating stint at an in-patient hospital. Her parents dropped her off there the month before college, after a year of cutting after a breakup with a different guy. The scattered scars—still slightly visible when her sleeves rode up on her forearms—served as permanent physical reminders of temporary emotional pain.

"I wound up in the hospital," Katy explained, "because I was on, like, ten different drugs in a year, and one of the antidepressants made me manic. At first, they thought I was bipolar, but that went away when they changed my medication, so they settled on saying I was border-line."

"Why were you on so many medications?"

"I kept telling my doctor my medication wasn't working, and then I'd get a different prescription or a higher dose of something."

"What did you mean by 'not working'?"

"The meds weren't making me happy, and I felt all this pressure to be happy. 'When you're unhappy, I'm unhappy,' my mom always says. She panics when I'm unhappy or upset."

We live in a culture, and Katy lived in a family, that fetishizes happiness. When feeling good is the highest good, we feel anxious about being anxious, stressed about being stressed, sad about being sad, and so on. That's a problem, especially for young adults whose jobs and schools, and relationships and cities, and friends come and go. It's no wonder that young adults are more likely to feel angry and anxious, and sad and bored, and irritated and frustrated than their older future selves. What is a wonder is why we expect them to be so darn happy.

"I just felt all this pressure for college to be great," Katy went on. "My mom was always talking about how great college was for her. And I was feeling anxious about it not being great. And now I feel all this pressure from social media, from the world, for my *life* to be great."

"Maybe it will be," I said.

"You don't know that," Katy said.

"No, I don't," I said. "No one does. And maybe that's part of what you're having trouble with."

She looked at me blankly.

"Let's think about this," I said puzzling it out. "You cut some just before college started . . ."

"Yeah."

"Then you didn't for a few years . . . until recently."

"This time it was more like scratching, but yeah."

"Okay, so why now?"

"This thing with this guy," Katy began. "I don't know why that upset me so much. I knew he wasn't really available when I started up with him, but I wasn't expecting him to dump me so suddenly."

"So, both times some kind of breakup was involved?"

"Well, yeah, but I've had other breakups in between, and I never went crazy."

"Okay, so why then and why now?" I asked again.

"Both times I was about to move and start something new—you know, school and a job—and that makes me feel anxious. I feel sick to my stomach not knowing how it's going to go," she explained. "I mean, I'm still on two meds, and I don't expect them to make me happy anymore, but I don't know . . . I thought my twenties were supposed to be fun. Like, these are supposed to be the best years of my life, but that's not what it feels like to me at all."

Let's clear something up. Contrary to what popular culture and social media may suggest, your twenties are probably not going to be the best years of your life—at least not emotionally. These may (or may not) be the years when you look your best, but they're unlikely to be the years when you *feel* your best. In fact, statistically speaking, your twenties are likely to be the years when you feel your worst.

As we already know, when we are feeling uncertain, negative thoughts tend to be "first and fast." Somewhat similarly, negative emotions are likely to feel, as I tell my clients, "strong and long." Uncertainty makes our emotions feel more intense, so compared to other, more settled times of life, our bad feelings are more powerful and long-lasting, which can make young adulthood not as fun as we thought it would be.

"If these turn out to be the best years of your life," I said to Katy, "then something has gone terribly wrong."

"Don't peak in your twenties," she paraphrased, with a laugh.

"That's right," I laughed back, noticing how likable—and how unlike someone with a personality disorder—Katy actually was. "Life is supposed to get better as you go."

One of my favorite studies on how life gets better looked at the everyday emotions of a diverse sample of nearly two hundred adults, ranging in age from 18 to 94. At random times throughout the week, each participant was asked to report on a variety of positive feelings, such as happiness, contentment, pride, excitement, interest, accomplishment, and amusement. Then they were asked to report on negative ones such as anger, fear, sadness, anxiety, irritability, frustration, and boredom.

The good news—for our future selves, anyway—is that there were no age effects for positive feelings. Older adults felt good about as often as younger adults, albeit maybe sometimes for different reasons. Younger adults might have been excited about a new apartment or an upcoming music festival, while maybe older adults were excited about a new grandchild or a trip to Australia. Whatever the case, good moments were enjoyed just as frequently—and just as intensely—across all ages and stages.

Not so much for negative feelings, though. Compared to older adults, younger adults were more likely to experience all sorts of ways of feeling bad. The frequency of negative emotions declined in a linear fashion across adulthood until around age 60, when there was a slight uptick. By far, however, 18- to 34-year-olds had the most bad moments and the most bad days.

Surely related to this outcome is that, compared to young adults, older adults in the study seemed better able to regulate their feelings. Their positive states hung around longer and their negative feelings passed more quickly. They were also more likely to report mixed feelings or moments when the good and the bad could coexist. For young adults, however, their bad feelings were more likely to outweigh, outlast, or overwhelm their good feelings.

Researchers in this and similar studies have concluded that, overall, life gets better as we age, in large part because we have more control over our emotions and over our lives. Work. Money. Friends. Love. Purpose. Time. Habits. We are more apt, and more able, to choose our situations wisely by selecting people and activities that make us feel better, not worse. And when our situations do go sideways, our negative emotions don't feel as strong, and they don't last as long. All this takes practice and perspective, which are two things young adults like Katy may not have—yet.

That doesn't mean they have a personality disorder.

In recent years, the number of young adults who think they're borderline has trended upward, just as the age at which young people are being diagnosed with the disorder has trended downward—a troubling shift that goes against what having a personality disorder is supposed to mean. By definition, *personality* is an enduring and consistent pattern of thoughts, feelings, and behaviors—an individual way of living that makes us "who we are." So, when we tell someone they have a personality disorder, we're suggesting that who they are is abnormal or unwell. Because of this, as Katy found out via Google, personality disorders are often seen as resistant to change and as difficult, if not impossible, to treat.

"So, *now* what am I supposed to do?" she wanted to know.

Historically, personality disorders were not diagnosed in those under 18, mostly because teen personalities were seen as still forming. How can we say someone's personality is disordered if it is not yet ordered? Now, however, according to the *DSM*, borderline personality disorder can be diagnosed in children or teens as long as the symptoms last for more than a year and are "pervasive, persistent, and unlikely to be limited to a particular developmental stage."

That last part—"unlikely to be limited to a particular developmental stage"—is why I still don't diagnose personality disorders in those under age 18. Nor do I diagnose them in clients under age 30. Not enough people know that our personalities change more in our twenties than at any other time in adult life. This is why I assume that much of what I see in my clients, especially much of what is problematic, *is* limited to a developmental stage—their twenties—and part of my job is to help make it so. Because I work with young people, I am in the business of *preventing* personality disorders, not diagnosing them.

Despite the long-held view that "borderlines" are lifers, recent research shows that those with the diagnosis do get better—and stay better—within about five years' time. Symptoms typically emerge in the teen and early adult years, but then they lessen with treatment, or life experience, or maturity. Impulsive acting out becomes less common. Interpersonal problems improve as problem-solving improves. Difficult emotions are not so strong and long.

Five years may sound like a long time to wait, but that's about how long it takes for some young adults' lives to settle down and for their brains and bodies to settle down, too. That's also about how long a developmental stage lasts. Besides, five years is a much shorter time than forever, which is how long many young adults—and their parents—are told personality disorders may last.

"Life can change, and you can, too," I explained to Katy, who was sure she couldn't be helped because the internet said so. "If you're still having drunken shouting matches on the sidewalk when you're forty, then, yes, maybe at that point you have a personality disorder. But you're not there yet. Let's not go labeling yourself for life."

Rather than diagnose someone with borderline personality disorder, I prefer to focus on the skills they may be lacking. And a big one, for Katy and for many other twentysomethings, is the ability to live with uncertainty and all the feelings it produces.

Perhaps not surprisingly, the staff at the hospital had once tried to teach Katy how to do just that. What was surprising, at least to her, was that they did so by having her concentrate on an apple: how it looked, how it smelled, how it felt, how it tasted. It's a classic mindfulness technique, the usefulness of which was lost on Katy. To communicate that, she told me, she'd thrown the apple against the wall. "What does a fucking apple have to do with getting my boyfriend back?!" she half-shouted at me as she recounted her stay.

Mindfulness interventions don't bring boyfriends back, of course. And they don't keep us from having tough times. Instead, they can help us get *through* tough times—like breakups and breakdowns—without hurting ourselves. Typically, they involve techniques, such as focusing on our breath or an apple, that bring our attention to the present moment. In doing so, they keep us from future tripping and time traveling. "None of your problems are here in this room," a yoga teacher crooned in a mindfulness training session I once attended.

Although I assume the folks at the hospital explained all this to Katy, I took a more brain-oriented approach. I told her about the default-mode and the task-positive networks: "I'm guessing what they were trying to do was show you how to get your mind off what was upsetting you by putting your mind *on* something else," I explained. "The apple."

"That's *dumb*," she said, still unconvinced.

"Actually, it's not that different from what you were doing with the razor blades," I explained. "When people cut themselves, they take all that scattered emotional pain they're feeling and they replace it with concrete, focused, physical pain—something they can treat, and bandage, and *do* something about. They give themselves an urgent and immediate task. Maybe apples aren't for you. But cutting can't be the way, either."

"So, what *am* I supposed to do?" she still wanted to know.

It was a fair question.

The word *emotion* comes from the Latin word *emovere*, which means "to move out" or "to agitate." It's fitting, because the evolutionary purpose of emotion is to spur action of some kind. And, especially when we're feeling uncertain, there can be a kind of urgency to do something *right now*. Self-injurers, and young adults in general, have less confidence in their ability to problem-solve, so when they feel bad, they're apt to thrash about feeling helpless and unsure of what to do.

So, I told Katy, when you're feeling uncertain, do something else—do *anything* else—besides hurt yourself somehow. Take a cold shower. Phone a friend. Walk around the block. Watch a show. Listen to music. Run an errand. Write in your journal. Figure out what works for you, but remember: Uncertainty can feel intense, but almost nothing is ever as good or

HOW TO FEEL ~ 81

as bad as we think it is, nor do our good or bad feelings last as long as we expect them to last.

Even just knowing that can help feelings pass.

A few years ago, I told Katy, I took a small group of young adults to a Zen center in Japan. There, in an understated fifteenth-century Buddhist temple, thin, sliding rice paper screens served as walls separating us from the damp, cloudy day outside. Our teacher was a reverend—a revered monk—who began the morning by leading us in a silent mindfulness meditation as we sat cross-legged on cushions on the floor. Our only instructions were to close our eyes and focus on our breath.

After a few minutes that felt like a few hours, the reverend rang a small bell and asked us how it was. One person said they were cold. Another person said their nose itched. Someone else said their back hurt, and they couldn't stop thinking about their ex-girlfriend. Most everyone felt annoyed they couldn't just clear their minds and be at peace, like (they thought) they were supposed to be.

"Why do you want to learn to be more mindful?" the reverend asked as a sort of friendly challenge.

A chorus of responses rang out:

"I want to be less stressed."

"I want to be happier."

"I have anxiety, and I want to calm down."

"A lot of people in the West," the reverend began with a bemused smile, "they use meditation as a pain reliever. But that's like taking aspirin. It might dull your pain, but it doesn't fix your problem. Sitting still and breathing are good for you, but they are not the same thing as being mindful."

My students were more or less stunned. Most, I think, were expecting some age-old wisdom about how they could feel good pretty much all the time. I, however, was nodding my head.

As the reverend spoke, I thought about college counseling centers and community clinics and office buildings around the country—places where mindfulness apps are routinely prescribed for nearly every stressed or anxious twentysomething who walks through the door. Like the newest stationary bike, it seems, such apps are helpful only if you use them regularly, which in my experience most people don't. Those who do are often dismayed that the apps don't quickly banish their bad feelings.

Discomfort is a part of life, the reverend went on to say. Maybe that discomfort is an itchy nose, or back pain, or a broken heart. Mindfulness is not about getting rid of discomfort; it is about accepting discomfort.

"Let's try it," the reverend said. "Don't try to feel at peace. Don't try to feel calm or happy. Just be aware of whatever it is you feel. Don't try to push it away. Don't try to cleanse it with your breath. There's nothing dirty about what you feel."

Quite unexpectedly, when we let our uncomfortable feelings just be, our noses were less itchy, our backs didn't hurt so much, and people's exes didn't hang around as long in their minds. This is what's called a *paradoxical intervention* because accepting our feelings—even the painful or unwelcome ones—without trying to avoid or suppress them can help us feel better, not worse. That might sound unlikely, but neurologically, it makes sense. In fact, MRI research shows—literally—that when we accept how we feel, there is less activity in the amygdala, that smoke detector part of the brain. We experience less fear, less pain, and less avoidance, and our heart rate lowers, as we don't feel so alarmed by how we feel.

Fortunately, you don't have to be a Buddhist to be more accepting, and it doesn't require apps, meditating, sitting cross-legged on a cushion, or even apples. In fact, while the concept of acceptance might sound very, well, Zen, accepting something as a normal part of life is what psychologists call *normalizing*. Normalizing is simply recognizing that something we're experiencing is common and expectable, rather than abnormal, or unacceptable, or bad.

In a 2018 study with a diverse group of more than a thousand young adults, those who saw their feelings as normal—just noticing and observing them without labeling them as good or bad—experienced lower levels of depression and anxiety, as well as higher levels of well-being and satisfaction.

Ironically, those who made normalizing a habit experienced fewer bad feelings in day-to-day stressful situations related to work and love.

Yet, accepting our feelings isn't the same thing as accepting our situations. In fact, normalizing is associated with enhanced problem-solving because when we're less afraid of our feelings, we feel more able to handle whatever we face. In another 2018 study, this one of nearly three hundred young adults, about half were given brief mindfulness training and the other half were not. Six years later, despite not having much kept up with their practice, those who had been exposed to acceptance were less likely to avoid their problems and more likely to try to solve them.

As I told all this to Katy, she listened skeptically. "I still don't see how any of this would have solved my two breakups," she challenged.

"I guess it depends on what you mean by *solve*," I said.

"The best treatment for anxiety and depression from a pending house foreclosure is renegotiating the mortgage," say two preeminent psychologists in a paper about evolution and emotion. "However, most pathological emotions arise from brains interacting with problems that have no ready solution." I take issue with the word *pathological*, but other than that, I could not agree more with this statement. The most vexing problems we face as adults are problems that have no ready solution and no quick fix.

"The solution to your love life may not be getting one of those boyfriends back," I explained to Katy.

"Probably not," she agreed.

"Problem-solving is one of the best ways to calm down, but who to love is a problem that may take some time to solve. You can make progress, but it can be months or years before you get to see the outcome. In the meantime, you're going to live with uncertainty around that, and it may not always feel good. But that's normal."

"I always want the perfect solution to every problem when I'm feeling bad," Katy observed after thinking awhile. "But I guess what you're saying is that a lot of my problems are just things I don't like or things that haven't been resolved yet."

I couldn't have said it better myself.

"I've got a list in my wallet of five things I can do besides cut myself when I'm feeling bad," Katy told me in our last in-person session before she headed to Washington, D.C.

"Your skills can come with you wherever you go," I affirmed.

"Sometimes I think I should stay here and get completely better before I go anywhere," she said, backtracking a bit. "But then I get worried that I *do* have a personality disorder, and I can't change, like this is who I *am*."

"Your personality can change—and it will change—because everything else about your life is changing, including your brain. But none of this is going to happen overnight or just because you're seeing me."

"So, what else can I *do*?" she asked, still wanting to problem-solve—and right now.

"Go start your new job," I said. "The best thing you can do to feel better is to get to work."

More on Katy in the next chapter.

SEVEN

HOW TO WORK

Getting up. Sitting down. Going back to work. Might not help. But still it couldn't hurt.

—Bo Burnham, *Inside*

The single biggest driver of positive personality change in adulthood is work. Across our twenties and thirties, we become more emotionally stable as we age, and believe it or not, we largely have our jobs to thank.

In a 2013 study of nearly 900,000 young adults from sixty-two countries around the world, work played a stronger role—even stronger than becoming a partner or a parent—in helping citizens feel more agreeable, more responsible, and more settled. And in countries in which work started earlier, young adults enjoyed these benefits earlier, too. Perhaps this is because, despite cultural variations in what being a partner or a parent may require, around the globe, work is work. Day in and day out, no matter the occupation, there are structured demands and structured rewards, and there are skills we must learn and master.

So, that thing we spend about half our waking hours doing—or not doing—has an outsize impact on who we are and who we become. That's why I won't work with young adults who don't have a job or who aren't willing to get one. Being unemployed or underemployed when we're young doesn't help us feel happy or healthy, and neither does being broke or dependent on our parents. Work forces growth and change in a way that few of us can accomplish on our own, or even with our therapists. Sure, we might all need to take a so-called mental health day once in a while, but showing up for work is, in fact, good for us—and maybe even better for us than anything else.

That's what I said to Katy—over Zoom—not long after she'd moved closer to that job in Washington, D.C.

Virtual sessions, especially with twentysomethings, are a whole new way of "meeting people where they are," as my clients don't bother to arrange themselves in front of tasteful backgrounds, nor do they care much about the lighting or their hair. "I can't even think about starting work next week," Katy said, looking a bit disheveled. "I've got so much to do this week. My mind was racing just thinking about it, so I made all these lists."

She held up sheets of paper with scribbles and scrawls, and it scrambled my brain even seeing them from afar.

"I've gotta get a parking permit for my new neighborhood. I've got stuff to take to the consignment place. I've got to find a vet for my cat," she read from one piece of paper before shifting her attention to another. "Oh, and here's a big-picture list for the stuff I feel like I need to understand, like taxes or cryptocurrency."

"Wait, why do you need to understand cryptocurrency?" I asked, trying to slow Katy down.

It didn't work.

"Check out all the things I'm not getting to just today," she pressed as she ignored my question and held up yet another list. "I don't know how starting a job on top of all this is going to help."

"I think you're spending too much time in your head, which is not always such a great place to be," I interrupted. "Work, I think, is exactly what you need."

There are lots of ways to shift our brains out of the default-mode network, but perhaps the most productive way is to go to work. To have an occupation—to be *occupied*—means to be busy and active, and this engages the task-positive network. When we have a job, we spend six, or eight, or ten hours a day working on tasks and problems, and this alone can be good for our mental health.

"Work is kind of like putting your mind on the apple . . ." I started to explain.

"Don't get me started on that fucking apple," Katy interrupted only somewhat in jest.

"But it's better than that," I added with a laugh. "Ideally, when you go to work you aren't just distracting yourself. You're also learning things, and you're earning identity capital, and that changes who you are."

I consider myself a sort of middleman. A big part of my job, as a therapist and as an educator and a writer, is to introduce people to information or concepts that might change how they think, or feel, or act. Most of the time, these concepts are not mine. They are the product of other scientists' hard work (and, please, look at the endnotes at the back of the book to learn and read more). I just happen to know the research and am well acquainted with a population—twentysomethings—that would benefit from knowing it, too.

One of the most popular concepts I've talked about to young adults is something called *identity capital*. This term refers to the things we've done that add value to the person we are. It is how we have invested in ourselves not just as professionals but as people, too. The most concrete way to think about identity capital is to consider what goes on a résumé—educational degrees, test scores, GPAs, previous jobs, club memberships, hobbies and talents, languages we speak, personal and professional accolades—but it can also refer to our interesting or important experiences or qualities. As a twentysomething, time is your most valuable resource, and identity capital is what you have to show for how you've spent your days and your years so far.

Sometimes, however, I think twentysomethings misunderstand identity capital, viewing it as something that makes a good story or that makes them look or sound good. But let's be clear: What actually makes identity capital valuable—to yourself or to anyone else—are the skills it implies you have. According to economists at the U.S. Federal Reserve, data from about 5 million workers followed across a forty-year span suggest the more skilled you become in young adulthood, the more you can expect your earnings to grow and grow over time, rather than stagnate. So, your learning curve in your twenties predicts your earning curve in your thirties and beyond—and it's not just about the money.

In a 2022 study of 3,000 employees from different industries, 83 percent of workers of all ages said that gaining skills was one of their top priorities. And 74 percent of young workers surveyed said they would leave their jobs if they didn't have adequate skill-building or growth opportunities—as they should. Workers imagine that having more skills will not only lead to higher incomes but also afford them a better work-life balance, more meaningful leadership opportunities, and greater purpose over time. And they're right. The more we learn—and keep learning—at work, the more competence, the more options, the more mobility, the more connections, and the more certainty we keep gaining, too.

According to the chaos theory of careers, twenty-first-century work will forever be uncertain, changing, unpredictable, and boundaryless. No one can plan for recessions, or pandemics, or inflation, or wars, or technological advances, or downsizing. What we can do, however, is acquire skills that no person or circumstance can take away. Remember that, on average, young workers will have about nine jobs by the age of 35. Most ultimately wind up in positions, careers, or specialties they never knew existed—or that maybe *didn't* exist—when they were in their twenties. So, whatever your current job might happen to be, your real job as a twentysomething is to get out there and get some skills. Personal, professional, and financial—and even emotional—stability comes from having identity capital that is transportable across jobs or locations; these are skills you can take with you into the future as your jobs come and go.

And jobs will come and go.

• • •

"I don't feel better at all. I feel like really, really anxious," Katy said somewhat accusingly a few weeks into her new job.

"I said work would be good for you," I clarified. "I didn't say it would feel good all the time."

"It is good to have somewhere to be every day and, you're right, it is better not to hang around in my apartment all the time," she said, softening a bit. "But the whole first week I had to leave for work an hour early because I wasn't sure about how the Metro would work out, and I was still late a couple of times. Then once I'm at work, there are all these things I don't know how to do. I can't figure out if I'm supposed to ask people or figure it out for myself. It's *stressful*!"

Work may be the biggest driver of growth in adulthood, yet it is also the leading cause of stress in adulthood, too. That may sound like a contradiction, but it's not. Growth and stress often go together because if we are going to learn how to do new things, we have to engage with things we don't yet know how to do. New contexts, such as new jobs or new workplaces, decrease confidence in the short run. They make us anxious and, in doing so, they increase attention and learning. And paying attention and learning is how we increase confidence in the long run.

"I was in a bagel shop the other day," I told Katy, "and there was a high school student who was training on the cash register. Everyone else in the store was going about their jobs like they could do it all in their sleep, and I'm sure they could because it wasn't their first day. But this poor kid looked so stressed and anxious, and he was watching his co-worker work the register like he was watching brain surgery. My heart went out to him, but I also knew he was learning. This is what learning looks like and feels like sometimes."

"I don't even have a key card," Katy went on. "So, every time I need to go in or out of the office, like out to the bathroom by the elevators, I have to ask someone to open the door. I feel like a fake employee, like a total imposter. I actually just spent the last hour reading all these posts about imposter syndrome. I totally have that."

Imposter syndrome isn't a real disorder, of course. It's a pop-culture malady that shows up a lot online, and I told Katy as much. "Imposter syndrome has a catchy name, and people identify with it, so it makes for some good clickbait," I conceded. "But I think that's the wrong way to understand what's going on."

She stared at me blankly.

"Let me ask you this: What do you think you're pretending to be?"

"Somebody who knows what they're doing."

"Well then, stop," I said. "No one expects young workers to know everything. In fact, employers don't expect them to know much of anything. Everyone knows you're there to learn. Or, at least they hope you are. So, stop pretending about what you do know, and start leaning into what you don't know. Lean into the uncertainty, and out yourself as someone who wants to learn."

I didn't do everything right in my twenties. But one smart thing I managed to do was to use graduate school as a place to learn as much as I could while I wasn't the one in charge. I asked for the hardest clients. I tried out different types of therapy. I had supervisors watch videotapes of my sessions (despite how embarrassing that was). I taught new classes. I worked in different labs. I wrote articles for different kinds of journals. I surrounded myself with the smartest classmates and co-workers I could find. I used uncertainty to my advantage, and that's how I got better at what I was doing. That's how I figured out what I liked and what I was good at. That's how, eventually, I became sure of myself and of who I am.

"I just wish I could work from home," Katy moaned a few months later.

"There's a default mode in your brain," I told Katy, "but there's also a default mode in your life. It's what you revert to when you don't have to get out and do something else. I think you need to stay out of your head *and* out of your house."

There's no one-size-fits-all, but especially for young workers, I caution against working from home full time. Of course, there are upsides: No commute! Better food! No annoying chit-chat! More freedom and flexibility! But, as with anything else, there are downsides, too: No boundaries between work time and free time. Less in-person interaction with colleagues and the world. Less physical movement. (Sure, some people may be using that reclaimed commuting time to run five miles a day, but most of us aren't.)

The data are only just coming in, but one of the first large studies of working from home suggests that remote workers miss out on what researchers call the *power of proximity*. Previously, the purported upsides of being physically close to one's co-workers have been difficult to quantify. Who you're in the building with impacts who you grab coffee with and who you bump into in the hall, people say. Or, we hear that seeing people face to face puts you on their radar, while being remote can keep you out of sight and out of mind. In this recent study, however, researchers were able to measure how being in the building with one's colleagues affects the feedback workers receive.

This 2022 study looked at software engineers, or workers whose jobs would presumably lend themselves quite nicely to being remote. Yet, even for them, the power of proximity played a role. Engineers who worked in the building received about 20 percent more feedback on their code than those who worked somewhere else. And this tendency to receive more comments, and more substantive comments, when being there in person was especially true for young workers. That is, young engineers who physically showed up for work—and who presumably had the most to learn—were likely to receive the most, and most useful, input of all.

Feedback matters because, according to data from the National Bureau of Economic Research, nearly two-thirds of on-the-job learning—and almost one-fourth of our total identity capital—comes from co-workers. And it's not just engineers. Studies show that when various professionals—such as inventors, teachers, and salespeople—are able to learn from more senior colleagues, they do better down the line. So, young worker, put yourself in a position to learn as much as you can from the people around and above you—even if this means showing up to an office at least some of the time.

Remote work may be a recent revolution, but wanting to get out of working in an office is nothing new. Working from home may be comfortable and convenient—like wearing sweatpants and like being in school—but, for those same reasons, it is not always conducive to growth. Getting out in the world and going in to work exposes you to more people and more situations and more feedback—especially the sorts that you may not choose or think of yourself—right when your career, and your brain, might benefit most. But, likely, that will mean doing work that is uncomfortable and inconvenient at least some of the time.

Still, to be transparent, I've been working from a home office for almost twenty years—though never exclusively. If, every day, I saw clients only in my private practice, my world would be pretty small. If, every week, I was the smartest person in the room, I wouldn't learn much. That's why I always make sure I'm working with a diverse group of colleagues and young adults from around the globe. I supervise in community clinics. I cover shifts in student health centers. I teach on study-abroad programs. I give talks at corporations and conferences. I go on podcasts. Sure, all those things are less comfortable and convenient than heading out to a coffee shop in my jeans to write. But new and different experiences give me new and different ideas. Hearing a wide variety of people's perspectives and questions—especially the ones I'm not expecting—is how I improve my work.

I should also say that I am in a position to do hybrid work from home—or from my laptop, or a coffee shop, or abroad in other countries—as much as I do because I wasn't able to do that when I was younger. The skills I often begrudgingly gained in the workplace then are what give me the know-how to be a free agent now. Without a doubt, working from home at least some of the time is a more forgiving, humane, and family-friendly way to do your job. But while young people usually don't have toddlers or sick kids at home, now is the time to get out there and learn how to work—probably from other people *at work*—as much as you can.

•   •   •

That's what Katy was trying to do when the company she worked for folded, about two years after she first rode the Metro there. "I've got a list for what I need to do to find another job," she said, getting organized again. "It's all a lot less overwhelming this time around; I need to update my résumé and send it to a few people, but it only has one job on it so it feels a little thin. Like I only know how to do one thing."

"You may have had only one job, but I'm not sure you're giving yourself credit for all the things you learned. You use lists to organize the outside world. What if you made a list to organize your inner world?" I suggested as we signed off from Zoom. "What if you made a list of everything you learned how to do at work?"

As only a twentysomething can, Katy thumb-typed this text in a matter of minutes:

> How to get up at the same time every day
> How to dress for meetings
> How to figure out breakfast
> How to get out of the house with all my stuff for the day
> How to ride the Metro and get somewhere on time
> How to sit down and start working even when I don't feel like it
> How to deal with clients
> How to handle difficult personalities and work drama
> How to be more comfortable on the phone
> How to work as part of a team
> How to make small talk on Zoom
> How to stay motivated after getting passed up for a promotion
> How to have conversations with my boss about my career
> How to network with people who aren't on my team
> How to keep doing my job while having boy problems
> How to say no when I've got too much on my plate
> How to manage my time
> How to run a meeting

How to live alone

How to stop saying "please" and "sorry" so much

How to coordinate with people in different time zones

How to set "hard stops" for meetings

How to mentor an intern

How to set up my monitor

How to set boundaries with colleagues who overshare (and want me
 to overshare)

How to not snap at my boss or my co-workers

How to do work emails

How to report to my boss and be part of a larger organization

How to write reports and proposals

How to manage deadlines

How having a good boss can make such a difference

How to ask for help

How to ask for time off

How to interview for new positions

How to balance so many different things at once

Still working on this one, but how to organize

How to speak up in a meeting and give presentations

How to give and get feedback

How to describe myself on a résumé or on LinkedIn

How to stick with something for eight hours a day

How to wait an hour before I respond to an email that makes my
 heart race

Still working on this one, too, but how to go to sleep without
 stressing about work

How to realize it's not the end of the world if something blows up at
 work (or if the whole company blows up)

It's a long list, I know, but other young workers—and employers out there—need to see it. I think we forget how much young workers are learning—or should be learning—on the job.

"I'm curious," I said the next time I spoke with Katy. "If you were talking to other young workers about your how-tos, *how* exactly would you say you learned how to do them? People often ask me questions like, 'What are the steps?'"

"I'd say watching other people and trying things," she offered up right away. "Getting things wrong the first time and then fixing them. I don't know how else you *could* learn."

Indeed.

"Making that list was really eye-opening," Katy reflected some time later. "It made me realize that I've spent a lot of time in my life making a big deal about all the uncertainty out in the world, when the biggest uncertainty was *me*. I really had to confront myself about where all the crazy was coming from a while back. I was pointing fingers at being borderline or anxious—well, I *was* anxious—but I was anxious because of all the stuff I didn't know how to do. I was avoiding all the things I didn't know how to do instead of just learning how to do those things. I didn't want to face how feeble and inadequate I felt."

I kept listening.

"I guess now that I don't feel quite as feeble, I can say it all out loud," she continued. "Maybe I can't put my whole how-to list on my résumé, but it still makes me feel better about finding another job. I feel more, I don't know, *real* as a worker. And as a person. Making progress at work feels like proof that my life will work out—that it will be okay—in a way that school never did. It even makes me think that I can eventually get off the medication I'm still on. I want to have kids one day, and I don't want to be on meds when I'm pregnant. That's a ways off but, it's weird, just feeling better about work, I feel better about dating and just being more social in general."

It wasn't weird at all. What Katy was talking about is why work is the leading driver of positive personality change and emotional stability in young people. It's because forty hours a week of surviving uncertainty at work helps us survive unknowns everywhere else. It's because showing up for work helps us show up for other new things in life. And it's because the skills we learn aren't just ones we take from job to job. They are the building blocks of competence we take with us everywhere—from relationship to relationship and from room to room—as we try to be, not just workers but also parents, and partners, and people, and friends.

EIGHT

HOW TO BE SOCIAL

I'm sick of not having the courage to be an absolute nobody. I'm sick
of myself and everybody else that wants to make some kind of splash.

—J. D. Salinger, *Franny and Zooey*

I am worried other people don't like me.

As of 2023, according to an ongoing, nationwide study of the mental health of college students, this is the single, fastest-rising concern
among young adults. Not far behind are feeling self-conscious around
other people, having trouble making friends easily, being uncomfortable
around other people, feeling anxious about public speaking, and feeling shy.

Somewhat unfortunately, these concerns are used as indicators of social anxiety disorder, the fastest-rising mental health complaint among
young adults. As we already know, social anxiety is a fear of social situations in which we might be evaluated or judged. Whether it's talking at a
party, going out on a date, interviewing for a job, giving a presentation,
playing pickleball, or making a phone call, social anxiety is worrying that
we'll say or do something embarrassing, or that we'll show symptoms of
anxiety, like sweating or shaking.

I say "unfortunately" because at the heart of social anxiety is the common and normal experience of social *uncertainty*—or, not feeling sure of how an encounter will go or how you'll come across. Almost everyone worries about being liked sometimes, so social anxiety is best thought of as a bell curve. At one end are people whose worries are crippling, while at the other end are those who don't seem concerned at all about what others think. In the middle, more than half of young adults are estimated to have at least moderate social anxiety that will, in general, get better with age.

Consider this meme a colleague sent me: "When you're twenty, you care what everyone thinks about you. When you're forty, you stop caring what everyone thinks about you. When you're sixty, you realize no one was ever thinking about you in the first place." So, age 40 or 60 can be a nice place to be.

But not necessarily. Social anxiety is still the third most common mental health diagnosis among older adults. The first and second most common are depression and alcohol abuse—and, sometimes, these three problems are related. Anxiety about being around other people can make us feel hopeless and sad, and that can lead us to avoid activities that might make us feel better. Or, our fears can cause us to stay home and drink, or to drink in order to brave going out. In fact, those with social anxiety are two to three times more likely to have problems with alcohol. So, how we handle social uncertainty in our twenties matters.

Although social uncertainty is common in both women and men, social anxiety is one of the few mental health concerns for which men are more likely to seek treatment. Here are five twentysomethings who came to my office for help:

Jonah started taking antidepressants for social anxiety when he was in college. "I used to start sweating when I talked to people at parties, so I'd pregame to be less anxious. But then I'd wake up the next morning with the worst hangxiety. Being hungover definitely makes my anxiety worse.

It was pretty bad, so I went on meds, and it shut down my symptoms, but it kind of shut me down, too. I stopped caring about what other people thought, but I also became brutally unmotivated at my first job, and I don't think I've achieved as much as I might have. I'd say my social anxiety is better, but I still feel very self-conscious about work."

"How so?" I asked.

"In college, I couldn't stop comparing myself to other people on Facebook. Everybody always seemed to be having a better time than me," Jonah explained. "Now, I'm doing the exact same thing on LinkedIn. Now, it just seems like everybody has a better job."

Isabelle had been a top student in high school and college, so she was used to knowing where she stood with her peers. In her twenties, however, she was not so sure. "I get hung up on whether some comment I made in a meeting or something was stupid. Or, I think, with all the advantages I have had in life, I should be doing better than I am, or I should have something better to say," she said. "I need to know people think I'm funny and smart, and social media, with likes or shares, is an easy way to monitor that. I need my self-worth to be tangible. Unless I see it confirmed externally, I won't trust it. I need the proof."

"Do you get it?" I asked. "The proof?"

"For a while," Isabelle said. "But I'm only as good as the last good thing I posted on Twitter."

Cruz was a student of mine who always sat apart from everyone else in class. He slid in and out of the last row with his earbuds in, signaling to other people he had no interest in talking or listening. So, I was surprised when he came to my office one day and asked for help. "I think I have social anxiety," he began. "There's a graduate student in the lab where I work who I'm supposed to have coffee with. I look away when I pass her in the hall. It's really getting bad. I can't initiate anything with anyone. I want to connect with people, but I don't know *how*."

"You initiated something with me," I replied, pleasantly surprised by how likable Cruz was once he started talking.

"No offense," Cruz said with a shy smile, "but you don't count."

Trina wore a face mask to her therapy sessions. "My acne is bad, so I don't want anybody to see my face," she explained through tears. "I have some friends, but I've been avoiding them because I feel like I look worse than I used to. A lot of days I just sit in bed and watch TikTok."

"Let's get you a dermatology consult," I said. "And let's get you out of bed and off your phone. Do any of your friends know what's going on?"

"I haven't told anybody," Trina explained. "A therapist is trained to say the right things, but you never know what other people are going to say."

Sam said he lost his confidence after he and his girlfriend broke up. "I have a lot more time on my hands now that I'm single again. I never know if somebody wants to hang out, so I wait for them to reach out to me. If I do go out, I don't know where I stand with people. The other guys always seem to have cooler shoes. They have funnier stories and better lines. They all seem to be in this awesome friend group, and I'm on the outside."

"How do you know?" I asked.

"I see them all texting each other," Sam said. "They're all on this group chat, and I'm not. I mean, why am I the only one not on the chat?"

"It's normal to feel left out, especially when you're in your twenties," I said. "But that doesn't mean what you're thinking is true."

"Yeah," Sam said, seeming disappointed by my professional opinion. "That's what my mom says, too."

In a 2005 television interview about this new thing called Facebook, a 21-year-old, baby-faced and nervous-looking Mark Zuckerberg dressed down in a T-shirt that read, "My mom thinks I'm cool." It was an ironic choice, really, for the man who was launching what would become the first worldwide social media platform. With Facebook, what Zuckerberg presumably knew—and perhaps was banking on—is that what our parents think gets us only so far in life. In our teens and beyond, what our *peers* think matters most. That unalterable reality is why, two decades later, social media is now the world's most widespread evolutionary trap.

An *evolutionary trap* is when a modern invention hijacks an ancient instinct—and not in a good way. Baby sea turtles leave their nests in the sand and walk toward the bright lights on beachfront homes, rather than toward the moonlight on the ocean. Albatrosses mistake pieces of brightly colored plastic in the ocean for their prey. Humans overindulge in sugary, salty, fatty foods that were once hard to come by but are now available everywhere. "Bad choices look like good ones," say scientists about such traps, "and animals are lured into an evolutionary dead end."

The ancient instinct that social media hijacks is our need to be liked. Because we have an evolutionary imperative to survive and reproduce, we have a fundamental drive to seek the shelter and comfort of others. In childhood, safety and belonging mean being part of a family, but in the teen years and beyond, our attention turns outward, toward our peers. That's because, by young adulthood, our survival no longer depends on our parents but, rather, on our ability to make friends and find lovers. Our days in the nest—or in the house—are numbered, and it becomes our turn to get out there and create communities and families of our own.

To help this process along—during the brain's second growth spurt, the one that takes place in our teens and twenties—our attention shifts from parents to peers. Here's a fun fact: A 2022 study showed on MRI brain scans that, while a mother's voice activates the reward center in a child's brain, by late adolescence it is unfamiliar voices that grab our interest most.

In our teens and beyond, as we tune out our parents, we become exquisitely tuned in to what's happening with those around us of the same age. We see ourselves through their eyes, self-consciously wondering what they think about our clothes, or our hair, or our job, or our shoes, or our body, or our personality. We have a whole new interest in tracking the hearts and minds of friends and acquaintances, as well as the fashions, trends, and gadgets they prefer. Meanwhile, as competition ramps up in sports, school, work, and popularity, we become more sensitive to rejection.

This developmental shift is as old as humankind, and it also shows up in some of our earliest research on child and adolescent development. In 1956, researchers asked more than a thousand participants, ages 9 to 18, to rate their worries and fears. Social evaluation was the least common concern for 9-year-olds, but it was the most common worry among 18-year-olds.

In our teens and twenties, then, it's common to care—a lot—about what other people think, and to have trouble discerning quite what that is. Sure, middle schoolers have long passed notes that read, "Do you like me? Yes. No. Maybe. (Circle One)." And, every year, high schoolers hold various forms of popularity contests, such as elections for class presidents and prom kings or queens. Historically, however, concrete social information has been hard to come by, so young adults mostly got used to never really quite knowing where they stood with other people—until the twenty-first century, that is.

Enter social media—the world's first real-time, grand-scale sociometer. Never before has it been so easy to measure how much we are liked or disliked. Never before has it been so simple to get data—in the form of snaps, shares, swipes, and pokes—about our relational worth. Never before has it been so possible to see how we measure up to so many people—too many people. And never before have we been able to do all this without risking rejection, face to face. So, like baby turtles marching toward beach houses, we check, and check, and check our devices, looking for information about how much people like us and about whether we belong.

But it's a trap. Social media may look like a less risky, more quantifiable alternative to unpredictable, in-person interactions, but for those who feel socially anxious—and remember, that's most twentysomethings—social media is no safe haven. That's because social media allows people to engage in the two most common—and most counterproductive—responses to social anxiety: avoidance and impression management. Many twentysomethings use their devices to sidestep anxiety-provoking social interactions, as well as to fixate on how they are perceived, and this only makes social anxiety worse.

In a 2019 study of Facebook users, young adults who were socially anxious became even more anxious when they used the app. They tended to overthink and overedit their posts and to closely monitor responses and followers. After 10 minutes of Facebook use, they were more likely to see themselves harshly, through the eyes of others, concluding that "People think I'm boring," or "People will unfollow me," or "Nobody will like what I add." And, they were more likely to interpret ambiguous situations—such as a post not being commented on—negatively rather than neutrally.

Because posting online can be stressful, many twentysomethings use social media to avoid not only offline interactions but online ones, too. In a 2022 study of Instagram users, although those who were more socially anxious spent more time on the app, they were less likely to use the platform to connect with others. Rather, they spent their hours scrolling, and surveilling, and comparing themselves to others, trying to discern where they stood. Indeed, multiple studies have shown that the more unsure we feel about ourselves, the more likely we are to compare ourselves to other people, both online and offline. And now, with social media we can make those comparisons hundreds or thousands of times a day.

In a 2021 study of Instagram users, the more insecure people felt in social situations, the more likely they were to have "Instagram-contingent self-worth." This is a problem because, whether we feel socially anxious or not, when we look at other people's online photos and posts, we aren't just engaging in social comparisons; we are mostly engaging in *upward* social comparisons. We are contrasting the lowly realities of our day-to-day lives against the curated highlights of others, and this makes people feel bad: "Look up and feel down!" or "Compare and despair," it is said.

"There is no faster way to crash a population than an evolutionary trap," says biologist Bruce Robertson, and to be sure, screens and devices are luring us in. So, in 2023, the American Psychological Association issued a rare health advisory about social media use for youth. Consistent with the research, the recommendations included using social media actively to connect, rather than passively to compare. They also suggested taking steps to limit exposure to harmful or hateful content pertaining to issues such as race, gender, sexuality, religion, and mental health—and to limit the time spent on social media in general. So, it's not *whether* we use social media, it's how we use social media and how much.

Besides, the only way to feel more sure of yourself socially is to spend more time being social. You have to have the courage to be a nobody—to know no one when you head into an office, or a classroom, or a party—to not know how things are going to go and to walk in the door anyway. Only experience can teach your brain that this isn't as dangerous as it feels. Only practice will help you get better at talking to people you don't know. Only repetition can help you feel more sure of yourself in uncertain situations. Then, rather than relying on external validation, such as what is constantly shifting and updating online, you carry within yourself a stable internal sense of generally being all right.

That's what I told Trina, when she said I was the only person she had talked to all week.

"What about coming to a group I'm running?" I suggested.

"I don't want to do something with other people," she said from behind her mask. "That's what I'm having trouble with."

"That's why you need to do it," I replied. "Avoidance is a symptom, not a strategy. That's why groups are more effective for social anxiety than individual treatment: You're actually confronting something you're afraid of, rather than just talking about it. Besides, these things usually go better than we think they will."

The group Trina reluctantly joined consisted of a rotating handful of young adults who met to talk about their own rotating list of social concerns. There was Isabelle, who always tried to come up with the perfect thing to say on Twitter. There was Jonah, who was spending too much time lurking on LinkedIn. There was Cruz, who came to meetings wearing his earbuds. And there was Sam who, without a girlfriend, felt left out by other guys.

"Your social media isn't your social *life*," Jonah said, serving as sort of the elder in the room.

"Yeah, social media is kind of a litmus test for me, which is funny, given how much I rely on it," Isabelle said. "If a guy asks me for my Snapchat, I give him my number instead. I don't want someone sending me photos of their face all day. If someone can't call or text and invite me to meet up, then I'm not interested."

Everyone in the group laughed.

"Social media has seriously fucked up our age group, I think," Sam said, adding to more laughs.

"Sometimes I think we blame social media for our social problems," Cruz said, with one earbud still in, "when the real problem is our own self-doubt. Do you feel anxious because of your phone, or do you hide behind your phone because of your insecurities?"

"I think it's both," Trina said. "I turn to my phone because I doubt myself, but then social media just makes me doubt myself *more*. Snapchat gives me FOMO. Instagram makes me feel bad about my skin. And TikTok is just so . . . *addictive*."

It didn't take long for the five members to notice—and point out—that, when it came to being social, each of them was hiding behind *something*: a mask, some earbuds, a girlfriend, social media, medication.

"What are you afraid of?" I asked.

Not being liked, they all agreed.

In 2013, I gave a TED talk, which is one of the most uncertain social situations imaginable. You have one chance to give a live performance that will be evaluated by thousands in the audience and by millions more online. It's a lot of pressure, and the best piece of advice I received before getting onstage was this: People want to like you, and they want to like your talk—so just let them do that.

I have to admit I'd never thought of it that way.

Maybe that's because it wasn't until 2018 that researchers identified what's called the *liking gap*. The liking gap is the now well-documented tendency we all have to underestimate how much people like us. Yet another instance of negativity bias, the liking gap is taking uncertain social encounters—a party, an interview, a conversation—and imagining they're worse than they are.

"I just keep feeling like this group of guys I know, like they don't like me as much as they like each other," Sam said. "And I keep thinking I need to hang out with them more so I can improve my standing."

"That was me five years ago," Jonah said. "All I could think about was how I ranked."

"What did you do?" Sam wanted to know.

"I went on medication, and I waited for all that social stuff to pass, and in a way, it did," Jonah said. "But now I have the same insecurities with the guys at work. Maybe because of the meds, maybe not, I haven't applied myself at work as much as I could have, so I wind up feeling bad about that."

"Oh my God, how does this *end*?" Sam asked with a groan.

"The medication did make my physical symptoms better," Jonah said. "But I think the biggest gains I've made have come from having to do things that made me nervous. I don't worry about presentations at work at all anymore, because I have had to do them so many times. A lot of other things—voluntary things, social things with guys at work—I've avoided, though. I need to say yes to more things like that."

"My worry is that I won't have anything to say yes to," Sam said. "Like, by Friday, I'm stressed if no one has reached out with something to do."

"Maybe you need to be the one who reaches out," Trina suggested from behind her mask.

"I don't initiate things because I'm afraid people will say no," Sam said.

"I don't initiate things because I'm afraid people will say yes," Isabelle offered, "because, if we wind up hanging out, I worry it won't go well, like I won't have interesting things to say."

"I don't know *how* to initiate things with people," Cruz broke in. "That's my problem."

"Well, you have to take the earbuds out," Isabelle said with a smile. "They scream 'Don't talk to me.' And they also keep you from having to talk *to* people."

"I don't know *how* to talk to people," Cruz said.

"I used to think that," Jonah said. "But what more is there to it than asking somebody to do something? Or saying 'Hi'? Or asking a question? Or finding some common ground to talk about? That's what we're doing now. What other instructions do we think exist?"

"Your homework," Trina said to Cruz, "is to reach out to that person in your lab and have the damn coffee."

"Yours," Isabelle said to Trina, "is to go somewhere without your mask. Your skin doesn't have to be perfect for people to like you."

Everyone in the group had good ideas about how to be more social, but in the beginning anyway, they were just ideas. If the members of our group wanted to close the liking gap, they needed to walk the talk.

It can take a while.

One 2018 study of college suite mates found that the likability gap persisted until nearly the end of the school year when, finally, after many months, friends felt confident about where they stood. So, even though people may like us more than we think they do, it may take time—and repeated experiences—to believe it's true. That's probably why forty-somethings and sixtysomethings think less about whether other people like them: They have more experiences of being liked—by the people whom they have decided matter anyway—and they probably also have other things in their lives that matter at least as much.

Not so—yet—for many twentysomethings, and that's what makes being social so difficult.

"I texted for coffee, and it was a nightmare," Cruz said, sometime later, building the suspense, "but probably a useful one. The person didn't message me back for almost a week, and I had to keep going to the lab, not knowing what that meant. When we finally got together, she said how sorry she was that she'd been so busy and forgetful. Her not getting back to me wasn't about me at all. After that, I don't even remember *how* we talked. We just talked. It was great."

"If I can tell Cruz and Trina they don't have to be perfect," Isabelle said, reporting on how she'd talked herself into going to a recent dinner party, "then I guess I don't have to be amazingly interesting, either. I just need to be myself when I'm talking to people, and they are probably going to like me just fine."

"They definitely are," Trina said, no longer from behind her mask.

"You know, Trina," Isabelle said. "It's nice to see your face these days. You honestly look a lot different from how I thought when we first met. And your acne isn't bad at all. It's definitely not as bad as you seem to think it is. You know, there's a gap there, too."

"Knowing about the liking gap . . . that has helped me realize that other guys aren't walking around trying to hate me," Sam said somewhere near the end of his time in the group. "I actually found out that I wasn't on the group chat because it got going when I had a girlfriend, and so I was always busy and had other things to do. It wasn't personal. I just had to ask somebody to add me."

"Yeah, the liking gap has helped me have this sort of basic trust that people are good. And that's helped me stop worrying whether *I'm* good when I'm talking to people at work and just assume that *other* people are," Jonah said to Sam. "The guys you're always talking about probably do like you more than you think, but if it turns out they don't, they may be good people but maybe they're not *your* people. So, maybe rather than trying to spend more time with them, you need to spend less. You wouldn't keep following someone on social media who makes you feel bad—or you shouldn't, anyway—so maybe you don't need to follow them around, either. Find other people to hang out with. Or, hey, I'll hang out with you."

There was nothing magical about our group that helped Jonah and the others, nothing that twentysomethings everywhere couldn't do on their own. There was encouragement, and accountability, and reality checking that helped people show up for the social interactions that worried them most—and only that can disprove our worries and fears and close the liking gap. And, week after week, by showing up for each other, Jonah, Isabelle, Cruz, Trina, and Sam were learning something about what is perhaps the most valuable social skill of all: how to be a friend.

NINE

HOW TO BEFRIEND

All of us, cradle to grave, are happiest when life is organized as a series of excursions, long or short, from the secure base provided by our attachment figures.

—John Bowlby, developmental psychologist

At the end of Sally's crossed legs were a pair of Golden Goose sneakers. It was our first meeting, and like her shoes, Sally appeared casual and relaxed but chic and on trend. Four days a week, Sally worked in New York City as a financial analyst on Wall Street. The other three days, she lived and worked from home in Virginia, not far from where her parents had retired on a farm. From where I sat, Sally came across as sharp and polite, and she seemed personable enough. She paid her own bills, did her own laundry, and generally knew how to "adult." Her problem? She did not have a single close friend and had never once been on a date.

"Reddit says I have 'insecure attachment,'" she said, using air quotes.

"What does Reddit say insecure attachment is?" I wanted to know.

"It's not feeling confident that people like me, or will want to be with me, or you know, be there for me," she explained vaguely. "It's not being close to people."

"It sounds like you're pretty close to your parents," I countered.

"But why aren't I close to anybody else?" she asked.

"I'm not sure you've given anyone else much of a chance," I said.

In the course of a day, Sally had told me earlier, the only people she spoke with at length were her mom or her dad and now, once a week, me. She'd called my office not long after her 25th birthday, an occasion that embarrassed and saddened her.

Because she had no other plans, Sally went to her parents' farm, where her mom and dad felt compelled to come up with something special to cheer her up. This was baffling and frustrating for them, which in turn only frustrated Sally: "My parents just don't get it. They met each other in college. They're really happy people, but why wouldn't they be? They have each other. They're set. They've *been* set. They want me to be happy, and not so lonely, but they don't realize how hard that is."

Young adults are the loneliest people in the United States. As of 2019, even before the pandemic, about 30 percent of them said they often or always felt lonely, compared to about 20 percent of middle-aged adults and about 15 percent of older ones. Although about 50 percent of young adults did report having close friends, about 50 percent did not, and 25 percent of them said they had no friends and no acquaintances. None. So, in a way, Sally wasn't as alone as she thought she was. The data, and my clients, say that twentysomethings everywhere are struggling with profound feelings of isolation that neither parental love nor social media can cure.

These are the sorts of things I hear every day:

I don't really feel like I have a group that I belong to.
I'd like to delete the Snapchats from my old friends who haven't
    been great to me, but then there would be nothing on my phone.
I don't know how to get close to people. There's not a handbook for
    that.
One of my best friends ghosted me, and the other one found a
    boyfriend.
I don't know how to take friendships to the next level.

I lost interest in my social life because I'm embarrassed I'm not going
   anywhere at work.
I enjoy meeting people, but I don't know how to take it further.
I don't know a single person in my life.
Life in my twenties is hard in all sorts of ways. I feel like what I
   really need is a friend.
I just feel like I have no one to turn to when I need something or
   when I have a hard day.

In the 1970s, psychologist Mary Ainsworth developed an experimental
method to examine attachment in young children, called the *strange
situation*. In the strange situation, researchers observe young children
from behind one-way mirrors and rate how they respond to being left in
an unfamiliar room with a stranger and some toys. As the theory goes,
securely attached children—meaning those with loved ones they know
they can depend on—feel free to roam the room and play. Insecurely
attached children—or those without loved ones they feel they can count
on—are more prone to scream, cry, or shut down. Since Ainsworth's
earliest strange situation experiments, countless studies have examined
the ways in which children use parents as secure bases from which to
explore the world.

Only more recently have researchers become interested in the
strange situation that many young adults find themselves in today.
Many wake up most days to some sort of unfamiliar setting—a new city,
a new job, a new roommate, a new relationship, or a new breakup—
and developmentally speaking, they're supposed to get out there and
explore. It's tough, though, not because twentysomethings like Sally are
insecurely attached but because they don't have secure bases to steady
them in times of need. Like Sally, they probably don't live with mom
or dad anymore. Yet, as the average age of marriage climbs, about half
of twentysomethings—or roughly two-thirds of twentysomething men
and one-third of twentysomething women—don't have a steady partner, either. Today's twentysomethings will spend more time single than

any other generation in history, and that's where friends come in—or should.

Hashim told me he was on an antipsychotic. When I asked him why, he said, "My doctor put me on it a few months back. I can be, I don't know, *moody*. And sometimes I don't handle things so well."

"Can you give me an example?"

"A couple of weeks ago, I got mad and punched a wall," he said.

"Well, that's a good one," I said. "What were you mad at?"

"It was stupid, I know, but I get so upset about not having a connection with anybody. My family came here from Egypt when I was younger, and I think my parents have always felt alone. I'm not sure I saw them make friends, so maybe that's part of it. All I know is that I don't have anybody to talk to when things go wrong."

I kept listening.

"My friends have always been my girlfriends, which is fine. Or, maybe it's not fine because, ever since my girlfriend and I broke up, I feel completely alone. I feel like everybody else has all these great friends, but then I look around and I see other guys I know doing the exact same thing— leaning on their girlfriends for friendship. It's not right, though," he said with insight and openness that seemed to come easily. "I don't want to put all that on one person."

"I don't think you should, either," I said. "You seem quite easy to get to know. Do you ever talk to other guys like you're talking to me right now?"

"No," he said definitively. "I'm hanging out with a guy I kind of know this weekend, and I wish I could talk to him, not just about sports and music, but I don't know."

"Maybe you can," I said.

"Don't you think he'd think that's weird?" he asked.

Fight or flight has long been considered our primary hardwired reaction to danger, and for our ancient ancestors, this meant either taking on the bear or running for our lives. In the modern era, however, neither of these two choices works so well. By punching a wall, Hashim was lashing out against his feelings of loneliness. And by hiding out, Sally was trying not to feel overwhelmed by hers. But, as different as they were, both Sally and Hashim wanted the same thing. They wanted to be able to tap into a different hardwired way of getting through life. They wanted to be able to tend and befriend.

According to the tend-and-befriend model—and the research that backs it up—when we feel uncertain or unsafe, it's instinctual to form groups and take care of each other. Banding together is protective, of course, as there can be safety in numbers. While some researchers suggest that tending-and-befriending is more common in females, attaching ourselves to others is innate in both females *and* males. We cling to our moms, or run to our dads, or huddle up with our siblings because when we're young this is our best chance for survival. Huddling up is our best chance for survival as we get older, too, but in the strange situation of young adulthood, it is friends whom we often want—and need—to run to most.

Both Sally and Hashim thought they'd be better off if they had friends, and of course they were right. Having friends we can count on means having secure bases from which to explore the world. On a practical level, friends are a crucial source of advice and encouragement, both of which foster healthy risk-taking and growth. And on an emotional level, whether it's sharing a laugh, a hug, a conversation, or a soccer match, connecting with another person, like Hashim wanted to do, is incredibly soothing. Having friends is associated with lower levels of depression, anxiety, and anger, as well as higher levels of confidence, relationship satisfaction, and quality of life.

As with most things, quality matters more than quantity in the realm of friendship. In a 2013 study, doubling the number of face-to-face friends had the same effect on happiness as a 50 percent increase in income, yet the size of one's online social network was generally unrelated to well-being. Similarly, research shows that youth who have strong peer relationships report better mental health and social competence, while those who are seen as "popular" are more likely to struggle with social anxiety—presumably because they worry about maintaining their status.

Although friends are often seen as less important than partners or parents, the data suggest that friends are *how* we move from parents to partners. Friendships are better predictors of healthy romantic relationships at age 30 than are our relationships with our parents—and they are even better predictors than our early experiences with dating and sex.

That's because friendships are our first experiments in "voluntary interdependence." Unlike family, friends are people who *choose* to spend time with us. These are the first nonfamilial relationships in which we practice sharing, caring, loyalty, sensitivity, hard work, and assertiveness. Friendships are where we learn how to solve problems and resolve differences out in the world. They are where we brave tough conversations, like the ones we may soon have at work or in love. Friends are the people who teach us that good relationships—and good jobs—aren't just one mistake away from ending. Good friendships show us what good, chosen relationships are.

All this is why, more and more, I do what's called *social prescribing*, or directing clients like Sally and Hashim to make some friends. Social prescribing is a movement in the United Kingdom, in which physicians refer lonely patients to the community for connection and support. Sometimes those referrals are to community centers, churches, or neighborhood clubs. But other times the referral is more symbolic. It's a doctor's directive to take seriously the health benefits of having people in our lives who care about us.

When I encouraged Sally to go beyond her parents for social support, she said, "I come here. You're helping me."

"Your parents wanted you to expand your social horizons, and you added me, which is a start," I said. "But if things end there, then I'm not doing my job."

"So, I'm a job," Sally said.

"That's the problem," I went on. "For better or for worse, this is a professional relationship. You schedule appointments for an hour of my time. And as long as you're paying me, you'll have trouble believing I actually like you. Your coming here placates your parents, and it gets you through the week. But it might also be getting in the way of your getting out there and making some friends."

"When you put it that way, it sounds so forced," Sally said, wrinkling her nose. "When I was growing up, I felt like friendships were more, I don't know, *organic*."

"I think that's a misunderstanding," I replied. "Your friendships probably *weren't* all that organic when you were younger. Other people were just putting in the effort for you. Schools and sports gave you opportunities to connect. Parents scheduled playdates or activities for you to join."

"I guess that's true," she said, clearly trying to remember how exactly those friendships came about.

"So, now it's your turn to make friends for yourself."

"I just don't know *how* to do that," she said with emphasis.

In his own sessions, Hashim had told me more or less the same thing.

A few years ago, I was interviewed for a national news story about Easter egg hunts for adults. To be more precise, the plastic eggs that would be scattered in parks around the country were filled not with chocolates and jelly beans but with condoms and Jell-O shots, so the egg hunts seemed primarily to be for *young* adults. The reporter thought this was yet another example of twentysomethings delaying adulthood.

I had a different take.

My guess, I countered, was that the egg hunts were less about not wanting to grow up and more about not wanting to be left *out*. So many holidays seem tailored for kids and their parents, but what about the twentysomethings in between? Sure, the egg hunts sounded like frivolous fun, but they also sounded like a way for young adults to connect with their culture, or their community, or their customs, or just each other. Maybe not surprisingly, my comments didn't make it into the article.

It's true, though. Without structured ways of meeting new people that parents and school and holidays once offered, young adults like Sally and Hashim often have a hard time figuring out how, when, or where to connect with others their age. And so do all adults. In 2022, the *Wall Street Journal* published an article about making friends in adulthood—and in the same year, *The Atlantic* and the *New York Times* did, too. The truth is that, as we age, and as we change jobs, or cities, or phases of life, we need to make friends, again and again.

The word *befriend* is a verb, and friendship requires action. Yet, almost without exception, clients who tell me they don't have friends don't seem to be doing much to make friends.

"But I don't even know where to start," Sally said helplessly when I told her as much.

"Well, I do," I said.

Remember the 2019 study that found twentysomethings were the loneliest people in the country? Although about 25 percent of young adults surveyed had no friends or acquaintances, about 75 percent of young adults—and an even higher proportion of older adults—did. So, we can all start by understanding how, or at least where, adults of all ages said they had made their connections.

Here are the percentages of adults who met at least one friend in the following places:

87% high school
76% work
70% college
61% neighborhood
44% church
38% informal setting, like a park or cafe
38% through their kids
33% fitness activity
32% social or hobby club
30% volunteering
24% event like a concert or a game (or an Easter egg hunt)

Looking at that list, you'll see that the most likely places to meet and make friends are the places we go again and again. So, the best way to make friends is to go live your life. That's how you'll meet other people with similar talents and interests who maybe, probably, are looking for friends, too.

That said, sitting next to someone at the office or in school does not a friendship make. As the amount of time we spend together *by choice* increases, the more likely it is that we'll become friends. It's about sharing not just oxygen and space but also interests, milestones, holidays, feelings, hobbies, information, Super Bowls, good days, bad moments, bike rides, confidences, or conversations. Maybe those conversations are about sports and music, or maybe they are about, as Hashim put it, "more."

Although some might say that true friends need to "go deep" or "be vulnerable," young adults are a diverse group, and there's no one-size-fits-all approach to friendship. Some friendships are shoulder-to-shoulder relationships, in that time is spent side by side in work meetings, or political rallies, or sporting events, or concerts. Others take place face to face, which means that time spent together often involves talking or sharing coffee or a meal. Still other friendships start off as shoulder-to-shoulder interactions but include more face-to-face sharing over time.

And almost always, friendships take time.

Hashim's antipsychotics were either doing one heck of a job or maybe he didn't need them. Week after week, when he came to sessions, he seemed open, cooperative, kind, and stable. So, after a while, I told him I was concerned about his being on powerful drugs he might be able to do without.

"Young adults can be moody, but you may not have a mood disorder," I explained. "Let's get a second opinion on your meds."

These days, I send as many twentysomethings to psychiatrists to come off medications as I do to go on medications. The psychiatrist Hashim consulted also thought he should try life without pills. It was my job to monitor him, and every week I checked on his sleep and mood, which seemed about the same as before.

"I'm not feeling *great*," he said one day.

"On a scale of one to ten . . ." I prompted.

"I'm probably a seven."

"That's not bad," I said.

"I guess I thought therapy would help me feel like a ten."

"That's a tall order!" I said. "Does your life feel like a ten? Is everything just the way you'd like it to be?"

"Not at all," he said.

"Then maybe it's unreasonable to expect your feelings to be a ten. Maybe your feelings are telling you something. What would make your life an eight or nine or ten?"

"My job could be better, but it's okay for now. I think I'm due for a new project later this year, which will be good. And I want to find people that feel like my people."

"Then let's keep working on that."

"I have been hanging out with a few guys here and there," he said. "I thought making friends would be faster, but it takes a while, huh?"

It does indeed.

There's no single formula, but studies suggest that casual friendships develop after spending around 50 hours together, close friendships after around 100 hours, and best friendships after around 150 hours or more. Yet, according to the U.S. Bureau of Labor Statistics, American adults spend only about 30 minutes per day socializing during the week and about an hour per day on the weekend. Compare this to the three hours per day we spend watching television or the several hours a day twentysomethings routinely spend on their devices. In fact, as of 2023, nearly half of young adults say they spend more time socializing online than they do in person. So, maybe we have more time for friendships than we think we do.

"I talked to my dad, and he said he hadn't found his people when he was my age. Knowing that maybe everybody doesn't have all their best friends already makes me feel better," Hashim said. "But I still think guys have a harder time with this, and it feels like a lot to try to change that."

"You have good instincts," I told Hashim. "Talk to people like you're talking to me. Go be the friend you wish you had."

"If you want to have a friend, you've got to be a friend," I told Sally in a similar session. "What would you like a friend to do for you?"

"Reach out to me. Invite me to do things. Hang out with me on the weekend, or go to a movie or something during the week. Talk about things. Be there when I need something."

"That sounds reasonable," I said. "So, what if you start by doing those things for *other* people?"

"I never want to text anyone first," Sally said. "That way, I don't feel so pathetic if nothing ends up happening. You know, because I didn't really try to put anything together. That's my insecure attachment thing."

"I don't know about insecure *attachment*," I said. "That sounds more like being plain old insecure, just being unsure of whether something is going to work out."

Like a kid sitting on the edge of a playground, Sally sat on the edge of life, not wanting to do something until she knew exactly how to do it and how to succeed. Indeed, in that same 2019 study in which so many young adults were lonely, shyness was the leading reason people said they had trouble making friends. I get that, but research also shows that, once they make connections, those who feel socially anxious are just as good as others at having friends. In fact, having friends is what helps them feel less anxious over time.

I knew, and maybe Sally knew, too, that the only way for her to feel less unhappy—and less anxious—about not having friends was to accept the uncertainty and try to befriend someone anyway. But because she was convinced she would never be able to do that, she soon stopped coming to sessions.

Two years later, Sally came back to my office, this time because she was having trouble with her love life.

"Your *love* life," I remarked with surprise.

"Yeah," she replied, like it was no big deal.

"The last time I saw you, you were having trouble making friends."

"Yeah," she shrugged. "That worked itself out."

"*How?*" I wanted to know, maybe hoping, like everyone else, there was some magical piece of advice that somehow I'd missed.

"I don't know," she shrugged again. "I had a new job in New York, and I made friends during the training program. I started spending time with them outside of work. And I got a roommate so I wouldn't be alone all the time. It was what you said. I just had to spend time with people I had things in common with. And once I started doing that, it actually did feel kind of organic in that we had things to connect over, like dealing with jobs and being in our twenties. So, it didn't feel so forced."

"And now you have a boyfriend, too?"

"Yeah," Sally said. "I actually think I have a boyfriend *because* I made friends. Hanging out with my parents all the time, that didn't exactly boost my confidence. I know my parents love me, but they have to. And you were right, I never really could get past the fact that you were paid to like me. Having friends, though, it made me feel like people might *choose* to like me. Then I guess it was easier to believe that someone could choose to love me, too."

TEN

HOW TO LOVE

There's a lot of talk about the positive aspects of love. We as a society downplay the danger, the anxiety, and the disappointment. We romanticize romance.

—Helen Fisher, anthropologist

Dev told me he was 30 when he fell in love for the first time.

For me to understand that, he said, he needed to explain where he had come from: a village in India, where he and his family were peasants. Dev described an upbringing in which his father was absent, and his mother grew his food and made his clothes but couldn't provide for him emotionally. "All I ever learned how to do was work hard in school," Dev said, "but that was all right because I did not want to be a peasant forever."

One of Dev's first memories was walking alone to the local school and registering himself for kindergarten. Another was seeing parents bringing lunch for their kids at midday. "No one ever came and brought me anything, so I was hungry a lot," he recalled.

A standout student in his province, Dev went away to high school in Mumbai, to college in the United Kingdom, and finally to work in the United States. Somewhere along the way, he realized he was gay. "You are only the third person to know this," he told me. "There was a guy in college I had a thing with, and then there is a guy right now—my friend I met on a dating app—who I think does not want to date me anymore."

Dev's language was confusing. The most recent guy he was referring to—was he a friend or a lover? And was their relationship over or was it still going on? When I asked for some clarity, Dev had a tough time providing it. "I'm confused, too," he said. "I don't know what's happening with my friend or with my health."

Recently, Dev had visited a general practitioner around the corner from my office, complaining of fatigue. Dev worried that he had cancer or Lyme disease or some other physical ailment. After a series of lab tests showed nothing amiss, the doctor diagnosed Dev with major depressive disorder and suggested that he try therapy.

Before I met with Dev for the first session—and every session thereafter—he sat in the waiting room and completed an electronic depression scale. The results popped up on the computer at my desk in the form of a graph, which showed a steep spike for depression. Dev had endorsed practically every item on the scale, from "I feel sad all the time," to "I don't enjoy things like I used to," to "I have thoughts of killing myself."

"I am my mother's only hope," Dev offered tearfully after we went over the items together. "My family depends on me, so it scares me to be sick. I went to the doctor because I was afraid I had a physical illness, but maybe I have a mental one."

Research suggests that about half the cases of first-time depression in youth are preceded by the end of a romantic relationship, and no other single life event accounts for more. So, far more often than not, when someone like Dev sits down and talks about feeling sad and hopeless, about crying a lot, about no longer enjoying the things they used to, about lacking energy, about sleeping or eating too much or too little, they also have a lot to say about a lost love. Sometimes the loss is the breakdown of a relationship with a friend, a parent, or a sibling, but most commonly it's the breakup of a romantic relationship.

This may seem obvious enough, but in my experience, most young adults are surprised by the ecstasy and agony that can accompany love. "Love is one of the most powerful sensations on Earth," according to anthropologist Helen Fisher. Love is universal (or arguably nearly so), its highs and lows well documented in songs, stories, myths, poetry, and legends spanning centuries and cultures. What love looks like—what form it takes—may be variable, but to the brain and the body, love is love. Still, love is not always what we expect it to be.

When we think about love, maybe we think about hearts and flowers, and great sex and constant (and constantly rewarding) companionship. To be sure, most people do find love to be a positive experience—euphoric, even—since it activates the same pleasure centers of our brains as do chocolate, money, and cocaine. But love is about more than just feeling good. Love is a drive every bit as strong as those for sex, water, and food. That may sound extreme, but as we already know, forming emotional attachments with others is crucial for our survival. We have a better chance of surviving and thriving if we don't go through life alone.

When I explained all this to Dev, it resonated: "Even when I was too busy with work," he said, "I'd make time to be with this person. It was such an out-of-control feeling. I guess I was hungry for love."

As pleasurable as love can be, romantic uncertainty—or not feeling secure about the status or future of one's relationship—leads to all sorts of unpleasant feelings that seem a lot like craving: anxiety, restlessness, sleeplessness, preoccupation, mood swings, possessiveness, obsessive thinking, risk-taking, and loss of self-control. "My friend gives me so many mixed messages about whether he wants to be together," Dev said. "Every time he changes plans with me, I feel like I am falling off a cliff."

There's a reason we talk about being "madly in love" or "falling in love": Love can be maddening and destabilizing. According to Sigmund Freud, "one is very crazy when in love." Freud wasn't right about everything, but he was spot-on when he said that, as well as this: "We are never so defenseless against suffering as when we love, never so helplessly unhappy as when we have lost our loved object or its love."

Emotionally, couples feel more stable when their relationships feel more stable. Longer-term committed attachments are associated with feelings of calm, security, and comfort because there is predictability, the sense that the relationship's future is somehow known. But not all relationships make it that far, and most in young adulthood don't. As young adults settle down and commit to long-term partnerships at increasingly later ages, more time is spent falling in—and out—of love. An estimated 95 percent of young adults have rejected someone, and 93 percent have been rejected.

So, heartbreak is about as universal as is love. Still, it's a terrible, painful experience, one that shows just how powerful our attachment system is. "The pain of grief is just as much a part of life as the joy of love," wrote British psychiatrist Colin Murray Parkes. "It is perhaps the price we pay for love, the cost of commitment. To ignore this fact, or to pretend that it is not so, is to put on emotional blinkers which leave us unprepared for the losses that will inevitably occur in our own lives and unprepared to help others cope with losses in theirs."

"You're grieving," I explained when Dev cried in my office once the breakup had been painfully confirmed via text message. "It's normal to be *really, really* sad after a loss like this. That means your attachment system— your heart—is working. To be honest, I'd be worried if you *weren't* sad."

That was easy for me to say.

I wasn't the one crying myself to sleep at night and dragging myself through my days fatigued, although I had done these things before. The alarming effects of a breakup were, at least in part, what had led me thirty years earlier to knock on my professor's door. When, at some point, he suggested I read a book about grief, it changed how I thought about how I was feeling. Rather than thinking there was something *wrong* with me, the fact that I was grieving seemed like proof of something right about me: I could let myself love someone. Around this time, probably also at my professor's suggestion, I went to a physician to rule out medical causes for my sadness and fatigue. When I mentioned I was grieving over a recent breakup, she chuckled dismissively.

Indeed, it can be difficult to take young love and loss seriously. Dev himself had a hard time believing me when I suggested that maybe his symptoms were the result of his breakup. I tried to explain it all to him—love, attachment, grief—but he scarcely seemed to notice what I was saying. He was in pain, and pain slows us down and focuses our thinking on what hurts.

Dev cried when he recalled the time his friend (as he still called him) told Dev he was uninteresting because he didn't have hobbies, like playing an instrument or video games. "My friend was born and raised in the United States. I never even saw those things in my village and never had the money to do them later on," Dev explained as he wiped tears away. "I remember the first time I saw a piano at my high school in Mumbai. It was so shiny I touched it. It was like a Lamborghini."

His face lit up at the memory, and he rubbed the tips of his fingers together lightly, like he could still feel the smooth surface of the piano. "The other kids in high school had lessons, but I'd never had the chance to play . . . anything," he continued. "I don't think I ever had the chance to *play* as a kid at all."

Maybe in hopes of showing Dev that his heartache was real, I told him that my heart ached as I listened to him speak. As he struggled to understand what happened to his relationship—and what was happening to him—he returned to the general practitioner again and again for more tests. Then, again and again, I would receive new results and new notes:

"Tests negative. Patient meets criteria for major depression but declines medication. He has been instructed to discuss medication with Dr. Jay," said one fax.

"Additional tests negative. Patient still meets criteria for major depression. Patient was told again about the benefits of medication," said another.

"Patient continues to ask for tests. Says Dr. Jay does not recommend medication because patient is functioning and getting his work done," said yet another.

Reading between the lines, it seemed that Dev's doctor was getting frustrated with Dev—and me. Why *didn't* I just recommend meds already?

Dev's physician and I were separated by two city blocks and a gulf of understanding. So, I picked up the phone to better collaborate on Dev's care. I explained that I was hesitant to recommend medication because, although Dev's depression was severe, it was also situational. He was grieving the end of an important relationship, and this was after growing up—and growing up gay—mostly alone. I was concerned about the effect that medication would have on his ability to work, which was an important part of his life that had always gone well. And I was hesitant about giving him the message that he was defective, or ill, or handling the breakup poorly. Rather, I wanted him to see this as an opportunity to learn something about how to love and how to cope with loss.

To be sure, it had been two hard months for Dev, and maybe even at times for the physician and for me. I often wondered how unhappy Dev needed to be before he—and I—felt medication was necessary. I sometimes worried, on weekends or holidays, that Dev might kill himself, or try to. But I knew Dev felt important to his family and to the people at work. I also knew that about one-fourth of those with depression remit spontaneously—without treatment—within about three months, one-third are better within about six months, and one-half are no longer depressed within a year. And that's if, other than wait for life to change or improve, you do nothing.

But, I assured the physician, Dev and I were not doing nothing.

Dev and I were doing what people do, especially after a loss: We were trying to work out what went wrong. Week after week, he seemed unable to do much of anything other than talk—again and again—about the broken promises, the hurtful comments, the unanswered texts, the canceled plans, the nights alone. Why didn't his friend want to be with him? Why had he given him mixed signals? Why had he been so hurtful? Why hadn't he returned his love?

This kind of ruminating can seem frustrating and fruitless to the listener—and, yes, too much is too much—but Dev was doing more than just dwelling on the past. When we think deeply, even relentlessly, about something like a breakup, our brain is desperately trying to solve a problem that can't quite be solved. We would never know exactly why things didn't work out between Dev and his friend. Some uncertainty would have to stand. However, there were still lessons to be learned. Dev's pain was forcing him to re-examine his relationships, his choices, and his life so that he might fare better next time.

From this perspective, distress isn't always a bad thing. Feeling bad after a breakup can lead to growth, while partners who don't feel bad often aren't motivated to change their ways. When we survive a breakup, we may emerge feeling more self-confident, more independent, and more emotionally stable. We may feel stronger, more capable, and more focused at work and school. Often, we are motivated to develop better conflict-management skills, better communication skills, and improved relationships with family and friends. In the long run, the positive changes that come from heartbreak have been found to outweigh and outlast the negative feelings we experience at the time. In one forward-looking study of nearly two hundred young adults, making sense of a breakup predicted positive mental health and relationship competence and satisfaction three years down the line.

So, young adults who work to understand their breakups learn more than those who can't or won't. But *how* exactly one makes sense of what happened has a lot to do with how we fare. Dev was sure that, physically or emotionally, there was something seriously wrong with him. "At first I thought I was really sick," he told me, "but sometimes I think I am going crazy."

This was a problem because one of the most significant predictors of whether a breakup results in depression or anxiety is whether those like Dev make catastrophic (mis)interpretations of their own reactions. They see their tears, sleepless nights, and obsessive thoughts as proof that they are, as Dev said, "crazy," or that they are the problem. When we see ourselves as broken, it's easy to conclude that, now and forever, we are unlovable.

"What if there is nothing wrong *with* you," I suggested to Dev. "What if this person is just the wrong person *for* you?"

"But what's wrong with me that I *chose* the wrong person?" Dev pressed.

"You haven't had a lot of practice choosing," I said plainly.

"You think I need to date more?"

"Not in the speed dating sense, no," I clarified. "I'm thinking more along the lines of going to the grocery store."

For most of his life, Dev had been, as he put it, hungry for love. So, I asked him to think about what happens when we go to the grocery store on an empty stomach and without a shopping list. We snatch up the first yummy-looking items we see, as we frantically rush up and down the aisles, not knowing what we're looking for. Before long, we dash out of the store loaded up with a random, unhealthy assortment of items that don't go together or that don't amount to much: a bag of cookies, a few sticks of beef jerky, a pint of ice cream, a couple of avocados, a jar of caramel sauce, some frozen hash browns. What looks good to you might be different from what looks good to me, but either way, we grab what's available rather than what's good for us.

To change this, I told Dev, he needed to feel less hungry. He needed to nourish himself with love from other sources—from friends, from family, from me, from himself. When twentysomethings don't feel so starved for someone who cares, when they believe their drive for love can and will be satisfied in a variety of ways, they can slow down and think about what they want and what they need from a romantic partner. This is important, because a big part of figuring out how to love is figuring out *who* to love.

So I asked Dev—as I've asked many clients before—to think about making some kind of list. By *list*, I don't mean a rundown of the qualities that, in your imagination, make for the perfect partner. Rather, I mean a list of what you know about *yourself*. Most of what I do to help young adults be more successful in love is to encourage them to articulate who they are. I help them become more aware of their values, priorities, plans, and strengths—all the good things they know about themselves so far. Too many couples connect over what's wrong with themselves and their lives when, hopefully, these are the aspects of our lives that will change. A better strategy is to look for someone who loves what's good, and strong, and right about us—because these are the things we should hold on to over time.

"But that's the thing," Dev said after my grocery-store lecture. "I don't know what's good about me or what's right for me. My parents didn't have a good relationship, and I haven't had a good one yet, either. My friend just kept telling me what isn't good about me. So far, I'm only learning from mistakes."

More often than not, of course, that's how it goes. Sure, a few twenty-somethings walk into the grocery store for the first time, knowing what they want or need, or they get lucky with what they happen to grab off the shelf. But that is rare.

If the grocery store metaphor is too, well, metaphorical for your taste, here's another way to think about how we learn to love. Remember that, on average, young adults will have nine different jobs by the age of 35. What those jobs are often about is determining what people do well, what they enjoy, what they need from the workplace, and what they need to improve about themselves. Something similar happens with relationships. Most people fall in and out of love more than once in their twenties. Those experiences are how we learn how and who to love.

"You've got work figured out," I reminded Dev. "Now, your job is to figure out love. Some people have it the other way around."

Dev's depression lifted about three months after he first came to my office and about a month after he started to make his list. He decided he needed someone who understood and respected how his upbringing in India made him who he was—in a good way. He wanted a partner who was as mature, and caring, and hardworking as he was. He wanted someone who would show up for him reliably, much like other kids could once count on their parents.

I know Dev was feeling better because he told me so, because I could see it on his face, and because it showed up in the data. His scores on the depression scale were no longer elevated—at all—and I motioned him over to my computer so he could see his week-by-week progress. "I'm okay," he said, breaking into a smile. "It feels official, hearing it from you, seeing it on a graph. Can I get a copy of that? I probably shouldn't need it, but I do."

When Dev checked in with me again after about another three months, he said he felt like his old self again. "But better," he said with a smile. "I got a promotion at work. I'm learning to play the guitar. I went on a trip to the beach with some friends. I joined an LGBTQ group, which has helped me see we're all going through similar things. I keep the graph of my depression symptoms in my drawer at home, and sometimes I pull it out and look at it. I don't feel like anything is wrong with me anymore. I got my heart broken, but I learned a lot about who I am and about how to love myself."

ELEVEN

HOW TO HAVE SEX

"Why are you facing downward?"

"Because that's how it's done." Beatrix twisted to look at him over her
shoulder. A twinge of uncertainty caused her to ask, "Isn't it?"
—Lisa Kleypas, *Love in the Afternoon*

Michael walked into my office wearing perfectly torn and weathered black
jeans. His white button-down shirt was fashionably untucked, and his
hair was mussed in all the right ways. His style was backed up with substance. At age twenty-four, Michael had a good job at a music-streaming
company, as well as a background as a strong student. He had always been
a bit of "a stresser," he told me, but in recent months his anxiety had gotten worse. With friends, he felt so self-conscious that, more and more, he
just preferred to be alone.

It's not unusual to hear a young adult, who on the outside looks like
he has it all, say that on the inside he is not feeling so great. It *was* unusual
that, as Michael told me about his life in his twenties and before, he didn't
once mention romantic relationships, or hookups, or even a lack thereof.

So I asked about them.

"Actually, that's sort of a thing," he answered, shifting in his chair. "I
think I've been wondering about my sexuality or something."

"What's got you wondering?" I wanted to know.

"Well . . ." he said cautiously, "I've had . . . performance issues . . . with women."

His vagueness told me he was nervous about talking to me about sex. So I decided to brave it for the both of us.

"Do you mind if I ask whether you watch porn?"

When I first started working with young adults in 1999, I didn't think I'd be asking about porn a lot, and it wasn't something that came up a lot, either. When clients in those years were coming of age, viewing porn meant getting their hands on a *Playboy* or a *Playgirl* or a *Penthouse* magazine, and having a place to stash it. Or, maybe it meant tuning in, late at night in the family den, to a risqué movie on HBO or Cinemax. However it happened, by their twenties, most of my clients had seen porn, but few had seen very *much* of it.

High-speed internet changed all this, making possible what are called the three As of online pornography: accessibility, affordability, and anonymity. Put simply, internet porn now is widely available, it's generally free, and it is easy to view in private on your devices. According to 2021 data on the most-visited websites on the internet—Google, YouTube, and Facebook are ranked one, two, and three—four porn sites are in the top twenty. And of those four, two are visited more often than Netflix and Zoom, with only Amazon's web traffic growing at a faster rate.

Although the numbers are constantly changing, an estimated 90 percent of young men watch pornography, and of that group, about 60 percent watch porn weekly and about 15 percent do so every day. That makes the multibillion-dollar porn industry the primary form of sex education in America. And it's not just males who learn about sex through porn. About a fourth to a third of porn consumers are female, although females are more likely to watch porn with a partner rather than alone.

Most viewers of adult websites began viewing before they were even adults. According to the research, most boys and girls get their first glimpse of pornography somewhere around the age of 13, and most say those earliest exposures were unintentional. They happened at a sleepover, or on a friend's phone, or as the result of an internet search for something else. Almost without exception, my clients who have trouble with porn—most of them male—describe use that drifted from coincidental, to curious, to casual, to compulsive. Often without realizing it was even happening, they went from being a consumer to being consumed.

This brings us to internet porn's unofficial fourth A: addiction. When watching porn is coupled with the pleasure that goes along with masturbation and orgasm, we're more likely to repeat those behaviors again and again, even when maybe we want to cut back or stop. Whether or not internet porn can truly function as an addiction is something I'll let the substance-abuse experts debate. What's tough to argue with, however, are the things my clients say about how porn affects their relationships and their lives:

I feel bored and empty, so I watch porn and jerk off. I feel better for
a minute, but then I feel more bored and empty.
My boyfriend just told me he has a sex addiction. He said it makes
him feel powerful to receive naked pictures from random girls.
Every time I see a woman, I think about her in all these sexual
positions. It makes me feel like there is something wrong with me.
It's tough to quit porn because the consequences aren't so obvious.
It's not like I'm getting sick or going broke.
My boyfriend watches a lot of porn. And I feel like what he wants
from me in bed is so hard-core.
I'd rather watch porn and masturbate than be with my boyfriend
because then I don't have to worry about how he thinks I look.
I've been watching porn daily for almost half my life now. Soon, it'll
be more than half my life. I'd like to quit but I doubt I'll ever be
able to.
I wish I could tell my 13-year-old self just to never start watching
porn—at least not regularly.

I often wish I *were* sitting with my clients' 13-year-old selves. It feels a bit daunting to help someone change a habit that has a five- or ten-year head start. Yet, with those like Michael, that's where we are.

Michael looked almost relieved to tell me he'd been watching porn at least weekly, and often daily, since he was about 13. For many years, he thought little of it because most of his friends were doing the same thing.

"We'd all brag about how much porn we were watching, like the more the better, especially in college, but now I'm starting to wonder . . ." he said, trailing off.

I waited.

". . . about a lot of things," he added cryptically.

"Like what?" I wanted to know.

"I wonder what's wrong with me sometimes. I feel like there's this disconnect . . . with women . . . and with myself. Like, I have this habit I don't like, and I don't like what I think about women when I see them. I feel weird walking around, like why am I watching people have sex rather than having sex with people?"

"Good question," I said.

"I feel like I've lost my confidence . . . about everything," he continued somewhat cryptically again.

This time, I waited him out for what seemed like a long time.

"Mostly I watch straight porn, but sometimes I watch gay porn," he finally continued, "so I wonder what it means about me that I get off on that, too."

"Maybe it means you're a sexual being," I offered.

"Maybe . . ." he began. "But, you know, like I told you, I had performance issues the last time I was with a woman so . . . I don't know."

"I don't know, either," I admitted. "But what if I told you that performance issues, as you're calling them, can be a side effect of watching a lot of porn?"

"I'd be surprised," he said, raising his eyebrows.

• • •

Internet pornography has been described as a "massive human experiment conducted on a global scale." For about two decades, it has offered millions of people effortless sexual engagement, instant sexual gratification, and limitless sexual novelty, at least in terms of imagery. Because habitual users tend to, well, habituate to what they see, it's common for consumers to need to shift the types of porn they watch in order to be turned on, often escalating from the erotic, to the exotic, to the extreme. Some say pornography is just about fantasy, but according to the research, the effects of this "massive human experiment" can be real.

Here are a few findings: Those who watch porn regularly are more likely than those who don't to prefer masturbation to sex with another person. They're more likely to think about porn during sex in order to maintain arousal. They're more likely to worry about their sexual performance and their body image. And they're more likely to experience anxiety both during sex and in other aspects of their lives. So, it's not surprising—although it was news to Michael—that the more a man watches porn, the more likely he is to experience erectile dysfunction, or to have what Michael called "performance issues."

At the beginning of the twenty-first century, the rate of erectile dysfunction in men under 40 was only about 2 percent. Yet, as the three—or four—As of porn have sharply increased, so has the percentage of under-40 males who say they struggle with performance. In a 2016 review of studies from around the world, rates of erectile dysfunction in young men ranged from 14 to 43 percent, and the desire for in-person sex was declining, too.

The more frequent one's porn habit, the longer it goes on, and the earlier it begins, the more likely it is to impact one's off-screen sex life. That's because those who consume porn regularly are training their brains and their bodies to enjoy one kind of pleasure that may not generalize to other kinds of pleasure. This may be especially true for teens and young adults, whose brains are just wiring up for sex. Unrealistic bodies and unrealistic depictions of sex are skewing norms and expectations, especially for teens and young adults who may not have much else to go on.

"I started watching porn when I was like eleven," singer Billie Eilish said in a 2021 interview for *Rolling Stone*. "I think it really destroyed my brain, and I feel incredibly devastated that I was exposed to so much porn. The first few times I, you know, had sex, I was not saying no to things that were not good. It was because I thought that's what I was supposed to be attracted to."

By the time clients first sit down in my office, many have had more experience with porn than with in-person sex, and as with Michael, the sex they are having may not be going well. "When's the last time you had trouble having sex when you wanted to . . . with a real live person?" I asked Michael after we talked about the connection—or disconnection—between porn and performance.

"It was a couple of years ago, I think."

"Oh!" I said, unprepared for how long it had been. "So, what's been going on since then?"

"I've been sticking to porn and just avoiding sex altogether. I'm so worried I'll try something with someone, and I won't be able to, you know, *do it*. And maybe that person will tell someone else. It's so embarrassing. I wasn't really planning on talking about this today. Actually, I was thinking of talking to my regular doctor about maybe getting some anxiety medication or, you know, some Viagra, so, like, I could be sure."

What Michael was suggesting might sound extreme, but as the rate of erectile dysfunction among young men has increased, so has the number of those who are taking medication for it. Although the "little blue pill" has long been seen as an older man's drug—the sort of thing you'd find alongside cholesterol medication in a medicine cabinet—sleek ads and spam emails now market such drugs directly to young adults. From there, it's easy to get a prescription, it's readily available on the internet, and in some countries, you can get it over the counter.

The use of erectile-dysfunction drugs is up even among young men who *don't* have erectile dysfunction. Some use drugs like Viagra not so much for performance *issues* as for performance *anxiety*, as they worry they may not be able to perform as well as they would like—or in the way that porn suggests perhaps they should. Because erectile-dysfunction medications can result in erections that are stronger, longer lasting, and that require less downtime between orgasms, more and more men are taking them as a sort of insurance policy or confidence booster. Ironically, however, more frequent use of drugs like Viagra is associated with decreased confidence in one's ability to get and keep an erection on one's own. When sexual confidence comes in the form of a tablet, users can be afraid to go without, setting up a sort of psychological dependence on the little blue pill.

In a 2020 episode of the YouTube series *High Society*, "The Viagra Epidemic Among Young Men and Its Dangers," a 24-year-old man talks about his experience with what he calls "popping the bluey"—a habit he says he'd like to stop. When, at one point in the documentary, he confesses to a sex partner that he took Viagra for their first encounter, the woman looked surprised and confused: "Why?" she wanted to know. Then, when he explained his rationale—"In my head I've been thinking that girls would expect me to fuck them like a porn star and, like, last hours in bed"—she looked even more surprised and confused. It turns out that wasn't what she was looking for at all. In fact, the woman said, the sex was better during their subsequent encounters when they knew each other—and each others' bodies—better, and when Viagra hadn't played a role.

All this is why, when Michael suggested asking his doctor for anti-anxiety medication or Viagra, I wasn't exactly on board. "Skills over pills," I told him, and I encouraged him to get some practice being intimate with someone instead.

He looked hesitant, if not downright panicked, and right away he catastrophized: "What if I go home with someone, and I try to have sex, and I fail?"

I pointed out that what he was describing has the same script as a porn flick. Boy meets girl (or someone). Boy has sex with girl (or someone).

"I'm not prescribing a hookup," I clarified. "What else could you do to practice being intimate with someone?"

Michael looked blank.

"How about you meet someone, and you get to know that person, and you kiss that person, and you gradually work your way up to sex?" I elaborated. "That way, you have some data points, some confidence along the way, about how things might go. Then, whatever happens happens in the context of a safe, if fledgling, relationship. You work it out together. What if those are the skills I'm talking about?"

"That never even occurred to me," he said, looking somewhat disturbed by this realization.

Sexual scripts are cultural messages about what sex is, what it means, and how it is supposed to go. And because sex is something that usually happens behind closed doors, internet porn is the most available, most explicit sexual script available to young adults worldwide. Although it's difficult to generalize about the hundreds of millions of web pages with unique adult content, content analyses show that mainstream pornography typically depicts sex that is casual and even callous. Physical encounters tend to be fast, recreational, unfeeling, unrealistic, risky, and uncommitted. Men are often dominant and even aggressive, while women appear submissive and up for anything. Little is shown about how to have safe sex, or how to ask for or give consent.

When Michael and I talked about sexual scripts, he said he thought the roles portrayed in pornography were similar to those in hookup culture, in which sex is also casual and sometimes callous. Some young adults are simply enacting what they've seen in porn and in the media in general. But neither porn nor hookup culture bears much resemblance to what many twentysomethings, including Michael, want or feel prepared to do.

"I mostly stick to hanging out with my guy friends because the pressure to perform, you know, like if I hook up with someone," he said, "it just makes me so anxious."

"But sex isn't a performance," I reminded Michael. "You're not a porn star."

"I'm not even close," he said, maybe missing my point. "I feel like I'm so behind, like I'm the only one having trouble with sex."

One of the most prevalent stereotypes about young adults is that they're all having great sex, and lots of it. But today's young adults are less likely to be married or partnered, and contrary to what we might have heard, single twentysomethings have less sex than do those in relationships. Economic insecurity makes many young singles look—and feel—less attractive as mates. For those who do have jobs, longer working hours and busier lives leave some of them too burned out to feel turned on. As more twentysomethings live with their parents, fewer have the privacy to bring someone home. On the couch, easier access to porn, gaming, and other electronic entertainment makes sex less appealing or less necessary.

For all these reasons and more, in the quarter-century I've been working with twentysomethings, they've been having less and less sex. According to a 2020 study of nearly 10,000 adults in the United States, about 30 percent of men and 20 percent of women ages 18 to 24 did not have sex in the past year; neither did about 15 percent of men and women ages 25 to 34. All these percentages are up since the year 2000. Maybe, from the perspective of unplanned pregnancies, sexually transmitted infections, and hookup regrets, this is a good thing. On the other hand, physical intimacy is a skill young adults are supposed to be learning, so those who aren't, like Michael, often feel inexperienced and unsure.

Here is what some of my other clients have to say:

I have never had sex before. No one has ever seemed interested in me.
I am in my twenties, and I've never had a girlfriend.
Every time my boyfriend and I have sex, we have to be drunk.
I shut down when things get to the point of kissing. There is a
general sense of, "No thanks."

I think maybe I'm bisexual, but I don't know. I've never fooled
around with a man or a woman.

I'm 29, I'm going bald, and I've never had sex. You don't get it. My
life is over.

Guys say that I'm closed off, that I'm not emotionally or physically
available.

Without a good job, I just don't have the confidence to go after
someone.

As a brown girl, I feel invisible to the white guys out there. And
those are the only guys I want, so I've never even kissed anybody.

There are so many categories about sex and sexuality. I just don't
know what I am.

I don't have time to worry about relationships and sex.

I did pelvic-floor therapy because I didn't like having sex with my
boyfriend. It took me two years to figure out that what I didn't
like was him.

I can't even imagine kissing someone without "liquid courage"—you
know, without drinking.

"I would kiss you, had I the courage," said painter Édouard Manet.
Courage is what we bring with us when we face uncertainty, including
the uncertainty of how to have sex. And usually, it takes more courage
to kiss someone—sober—than it does to get drunk and have sex. And it
definitely takes more courage to brave being intimate with someone—
a real person who may have thoughts and feelings and preferences and
reactions—than it does to stay home and watch porn.

Michael stopped watching porn regularly. I didn't ask him to, but after
many conversations and, somewhat to my surprise, he just did. What
didn't surprise me was hearing how much better he reported feeling as a
result. Correlation is not causation, so it's difficult to prove that a porn
habit *causes* problems with performance and anxiety. What studies—and

stories like Michael's—do show is that when habitual users cut back on porn, their mental and sexual health tends to improve.

"I feel less anxious and just *happier*," Michael said. "I think porn was causing some static in my brain, and I was turned on by, you know, pretty much anything. I didn't tell you this before, but at one point I was jerking off to my female friends' Instagrams. I think that was why I was feeling so weird around women—because I was embarrassed by some of the things I was doing. I'm not judging and saying porn is *bad*. I'm just saying that— watching it all the time—it didn't make me feel *good.*"

Michael and I weren't done, of course.

Sometime later he said this: "I've actually been thinking about my sexuality a lot. All the labels out there. I was thinking that I was gay because I was watching gay porn or that I was asexual because I was avoiding sex. I mean, being gay, being asexual—those are real things, but I don't know if they are true of *me*. I never see a guy walking around and I think, 'Oh, I want to hold their hand or something.' But I do think I want to know what I am or who I am, exactly, right now, and then I'll know exactly what to do and who to do it with."

"This may not be something you figure out today," I said. "And it's probably also not something you figure out in the abstract. I think you have to live the questions and see what you find out."

Then sometime later, Michael said this: "I went to this thing about consent with a group of people the other night. It was supposed to be this fun, cool event at this comedy club, but it really stressed me out. I feel like all I hear about, as a guy, is what I'm *not* supposed to do. I don't know much about what I *am* supposed to do when it comes to initiating sex. I feel like, as a guy, I get put in this position of being in charge of sex—which *is* comedy actually, because it makes me so anxious—and the burden is on me to get it right, or else I hurt someone, or face major consequences, or something. That makes me even more anxious, and it makes me want to retreat and watch some porn."

Michael's point was well taken; even in our sessions, I'd probably suggested more about what not to do—Don't replace people with porn! Don't try to figure this out in the abstract!—than I had about what *to* do. At the same time, I didn't have a script for Michael because, outside of porn or the movies, sex can't be scripted. There's another person involved, and I don't know who that other person is or what, moment to moment, that other person might want.

As I thought this over, it reminded me of back when I was learning how to do therapy—another intimate encounter that usually takes place behind closed doors. When I asked my first supervisor what to say in session, she said she could tell me how to begin the hour and that was about it. From there, therapy sessions—like all conversations and like sex—can unfold in an infinite number of ways. My job was to pay attention to how the person across the room responded to me and then respond to *that*. To imagine that I could go into session with a script would be to deny the other person's individuality and humanity.

"You talk a lot about performance," I said to Michael in session one day. "So, what if you think about sex as a different kind of performance, not the movie kind of performance in which you're playing a role. What if you think of it more like a musical performance . . ."

"I'm listening," he said with a smile.

"You're in the music business," I went on. "What if you think about sex like improvisation—even collective improvisation—like in jazz? You know, when two people are together, connecting through music, deciding minute by minute which notes to play, whether they want to take the song this way or that way, how long the song will last. That way, each time you have sex, it's like you've never had it before. You start with one note—one gesture—and you go from there."

"I just feel so blocked whenever I even think about kissing somebody," Michael told me, still struggling weeks later. "But I do want to have someone in my life. I want a family one day. I need to figure this out, but I just feel so *nervous*."

"Let's not worry about having a family right now," I said, slowing him down. "We are talking about kissing, remember? What makes a kiss seem so scary?"

"I don't even *know*," he emphasized. "That it'll be wrong? That it won't go well? That it'll be awkward? That I'll get rejected?"

"That's a lot of uncertainty," I said.

"Maybe I'll meet someone who has all the answers," Michael sighed, suggesting that he wished I did.

"No one has the answers to your life," I said. "The answers are going to come from your experiences and, in this case, from your experiences with other people. That's the only place they *can* come from."

Sometime after this conversation, Michael shared a kiss—and more— with someone. "It felt good," he said with a smile. "Really natural actually, once it happened."

"It is natural," I said.

"I think it helped that I got to know this person *personally* before we got together *physically*," he went on. "That did make me feel more comfortable. And, starting off just with kissing helped a lot. It made it easier than thinking about sex right away and about how everything was supposed to go. We were talking throughout, and it felt really connected. We were just making it up as we went."

TWELVE

HOW TO MOVE

Dancing and running shake up the chemistry of happiness.
—Mason Cooley, professor of literature

I woke up, aware that we were not moving.

It was February 2020, and I was on a ship with five hundred twenty-somethings somewhere in the South China Sea. We were together on a one-hundred-day educational journey around the world, with planned stops in ten countries: Japan, China, Vietnam, Malaysia, India, Mauritius, South Africa, Ghana, Morocco, Netherlands. I was there to teach positive psychology, which I thought would be a bit of fun.

So far, however, we'd spent three turbulent, seasick weeks crossing the Pacific. Then, we'd made it as far as a long weekend in Japan, when a mysterious flu-like illness in a city in China began to gain worldwide attention. For three weeks more, we'd sailed past China and hunkered down in Vietnam, hoping that rumors of an impending pandemic would subside. Instead, stories of more and more deaths crept across the shared border, and cases of the flu-like illness did, too. Soon, we set sail again, thinking we might outrun whatever was going on.

So, on this particular morning, floating immobile in the middle of the ocean didn't seem part of the plan. Still, I began the day the way I usually did. I walked about five steps from the bed to the desk in my small cabin, and I sat down to write the lecture I would be giving that afternoon: physical activity and mental health. The ship bobbed in the water, which made typing difficult. I missed the familiar hum of the engines and the steadiness that came from cutting through the water. All was strangely quiet.

Before long, the voice of the ship's captain boomed over the intercom. The mystery illness had been given a name, he informed us: COVID. It was unclear what COVID was, whether it was on board, or how it might spread. It was uncertain where we would go next—if we went anywhere at all. Countries everywhere were closing their borders and ships were being placed in quarantine, too. Classes, however, would go on as scheduled.

Shouts and raised voices wafted through the hallways and slipped under my door, and I felt like shouting, too. My cabin felt even smaller than usual, and I stood up from my desk to make a break for the top deck. *Not so fast.* Besides being in my pajamas, I was a professor—a professor of positive psychology! So, I would need to keep my chin up. There were five hundred students on board, and a lot of them were going to need some help.

I put on some jeans, stole my way up the back stairs, and grabbed a few minutes to myself along the ship's railing. All I could see in every direction was water, and I thought about the client who once told me that being in his twenties was like being in the middle of an ocean and not knowing which way to swim to shore. For the first time in a long time, I felt what it was like to be in my twenties again. Just last night there had been an itinerary for our hundred-day journey. Now, there was nothing but ocean and uncertainty—and upset twentysomethings—all around.

I turned around to face them. Confused and distressed students had begun to huddle on deck in twos and threes, and I mingled with them as they tried to make sense of the news. Most thought that maybe I knew something they didn't—like what would happen next. When, a short time later, the ship's engines were turned on, these same confused and distressed students erupted with applause and cheers. When we got underway, the breeze felt like an enormous sigh of relief. We may not have known where we were going, but it was good to be on the move again.

• • •

"God, I need this class today," one student said to no one in particular as she walked into the room where I taught. The Beastie Boys' song "Body Movin'" was blaring as others filed in with looks of dejected resignation. As I looked around the room, I knew I was there to be a professor, not a therapist, but I also knew I was probably the first older adult many of my students had seen since getting the news.

"So . . ." I began with a wince. "How's everybody doing?"

"It's confusing!" one young man began, sounding angry. "I don't know *why* we can't go to any countries! Are countries blocking *us*, or are we staying away from *them*? Why won't the captain tell us more?!"

"I just feel so guilty," a young woman cried, shifting the room's emotional tide in another direction. "I'm the first person in my family to leave the country. My parents and my grandparents sacrificed a lot for me to be here, and I'm not doing any of the stuff they thought I'd be doing. I feel like maybe it was all for nothing."

"I waited seven years to go on this trip," another young woman said, dabbing tears with her sleeve. "I opened a baking business on the side to save money for it. I broke the lease on my apartment . . . left all my furniture in storage . . . sublet my car. I went through major stress to get my visas. I'm so upset."

"I feel like I really fucked up doing this," groaned another. "I just keep thinking I made the wrong decision. I feel like I've done something stupid and I'm going to wind up getting sick."

"I'm totally freaked out that we're going to get this virus, and we're out here in the middle of nowhere," said yet another. "What if we all get sick and no one lets us into their country?"

"We've been on this ship *a lot*," a young man said. "I counted it up this morning. We've sailed like 10,000 miles already. If Asia is out, it's another 5,000 miles to Africa. After that, it's 10,000 *more* to Europe or North America. I don't know if I can do this!"

"We're just tired and emotional," a student summed up, fanning her tear-stained face with a book. "It's a lot."

"It *is* a lot," I said. "I'm not going to tell you to turn that frown upside down. This is scary and sad, and I don't expect anyone to put on a happy face about it."

My students' faces did not look happy, but they did look maybe a bit less distressed than when they'd first come in.

"That said, it's my job to keep on keeping on, so I've got a lecture about physical activity for whoever feels like that would be helpful."

"I really need this class today . . ." said the same student I'd overheard before, but loud enough this time for all to hear.

I hadn't prepared much to talk about because, fortunately, the topic is pretty simple: The more you move, the better off you'll be. Around the world, study after study has shown that people who are physically active feel better than those who are not. You don't have to be an athlete or even exercise to enjoy the benefits of movement. Maybe you go dancing on the weekends, or play frisbee with a friend, or throw the ball with your dog. It doesn't take a whole lot to be happier and healthier. About 30 minutes of moderate-to-vigorous activity, three to five times a week is all you need. But don't let the numbers discourage you. In recent years, experts have shifted toward the message that "anything counts." Maybe you take the stairs rather than the elevator, or you walk to the store instead of drive, or you play basketball rather than Fortnite. Any increase in your activity level is likely to improve your physical and mental health.

Yet the World Health Organization estimates that 80 percent of youth do not move enough. Maybe, in part, that's because we talk about physical activity the same way we talk about eating broccoli. It's something you know you *should* do, but it's probably not something you *want* to do. It's something that will do you some good later, but it tastes bad now. Or does it?

Yes, it's true that people who are active in the short run are happier in the long run—but they also feel better in the moment, too. When we get moving, our heart pumps and our breathing quickens, and this oxygenates the blood and the brain, which immediately calms us. The more vigorous the activity, the more it stimulates the release of our "happiness hormones"—endorphins, dopamine, oxytocin, and serotonin—which help us feel more pleasure and less pain.

Not surprisingly, then, physical activity has wide-ranging mental health benefits. In the most comprehensive analysis to date, a 2023 review looked at more than 1,000 randomized controlled studies that included more than 125,000 participants. The unequivocal conclusion was that all modes of physical activity studied—from running, to weight lifting, to yoga—were beneficial for reducing symptoms of depression and anxiety. What made headlines, however, was the conclusion that physical activity was *as effective as—or more effective than*—psychotherapy or medication. This makes exercise a clearly viable alternative or adjunct form of treatment for our most common mental health complaints.

Some professionals go further, arguing that, given its highly favorable cost-benefit ratio, exercise should be the *first-line* treatment for most cases of depression and anxiety. That's because movement not only has no negative side effects but it also has important positive ones. In a 2016 meta-analysis, activity of varying levels was found to have a positive impact on stress levels, energy levels, body image, self-esteem, social skills, and substance use.

Exercise is an affordable, accessible, nonstigmatizing intervention that can be carried on indefinitely. On the front end, physical activity acts as a preventive: Those who exercise regularly today are less likely to struggle with their mental health down the line. On the back end, those who use exercise to combat symptoms are less likely to relapse than those who use medication. Along the way, physical activity doesn't just help us feel better; it also helps us sleep better, and it's good for our hearts and waistlines, too. So, in stark contrast to psychoactive medications, exercise has positive effects on both our bodies and our brains.

Scientists have long known that physical activity is good for an aging brain, and now we know it helps the growing brain, too. A 2019 meta-analysis of more than 1,200 healthy young adults examined the relationship between physical fitness and white matter, or the connectivity among brain areas. In a simple fitness test that measured the speed and distance subjects could walk in two minutes, some young adults went farther and faster than others. Those who were in relatively good shape performed better on cognitive tasks, and MRI scans showed their white matter was more connected and less frayed.

But it's not just the connections in our brains that matter. Depending on what kind of activities we do, moving may connect us to our breath, bodies, strength, drive, creativity, spirit, hobbies, neighborhoods and cities, and to nature and music. When one of my clients who didn't have a car asked if he could do Zoom sessions, I suggested that he walk to my office instead; before long, he was starting his day—every day—with a long stroll around town. "How did I *not* know how much better this would make me feel?" he asked.

When another told me he spent six hours a day watching sports videos on his phone after his girlfriend moved away, I prescribed some basketball at the gym; just a few sessions later, he said he didn't need therapy anymore. "I think I'm good," he reported, and I believed him. From a mental health perspective, then, rather than thinking about moving as a way to prevent illness or death, maybe it makes more sense to think about it about it as a way to connect with wellness or life.

Studies show that group movement can be especially beneficial, as it connects us to each other. But, that doesn't mean you have to play some kind of team sport. One of my favorite students—someone I sailed with on yet another round-the-world voyage in 2022—struggled to find a friend group in high school until he created one through SpikeBall. "When I played SpikeBall, I would lose track of time, allowing myself to enjoy the game with people I really loved," he says in a TEDx talk on the topic. "As afternoons turned into dusk, SpikeBall pushed me out of my comfort zone and into my community."

For some, none of this information may be particularly new, but neither is the tendency to dismiss it. On its website, the Centers for Disease Control does not even mention exercise as a treatment option for mental health problems—nor do many physicians.

Consider this 2005 report from the Mental Health Foundation, in the United Kingdom. Of 200 general practitioners surveyed, 92 percent said antidepressants was one of their top three recommendations to patients with symptoms of depression, while only 5 percent suggested exercise as a leading strategy. And 43 percent said this was because they aren't convinced physical activity is an effective treatment—yet an almost equal share, or 42 percent, said they would try exercise as one of *their* top three strategies if they themselves became depressed. So, nearly half of doctors surveyed didn't believe the evidence about physical activity, and most of the other half did believe in exercise but didn't recommend it—perhaps because they didn't believe their patients would do it. Related to these findings is that 33 percent of the physicians in this same study said they prescribed antidepressants, even when they thought a different form of treatment would be better, because a patient asked for them.

The mental health benefits of physical activity are becoming more recognized—by doctors and patients—but there is still a long way to go. In a 2018 study in New Zealand, about one-third to one-half of doctors reported prescribing either daily or weekly exercise to patients for stress, depression, or anxiety. Yet, that still means that about one-half to two-thirds of the surveyed doctors *don't* regularly recommend exercise. As in previous studies, the biggest barriers were physicians' lack of knowledge about and confidence in exercise as an effective intervention, as well as their belief that patients are unwilling or unmotivated to move more.

It's ironic. At a time when so many people want to feel better right now, moving is one of the few things we can do to shift our mood within minutes. So, when doctors everywhere—including myself—hesitate to prescribe movement, we may be underestimating not only its benefits but also others' willingness to give it a try. "Don't *not* suggest something that works because you think your client won't like it or won't do it," a supervisor told me once. "It's your job to give them the best of what you know. It's your job to tell them the truth."

Back on the ship, I was struggling with this very thing: whether I should tell my class to get up and move.

• • •

"I don't know what to do here," I admitted to the class after my short lecture. "This course is supposed to be a living laboratory, so to experiment with movement, we were going to go up on deck and dance. But I know people are feeling pretty awful, and I don't expect you to just dance it off. We can stay here and talk about the disappointments and the worries. Those are real. That said, this is a class about positive psychology, and this is an opportunity to find out if moving around helps us feel even a little better."

As I weighed our options aloud, I noticed how comfortable I was giving voice to the bad and sad feelings. Yet, as I looked around at the students who had and had not yet spoken up, I sensed they were hoping for something else from me.

I decided to ask.

"What do you think?" I asked the young woman who, weeks before, had volunteered to lead the group. "Can you even do this today?"

"*Yeah!*" she replied more gamely than I expected.

"What about other folks?" I asked. "Do you want to go outside and get moving?"

Hands shot up to vote for outside.

"Okay, then, for those who want to give it a try, let's head up to the top deck. For anyone who needs to do something different, that's all right, too."

A couple of students slipped out the back of the room as everyone else filed up the stairs, and we spilled out into the sun. Up on deck, our fearless leader got us into formation and taught us moves in counts of eight: 1, 2, 3, 4, 5, 6, 7, 8. . . . There was music. There was movement. And before long there were even smiles. I'm not sure when it felt better—when we got everything right and danced in unison, or when we bumped into each other with our various missteps and laughed so hard we cried. If all this sounds a bit campy—in every sense of the word—it was. No, dancing around didn't fix any of our problems. But it did, for a moment, feel good. (And, years later, dancing on deck with my students is one of my happiest memories of the voyage and of the pandemic.)

In our next class meeting, I told my students how impressed I was with how they'd rallied. "I have to be honest," I said. "I thought it was a lot to ask of you to get up on the deck and boogie, given how everyone was feeling. I kind of dreaded coming in here and talking about movement, and trying to get up and dance. Did anyone else?"

Heads nodded, and hands went up halfway.

"But when I saw all of you," I went on, "the energy was incredible. And I mean that literally. I could hardly believe how you showed up in every way. Thank you for that because I was having a tough morning myself, but it ended up being a really wonderful day."

Now, there were more tears in the room again, but this time they felt like tears of connection and care.

"Dancing might seem silly, but it taught me something important. As a therapist—and as a person—I've struggled with telling people who are having a hard time to get out there and go for a walk, or pull out a Hula-Hoop, even though I know it's good advice. I never want people to think I'm trivializing their pain or their struggle. But you know what I thought after dancing with you?" I asked rhetorically.

The students waited.

"Excuse my lack of eloquence," I continued, "but I thought, 'Damn, this shit works.'"

"2020 was a year like no other," said the annual World Happiness Report when it was released. To no one's surprise, in almost every country around the globe, it was a year during which citizens reported feeling more anxious, and depressed, and stressed than before. Yet, despite all the suffering—or maybe even because of it—those of all ages looked for ways to feel better, including movement.

To learn from the moment, some nimble scientists quickly mobilized to study physical activity and emotional well-being during the worldwide lockdown. In one study, researchers collected data from more than 13,000 respondents in eighteen countries. Those who did some exercise almost every day reported the highest levels of feeling good, regardless of whether they had exercised regularly before the pandemic. Those who cut back on physical activity owing to lockdown restrictions reported worse mental health than those who were able to maintain or increase how much they moved. What this means is that it's never too late to get moving as the positive effects kick in quickly.

And we don't even need high doses of physical activity to feel these effects. More may be more when training for a marathon, but when it comes to bolstering mental health, moderate exercise is best. Intense workouts are physically and mentally taxing, so when we're struggling, it's wise to choose workouts that lift us up without wearing us down. Researchers have found that, whether we're in the throes of final-exam stress or pandemic stress, exercise that allows for some movement—but not too, too much—is what helps us feel good and strong. The best form of activity is something you enjoy or can incorporate into your day. Maybe it's dancing, or weight lifting, or hiking, or biking. Even plain old walking does the job.

In the spring of 2020, plain old walking was just about all many people, including myself, could do. One month—and 5,000 more miles of sailing—after my students and I danced on deck, I was back in the United States. After being cooped up on a ship for the better part of three months, I felt winded just trying to make it around the block. But day after day, I got out there—rain or shine, warm or cold, and went a little farther than before. It was a way to spend time with my family and my friends. It was a way to see the sun or the stars, and to feel fresh air on my face. It was a way to create momentum in my now otherwise slow-moving life. It was a way to boost my heart rate and my mood. Of course, I knew walking was good for my brain and body, but maybe even more important, it was a metaphor for putting one foot in front of the other, no matter what.

One year later, in the spring of 2021, I and many others were still regularly trudging about town when a massive cargo ship the length of the Empire State Building became lodged sideways in the Suez Canal. That was a metaphor, too. For how stuck so many people still felt. For just how much had ground to a halt. For the tragicomedy that life in a pandemic had become. When a photo of a minuscule excavator seemingly tasked with freeing the gigantic ship appeared, memes predictably swept the globe. "The work I need to do versus the motivation available!" said one caption. "Greenhouse gas emissions versus carbon capture!" said another. "The size of my bills versus the size of my paycheck!" said yet another. My personal favorite was the words "My COVID depression and anxiety" emblazoned across the giant vessel. What was written under the tiny excavator? "Going on a daily walk."

It's true. Our problems often seem far, far larger than the solutions in front of us, and many times they are. But that doesn't mean the small things don't do any good. That tiny excavator did play a role in freeing the cargo ship by removing soil from the bank of the canal, although it did not do the job by itself; there were also dredgers and tugboats, and a boost from a high tide.

Likewise, movement alone likely won't fix all, or maybe even any, of your problems. It's not going to cure a pandemic, repair a bad relationship, or make a dead-end job worth keeping. What it will likely do is put you in a better position to solve, or tolerate, those problems yourself. For some people, exercise is all they need to shift their mental health. For others, physical activity is one of several strategies or skills that they can put to good use. Whatever the case, we need to say it more: in one way or another—or in multiple ways—moving will *almost certainly* help.

THIRTEEN

HOW TO COOK

It's a life lesson they need to have, a skill everybody needs—to cook.

—Guy Fieri, restaurateur

No one comes to my office to learn how to cook, so it's not a topic I usually lead with. Just like no one with a tissue in hand wants to hear, "Have you tried going for a run?," they don't want me to suggest too early, "How about making a salad or whipping up a meal?" That said, how we eat—and even whether we can cook—does impact our mental health, so I would be remiss not to bring these matters up. It's like I have learned to ask about social media, and porn, and exercise, and drugs: Whether or not twentysomethings raise the issue with me, I interrupt and inquire about food.

Angela has attention deficit hyperactivity disorder (ADHD). She'd received the diagnosis after an extensive evaluation many years before, and had long taken stimulant medication to help her focus at school and work. "It definitely helps," Angela said, and I'm sure it did.

"The problem," she told me, "is that my meds wear off by the time I come home from the office, and I feel so overwhelmed. There's all this stuff I need to do when I walk in the door, and I don't know where to start, and it makes me really anxious. Plus, I'm starving. I get totally 'hangry,' so

I microwave a whole bag of dumplings, or whatever I have. Then I'm in a food coma, so all I can do is stumble over to the couch and watch TV for the rest of the night, or maybe I . . ."

"Wait," I cut in. "Why are you starving?"

"My medication kills my appetite, so I barely eat all day, but then I have major food stress by the time I get home. I need food and I need it fast. There should be, like, an app for that," Angela chuckled.

There was, of course.

Angela's apartment was often littered with food containers delivered by DoorDash or Uber Eats. "That makes me stressed and anxious, too," she explained. "I look around my kitchen and my living room, and it's such a mess. I'm embarrassed to have people over, and it just makes me feel worse about myself. So, I honestly think that makes me eat even more."

Most young adults have an unhealthy relationship with food, and they know it. In a 2018 survey by the American Psychological Association, nearly 60 percent of 18- to 21-year-olds reported coping with stress by eating too much or eating unhealthy food. This is called *emotional eating* or *stress eating*. It's having a bad day and scarfing down a bag of dumplings or chips. It's polishing off a pint of ice cream or a sleeve of cookies while you watch a movie. Of course, almost everyone reaches for the dumplings, or chips, or ice cream, or cookies from time to time, but if eating is your first—or only—way of handling stress or other difficult feelings, then you may be an emotional eater.

To be clear, emotional eating is not the same thing as having an eating disorder. Although eating disorders—such as anorexia, bulimia, or binge-eating disorder—do tend to emerge in teens and young adults, they're relatively rare, each one affecting only about 1 percent of the population. Emotional eating, on the other hand, is quite common, because the negative feelings that often spark it—anxiety, irritability, boredom, frustration, sadness, uncertainty—are quite common, too.

When we try to "feed our feelings," as psychologists say, not just any food will do. Negative feelings stimulate cravings for high-sugar, high-salt, or high-fat items that often come in the form of snacks, processed, packaged, or otherwise fast foods. That's why we reach for them: because they're easy to get and because they taste and feel good. Fatty foods like bacon and dairy products, sweets like chocolate, and starchy foods like pasta decrease stress hormones and increase happiness hormones—in the short run, that is.

Of course, sometimes it can be difficult to distinguish between young adults who are emotional eaters and those who eat unhealthfully because they don't know how to feed themselves any other way. Unfortunately, unhealthy eating is so widespread among young adults that it has become downright normalized. Remarkably, a 2020 article in *American Psychologist* about the stages of adult development identified unhealthy eating as a defining characteristic of those in their twenties, while according to the article, healthy eating is something we figure out in our thirties and beyond. Not long after, a 2021 story in the *New York Times* outlined the relationship between nutrition and mental health, or how what we eat affects how we feel. If this is news to *New York Times* readers, 70 percent of whom are over age 30, then clearly we need to get the word out sooner.

As it is, conversations about nutrition largely focus on how what we eat affects our physical health, rather than our mental health. Yet, around the world, an unhealthy diet is a risk factor for mental health problems, while eating healthfully is a protective factor. What it means to "eat healthfully" may look different in different countries and different cultures, but no matter where you are, diets higher in plant-sourced foods—such as vegetables, fruits, beans, nuts, and whole grains—and in lean proteins, such as chicken and fish, are associated with better physical *and* mental health. In contrast, a 2022 study of more than 10,000 adults found that the more processed foods people ate, the more likely they were to feel anxious and depressed.

That's because the digestive system functions as a so-called second brain, in that the gut is *second only to the brain* in terms of the number of neurons it contains. The brain and the gut are in constant communication, such that when we talk about a nervous stomach or having butterflies, that is the gut feeling anxious and registering that stress. Although we tend to think about mental health problems as residing in the brain, more and more we are learning they may also reside in the gut. A few small studies have shown that transferring the microbiome of a depressed person into the digestive tract of a healthy person can induce depressive-like behavior in the recipient.

One proven, but rarely discussed, way to change how you feel is to change how you eat, day to day. Here are two examples. In a 2016 study of more than 12,000 Australian adults, increased daily consumption of fruits and vegetables was associated with increased life satisfaction. The least happy people ate little or no fruits or vegetables, while the happiest folks ate about eight servings per day. The estimated effect of eating more plant-based foods was found to be about equal to that of moving from unemployment to employment. That's right: Improving one's diet had about the same impact as getting a job.

A 2017 experiment, also in Australia, included almost 70 adults with major depression. Half the adults were assigned to a 12-week healthy-eating program that included nutrition and cooking workshops, while the other half were assigned to a social support group. Both groups improved over the course of the 12 weeks, as would be expected, but the healthy eaters improved more. After six months, 30 percent of the healthy-eating group no longer met the criteria for depression, compared to 15 percent of those who had attended the support group. And despite the perception that fresh foods are more expensive than ready-made items, those in the healthy-eating group spent less money on food.

And money matters.

A 2018 study, this one of almost 2,000 college students in Appalachia, looked at the relationships among diet, food insecurity, and mental health. On average, students reported feeling depressed about 10 days per month and anxious for about 15 days. About one-third said they experienced food insecurity, meaning they were unsure about how to obtain healthy, affordable food. A likely related factor was that the mean number of servings of fruits and vegetables was around two per day, which was about equal to their average number of servings of added sugars. All three factors—food insecurity, low plant consumption, and high sugar consumption—were associated with depression and anxiety in the group.

In twentysomethings, food insecurity takes many, often related forms. Young adulthood is typically the least financially stable time of life, a period when millions opt for the cheapest meals they can easily find. Ramen. Frozen pizza. Microwave burritos. But money isn't the only uncertainty that comes into play. Far too many young adults don't know enough about food—or how it impacts their bodies and their brains—so they end their days, or their late nights, with alcohol, or sugar, or takeout. They aren't sure how to feed themselves, and they don't know how to cook.

Noah had always stayed out of the kitchen. Growing up, it was a room where his dad sat and drank while his mother cooked; and on more evenings than not, the two wound up fighting. Sometimes the fights were limited to screaming and yelling. Other times, Noah said, "things got physical."

"My dad was a cop and I think he had PTSD [post-traumatic stress disorder]," Noah explained, "although it wasn't right that he came home and got drunk and took his problems out on us."

I agreed.

"It was so stressful to be with my family," he went on. "I would eat, and eat, and eat. My dad shamed me for it. He would call me a pig, so I started to hide what I ate. I would buy candy and junk food, and eat it out of the house or in my room. I got pretty chubby."

"Then what happened?" I asked, noticing that Noah didn't look chubby to me.

"I took a nutrition class in high school," Noah said. "I liked my teacher a lot, and I lost a lot of weight. But now I feel like I have mostly forgotten what I knew. The weight has been creeping back up, because when I get stressed I still sneak off to eat."

I kept listening.

"I've never touched alcohol because of my dad, but now I realize I've probably always been an emotional eater. I guess food is better than alcohol, because I'm not going to wind up hitting someone because of it. But I don't feel good about myself or about how I handle things. I need to work on that."

Noah started a food log so he could keep track of what, when, and why he ate. Soon, some patterns emerged. He skipped lunch when he was busy at work: "I just try to push through because I don't feel like I have the time or the money to get something." He raced out for fast food at night when he was overly tired and hungry: "I feel better for a minute but then I feel worse. I feel like I can still hear my dad calling me a pig."

He ate when he was lonely, too: "I have a lot of good friends but having a girlfriend hasn't happened yet. When I get down about that and eat, I feel like that chubby person again, and I think no one will ever want to be with me."

It soon became clear that, like most twentysomethings, Noah needed to eat more regularly, more healthfully, and more affordably. So, I told him what I had told many clients and students before, whether they were emotional eaters or not: "I think you need to learn how to cook."

I suggested that Noah buy a five-ingredient cookbook and start by cooking one or two nights a week. This, I told him, would help him build up his "cooking confidence," which is knowing how to shop, how to follow a recipe, and how to prepare a meal with basic ingredients. Eventually, of course, cooking confidence is feeling relatively sure that what you make will (usually) turn out well.

Some of my clients don't feel confident in the kitchen because their parents did all the cooking when they were growing up. They didn't have to think much about how to go grocery shopping or how to make a meal. Others don't feel confident because their parents were working long hours and weren't at home to show them what to do. Cooking confidence, or lack thereof, cuts across race, class, and to some extent, gender.

In the 1920s, 85 percent of Americans' food purchases were for meals to be made at home. A century later, only about 50 percent are. A lot has changed in the last hundred years. Both women and men are now part of the workforce. Workdays and commutes can be long. Ready-made foods are widely available. For these reasons and more, Americans are eating out—or taking out—more than ever before, despite the fact that home cooking is associated with better physical and mental health, as well as other good things. Adults who have cooking skills are less likely to eat unhealthy, processed foods. And cooking confidence is associated with higher self-esteem and quality of life, as well as lower levels of anxiety and depression. Knowing how to cook is even good for our social lives.

When we know our way around a kitchen, we're more likely to cook with and for other people. Maybe we have a group over and grill burgers or barbecue chicken. Maybe we bake a cake for a birthday party. Maybe we go to a sick friend's house and make them a meal. Maybe we host a potluck and encourage others to work on their cooking confidence, too. Many of my clients would like to do these things, but they don't know how.

Fortunately, cooking confidence can be relatively easy to develop. A 2022 study of almost 700 Australian adults examined the effect of a seven-week cooking program in which participants attended hands-on sessions that included nutrition information, recipes, and knife skills. After the seven weeks, and at a six-month follow-up, the participants reported feeling more confident in the kitchen as well as having better mental health. At the beginning of the program, the women were more confident about their cooking than were the men, but by the end of the program, both groups felt equally sure of themselves in the kitchen.

This is important. Despite women and men being equally represented in the workforce, women still do more of the cooking in the home, a disparity that often causes problems in modern relationships. Indeed, there's something wrong with a culture in which only some people see the need to know how to cook. If you plan on eating, then you should plan on cooking. "I've always wanted to do everything different from my dad, which is why I've never been a drinker," Noah said. "And I don't want to be the guy who sits in the kitchen and watches his wife do all the work, either."

Within a year, Noah had made nearly every recipe in his cookbook, and he'd invited a date over for dinner, too. "The recipes aren't exactly difficult," he said at one point along the way, "so I'm surprised by how good they make me feel. I don't know if it's the cooking that makes me feel better or if it's not bingeing on junk food. That always made me feel so ashamed and out of control. Cooking is one way I feel like I have something concrete I can do to improve myself. I feel like I have instructions for how to have my shit together in one area of my life."

Noah was right. Cooking is one of the few areas of twentysomething life where there *are* instructions. Almost like being in school again, there are recipes and ingredients, and step-by-step descriptions of what to do when. If you can follow directions, you can cook. Then, within minutes or hours, you get to be done with something and see the results.

A win in the kitchen may seem like a small victory, but according to psychologist Albert Bandura, "such personal triumphs serve as transforming experiences. What generalizes is the belief that one can mobilize whatever effort it takes to succeed in different undertakings." When we gain more cooking confidence, that generalizes to a lot more: the belief we can do what it takes to keep ourselves healthy, the belief we can manage our day to day, and the belief we can accomplish the things, big and small, that we set out to do.

When I explained all this to Angela—my client with ADHD who favored DoorDash and Uber Eats—she looked at me skeptically. Then, she sent me TikToks and Reddit posts that highlighted how differently her brain worked from the "normies," as she called them, and how day-to-day chores were just never going to be her thing. "Chores never end. But arts and crafts," said one social media thread she showed me, "you can hold it up and say 'Look, I made this. I did the productivity today,' and nothing quite beats that rush."

Angela's mind did work differently from the so-called neurotypical brain, but I think she sometimes overestimated those differences. And she had a tendency to use her ADHD diagnosis as an excuse for why good advice didn't apply to her. The truth is that most young adults—and adults of all ages—struggle with repetitive labor. No matter what you do, there is always more cleaning, more laundry, more errands, more cooking to figure out, somehow. There's never a sense of being done.

"One time when my kids were little," I told Angela, "I was packing yet another lunch box and feeling put out about making both breakfast and lunch before 8:00 a.m., when I've never been much of a breakfast person. So, I was feeling sorry for myself and I looked out my kitchen window where a bird had built its nest. I saw it flying back and forth, bringing food to its babies. Later that day, and on other days, I noticed that this went on for hours. And I realized, there's nothing *wrong* with my life that I have to pack another lunch box. Feeding ourselves. Tending to our spaces. Tending to our loved ones. That *is* life, or at least part of it."

"So I'm supposed to be happy about it?"

"Well, I'm thinking about the post you sent me about crafts," I said. "About how good it feels to produce something. Cooking may not be like that all the time, but it can feel rewarding to make something in the kitchen. You do get to say what that post said, 'Look, I made this. I did the productivity today.'"

Angela didn't seem convinced.

Sometime later, one of the videos Angela sent me was about nutrition and ADHD, and especially about how reducing sugars and artificial ingredients could help reduce her symptoms. "My medication has made a big difference in my life, and that has made me a big believer that what I feed my brain affects me. So, I'm kind of into the idea that what I eat might affect me."

I listened, waiting to see where she was going with this.

"Here's the thing, though," she continued. "I think the only way I can reliably eat well is if I cook for myself a lot more than I do."

"Good idea!" I said, like I had never suggested it before.

Angela took a weekend cooking class with a friend, and she gradually began to put what she'd learned to use. "Now, when I come home all 'hangry,' I eat something decent," she said a couple of months later. "I'm taking leftovers to work and making myself eat something, even when I'm taking my medication, so I don't get so 'hangry' in the first place. What actually works best for me is cooking stuff on Sundays that I can put in the fridge and heat up at night. That way, I start my week feeling ahead rather than ending every day feeling behind. Plus, I don't have takeout containers stacked up everywhere, so I can have people over and not be embarrassed."

"Good for you," I said.

"It *is* good for me," Angela said. "I don't know if eating better is helping my ADHD or if being more on a schedule with cooking and eating is helping, but whatever it is, I do feel less scattered and anxious."

Eating something healthy, or making something healthy, may not cure anxiety, or depression, or ADHD, or a tough childhood. But, given that eating is something we all need to do, it's strange how much we underestimate the role that cooking—or not cooking—plays in our lives. Feeding ourselves is an everyday problem that has to be solved every day. How you solve that problem matters, so it might be time to change what you put in your body—and in your brain.

FOURTEEN

HOW TO CHANGE

There's a reason that so many people use binge drinking and runaway eating to support their mental health: because the effects are reliable. Because they don't require a prescription. And because they're available, right *now*.

—Benedict Carey, *New York Times*

Robert had been having panic attacks for about six months.

"The first time I had one I didn't know what it was," he told me from underneath the bill of a baseball cap. "I started sweating for no reason, my heart was racing, I honestly thought I was going to die. After that, it was like a switch flipped, and I had a panic attack sometimes every day or two, sometimes every week or two. I never knew when one was going to come on. So I started panicking whenever my heart rate went up or I started sweating, even when it was for a good reason, like when I was working out or, you know, talking to people at a party. I started panicking about panicking. So, for a while now, I feel like I've either been *having* a panic attack or I've been *anxious* about having a panic attack."

"Do you have a history of anxiety?" I asked.

"No," he said with a definitive head shake. "I've actually never been an anxious person at all. I've always been normal . . . fine . . . you know, no problems with anxiety outside of the usual public speaking stuff you would expect."

"Anyone in your family have problems with anxiety or panic attacks?"

"Nope," he said.

"Huh. So I wonder what started all this," I puzzled out loud.

"I know exactly what," he offered. "I was headed out for a long night of drinking with some friends, but I wanted to be able to stay awake for it, so I had an energy drink. And the next day, I thought I was having a heart attack, so I went to the hospital. The doctor said it was a panic attack, like probably from the energy drink."

"What kind of energy drink was it?"

"I don't know exactly," he said sheepishly. "It was one of those you get at the gas station. I do remember it had, like, a thousand milligrams of caffeine."

"One thousand milligrams . . . ," I began, as I reached for my phone and looked up caffeine equivalents, "so let's see . . . that's like . . . ten cups of coffee . . . or thirty Cokes . . . in one shot."

"Yeah, I'm a dumbass," he grimaced as I let that hang in the air.

"It sounds like you overdosed on caffeine," I went on, calling it what it was. "Not to mention that alcohol is a depressant and caffeine is a stimulant, so you were trying to get your brain and your body to do two extremely opposing things. It probably didn't like that."

"No, it didn't," he said, grimacing again, "and I've been having panic attacks ever since. Well, until recently. I made an appointment with you because I was hoping you could make all this stop. But for the last couple of weeks or so, I've actually been about 85 percent better."

"Oh yeah?" I said pleasantly surprised. "Why's that?"

"I started taking these CBD gummies every day, and they seem to be doing the trick."

Alcohol. CBD. Mushrooms. Caffeine. LSD. Ecstasy. Cannabis. Cocaine. Nicotine. Of all ages, young adults are the ones most likely to use nonprescription psychoactive drugs either regularly or recreationally. By regularly, I mean daily or almost daily. Recreational use is taking drugs on the weekends or once in a while "for fun." Either way, substance use is so normalized among young adults that, often, little thought goes into what they put into their bodies and their brains.

That's why even, and especially, if clients don't raise the issue in a first session like Robert did, I always ask what substances they use. I also ask when they use them, and why they use them, and how much they use them, and what exactly they've heard about their effects. Most twenty-somethings hold a somewhat paradoxical view of their drugs of choice. They see them as powerful and benign at the same time. They see them as both affecting and not affecting their brains.

By definition, all psychoactive drugs affect our brains, and that is typically why we take them: because we want to change how we think or feel or act. Maybe we want to have limitless good energy at a rave. Maybe we want to feel less tired so we can stay up and drink. Maybe we want to be less self-conscious when we go out on the weekend. Maybe we want to feel less stressed after work. Or maybe we want to feel less anxious day to day. Whatever our intentions, as with prescription drugs, we don't always get the effects that we want, nor is it always clear how exactly these substances will affect our mental health down the line.

Still, when I work with twentysomethings, I don't talk about substance problems per se. I talk about dosage problems. That's because I generally don't have an opinion about *whether* people like Robert use substances like caffeine, alcohol, CBD, or any other legal or illegal drug. I do have opinions about *how* they use them, depending on how their dosage might affect their lives. The most common problem young adults have with substances is that they use them too often or too much.

By and large, research shows that the younger we are when we start using drugs, or the more regularly and heavily we use them, the more likely this will result in unintended and undesirable consequences, including but not limited to dependence. Yet, even recreational drugs are not always fun and games, since one-off use can carry one-off risks. The high-potency cannabis that triggers psychosis or other psychiatric problems.

The night out on Ecstasy that kicks off a manic episode and maybe even lifelong bipolar disorder. The pill bought for studying or partying that unexpectedly contains fentanyl. The gas-station energy drink that brings on a string of panic attacks. With unregulated drugs, we often don't know what we're taking, what the dosage is, or what the positive or negative effects of even a single dose may be.

To be clear, the only risk-free dose of any substance—legal or illegal, prescription or nonprescription—is zero. That is likely why, when my mental health was at its worst, my professor suggested I not add drugs to whatever else was going on in my brain. It was good advice, and I took it instead.

But, yes, I did use drugs when I was a young adult. I recreationally took some and somewhat regularly used one or two others, for a while anyway. I moved on when life moved on, when it was no longer convenient or cool to lose nights to substances, or to wake up in the morning feeling like hell. I moved on when what I wanted out of life was more important than what I wanted out of an evening. This is a pretty common trajectory.

Young adulthood is not only the age when drug use is likely to increase—it is also the age when drug use is likely to decrease, or not. A nearly twenty-year study spanning the teen years to middle adulthood showed that most nonprescription drug use begins by the late twenties and subsides by around the mid-thirties. As might be expected, the substances most likely to be used into the thirties and beyond are alcohol, nicotine, and marijuana. Some people have dosage problems with these and other drugs, and some people don't.

The tricky part of talking to twentysomethings about substances is that dosage problems tend to take hold precisely when they're most likely to be shrugged off. Because a fair amount of risky behavior is expected from young adults, these are the years when, often, we don't realize how serious our—or our partners'—dosage problems really are. Consider this email I received:

"I'm twenty-seven and have been with my loving boyfriend for eight years. My concern is that he has addictive qualities that have cost him thousands of dollars (gambling) and several bouts of stitches (drinking), and he can be really moody. He doesn't handle stress well and can be dependent. This makes me nervous for our probable lives ahead together. Aside from that, our relationship is wonderful. We are committed, loving, alike in many ways, make each other laugh, and strongly support each other's aspirations."

You probably don't need a doctorate in clinical psychology to see that there is no "aside from that." Bad habits—such as with alcohol, or drugs, or food, or gambling, or devices, or pornography, or shopping—matter more than good ones. That's because it is easier to tear down a relationship or a career or a life than it is to build one up. So, either this woman's boyfriend needs to quit his excessive drinking and gambling—and probably do some other work, too—or she needs to quit the relationship before one or both of their lives are ruined. The woman already knows she has good reason to be nervous about their "probable lives ahead together," of course, and that's why she wrote to me.

Not every young adult who uses a substance has a dosage problem, of course. But, of adults who *do* have dosage problems, those problems most likely began in their twenties. So, that's what I tell my clients. I take their substance habits seriously, even if they aren't. I ask if perhaps their lives would be better if they leaned less on their drug of choice. I ask them about the people, places, and things that get them wanting more. I help them examine what effects, if any, their usage has on their relationships, careers, and lives. That's if I can get that person into my office. But, as with the email I received above, often it's a partner or a parent who reaches out.

Nisha's father barked at me to "close the deal." Those were his words when he berated me for not calling his daughter, as requested. Some days earlier, he had contacted me from Chicago to say that, much to his chagrin, his 26-year-old daughter was irresponsible with money. "I'm not going to pay for her to go to graduate school forever," he said angrily.

When I heard from Nisha's father the second time, I explained that I am not in sales and I don't "close deals." I am a psychologist, and I do my best to help people who walk through my door or pick up my books. Whether or not Nisha would ever be one of those people was up to her. "Give her my number again or give her a copy of something I've written," I suggested. "Maybe it will get her thinking. Maybe she'll call."

"Can't you go see her?" he asked, now sounding more like the scared father he was. "She goes to school right down the street from you. How can I *make* her call?"

There's an old joke, for lack of a better word, among therapists: How many psychologists does it take to change a lightbulb? Just one, but the lightbulb has to want to change.

In an indirect way, this joke references what are called the Stages of Change. This five-step model is a useful way to think about not only substance use but also *any* other sort of behavior we might like to be different. Here are the five stages:

Pre-Contemplation: We are unaware we need to change or are uninterested in doing so.

Contemplation: We start to think about changing and we listen to advice.

Preparation: We decide we want to change, and we make plans to do so.

Action: We put our plans into practice, and we start doing things differently.

Maintenance: New behaviors become our new normal.

When Nisha's father called me the first and second times, Nisha was in the pre-contemplation stage. Presumably, that's why her father got in touch instead. When we're in the pre-contemplation stage, we don't want to do things differently, nor do we see a reason to. Even if friends or family complain about our choices, we may see other people as the problem rather than ourselves. And, who knows? Maybe they are the problem or at least a part of it. In the pre-contemplation stage, it may not be clear what the problem even is.

My best advice for moving someone from pre-contemplation to contemplation is this: give them something to contemplate. Tell them that you care and are concerned. Let them know how their choices are impacting people's lives, including their own. Send them a thought-provoking article or a video. Gift them a book you hope they'll read, even if it sits on the shelf . . . until it doesn't. Let the consequences of their choices speak for themselves by resisting the urge to bail your loved one out. Whatever someone's bad habits are, they will probably never be easier to change than in their young adult years. But, still, the lightbulb must want to change.

Nisha came to my office about a year after her father challenged me to "close the deal."

"My dad told me I should either read your book or be your client," Nisha explained. "I finally read it, so I wouldn't have to meet with you. But then, once I finished it, I decided that maybe you weren't so bad."

That first day we met, I was struck by how forthcoming and reasonable Nisha was. She was in the contemplation stage, to be sure, thinking about making some sort of change. She talked some about finally finishing her dissertation so she could start to earn money and get her parents off her back. She also talked about trying to be more responsible with her spending. Either way, Nisha said, she came to see me because she would prefer to stay away from, as she put it, "more meds."

When I asked what she meant by that, Nisha explained that her general practitioner had recently given her a prescription for an antianxiety medication—a benzodiazepine—which she reluctantly filled. The one and only time she'd used her new prescription, she told me, was when she'd "drunk fought" with her boyfriend. Afterward, she felt panicked and unable to sleep, so she took two pills.

"Mixing alcohol and benzos can be dangerous," I said. "Are you trying to kill yourself?"

"No, I know," she said. "I didn't have good judgment that night because I had too much wine after being at school all day."

"Like how much, exactly?"

"You know, one or two . . ." Nisha said before trailing off.

"One or two what?" I asked.

"Bottles . . . ," she replied with a grimace.

"Bottles," I reflected. "On a weeknight. . . ."

"Yup," Nisha said grimacing again.

"The doctor who prescribed your meds," I began, "does he know how much you're drinking?"

"He doesn't ask a lot of questions," Nisha said.

"Well, I do," I said. "So what's up with all the drinking?"

"I feel really edgy sometimes after I take my ADHD meds . . ."

"Wait," I interrupted. "What ADHD meds? I didn't see an ADHD diagnosis in your medical history."

"I never really got a diagnosis, but in college I kinda had trouble getting all my work done, so my doctor gave me stimulants. I still take them sometimes if I need to jam on my dissertation. *Not* that I'm exactly finishing it," she added.

"So, you don't *know* you have ADHD," I clarified. "You just take ADHD meds sometimes."

"Actually, I know I *don't* have ADHD. I've never really had big problems in school or anything. I just use the stimulants to get more things done."

"And then what happens?"

"They make me so edgy during the day that I need a glass of wine to settle down at night. But once I have one glass, I keep going."

"So, it starts with the stimulants . . . ," I said trying to puzzle it out, "and then comes the wine. Then what happens?"

"I go on social media, and Instagram is just, like, a trigger for me. I see all these people who are further along with their careers and their lives. I wind up buying stuff, or I fight with my boyfriend. Then I end up tossing and turning and feeling bad all night."

"Or, now that you have benzos, maybe you take some of those and wind up in the hospital or worse?"

"I know," she said. "That's why I'm here. I don't like taking the benzos, and I don't want any more meds. My parents keep saying that maybe I need antidepressants, that maybe I'm depressed because I'm always telling them about how bad I feel."

"What do you feel so bad about?" I asked.

"Everything," she shrugged. "I feel like I'm behind my parents. They're so successful. I feel stressed that I *won't* be, that I won't end up with a good life."

"What's a good life to you?" I asked.

"Having a job and a partner I love. I have a great relationship, so that's good. But I feel so far away from having a job."

"So, you need to finish grad school and get a job," I agreed, "but still, by your definition of the good life, you're about halfway there."

"I just want to be done already," she complained. "I want to be done now."

"I get the feeling that your dad likes things to happen right now, too," I said. "But it takes time to build a good life."

"I *know*, and that's what makes me feel so behind," she said. "And it's not just my dad. I go on Instagram, and I feel like I'm behind on traveling. I feel like I'm behind on fashion. I feel like I'm behind on everything."

"And a new outfit or a bottle of wine makes it better?"

"It *does!*" she replied, keeping up her disarming streak of honesty. "Buying something gives me something concrete to be happy about. It's something I can do that feels like progress. Drinking may not feel like *progress*, but it does make me feel better, yeah."

Various forms of consumption—for Nisha, it was drinking, shopping, and pills, while for others maybe it is eating, or porn, or getting high—are tried-and-true ways to shift our moods. Food and drugs change our brain chemistry, as does gambling, swiping on our phones, or buying something new. That's why, as cliché as it may sound to say that someone like Nisha was self-medicating, that's exactly what she was doing. She was using substances to change how she felt.

The problem is that what feels good in the short run often feels bad in the long run. Too many stimulants made Nisha feel edgy by the end of the day. Too much wine led to arguments with her loved ones by the end of the night. Too much retail therapy led to large credit card bills by the end of the month. All this ultimately led to that "behind" feeling that she was trying to get rid of. Nisha's dosage problem made her feel like she didn't have her life or her mental health together—and she didn't. Disarmingly charming in her ability to own up to her poor choices, she seemed to be saying all the right things. The question was what she would say—or *do*—next.

When Nisha dropped her medications in the disposal box at her pharmacy—"I didn't like taking them anyway," she said—I thought maybe our work was about done. She was in the preparation stage, to be sure, making plans to change her ways. She told other people—her dad and her partner, and even me—that working with me was changing her life.

But it wasn't.

Even without the pills, Nisha's spending continued, and so did her drinking. Wine was referenced when she talked about shopping online: "It's just so easy to click on something I like when I'm hanging out at home having drinks." Tequila was involved when she described laying down her credit card for a night out with friends: "When I'm drinking, I'm not thinking." Champagne preceded an argument she had with her partner: "I don't even remember what that was about."

"I may be a bit late to the party here," I said in session one day, "but it seems like every time something goes wrong, alcohol is involved. I know you got rid of your medications, but maybe you need to think about how much you're drinking."

Popular culture normalizes, and even trivializes, drinking as a way of coping with stress. As with many habits—watching porn, scrolling through social media, shopping for the latest trends—drinking seems like such a classic pastime of youth that it can be difficult to critique without receiving an eyeroll in return. Often, we assume that we or our loved ones will grow up and grow out of a bad habit, such as drinking too much, before it becomes a so-called real problem. Many do. Some don't. But *when* we do or don't is right about Nisha's age.

"So, you're twenty-seven, correct?" I asked her.

"Yes."

"I'm not sure that drinking the way you are is as cute as maybe you thought it was five years ago," I suggested.

"Maybe not," she chuckled.

"You give that a maybe," I clarified. "Let me ask you this: Do you want to be drinking this way in five years?"

"*No*," she said firmly. "Definitely not."

"Then why are you doing it now?" I asked.

When, a few sessions later, I gave Nisha the information for local AA meetings, she looked at me like I was the one who needed help.

"You think I'm an *alcoholic*?" she asked incredulously. "I don't want to go to some meetings in a church basement somewhere."

"I don't know if you're an alcoholic," I admitted. "But I do know you have a dosage problem—you're drinking too much—and you don't seem to be able to do much about that on your own."

It can be confusing, to be sure. Even for me, it can be difficult to tell when I'm sitting across from someone whose college-age partying has simply gone on too long—or when I'm sitting across from an addict in the making, and I'm letting it slide. But I'm not sure the label matters much. What matters is whether someone would be happier or healthier if they used a substance less or not at all—and whether they are willing to do what it takes to make that change.

Finally, I told Nisha I couldn't work with her anymore until she addressed her drinking. "Everything we're trying to do goes out the window when you drink too much. And my helping you clean up the messes every week just keeps it all going."

I wasn't helping Nisha change. I was helping her stay the same.

• • •

The AA meetings in the church basement never did happen. What did happen was a pandemic, and that's what moved AA meetings online and Nisha into the action stage. "It was so easy to listen in, and what people said about their drinking really got me thinking about mine," she told me later. "Plus, everything was different when the world shut down, which gave me a chance to be different, too. People weren't going to bars, and they weren't posting all this amazing stuff on social media. I used lockdown as a way to focus and finish graduate school, once and for all."

It is tough to change your behavior when everything in your environment stays the same. The flip side of that, of course, is that if you want to change a habit, then change something—or several things—about the way you live. Most people, like Nisha, lean on substances or other bad habits because they're easy and within reach, and available right now. So take some pressure off your willpower by making those temptations less easy and less available.

If you want to stare at your devices less, get a flip phone. If you want to watch less television, cancel your streaming subscriptions. If you want to binge less on sugary foods, be mindful of what you keep in the pantry. If you want to watch less porn, keep your phone out of your bedroom. I'm not saying it's as simple as that, but major changes almost always start by changing what's within reach.

That said, fixing a dosage problem can't just be about doing something less. It also has to be about doing something else *more*. Nisha spent less time despairing about not having a job when she spent more time working on her dissertation. She had fewer glasses of wine—or none at all—when she started spending time with friends who had moved on from drinking. She stopped looking at Instagram and listened in on AA meetings instead.

Traditionally, these sorts of novelties—new jobs, new friends, new activities, new ways of coping—have been called *replacement behaviors* because they replace substances or other bad habits. Really, it's the other way around. Every one of my clients who has a dosage problem is doing the same thing: using substances as a *substitute* for the action they already know they need to take. But when we let substances do the work, whether they be prescription or nonprescription, we often don't do much else. We let pills—or alcohol, or gummies, or gambling, or social media, or porn—take the place of skills.

Post-pandemic, the world opened back up, and so did the bars, but Nisha wasn't much interested in going. She had new ways of having fun and new friends to have fun with. Besides, she was busy getting ready to go on the academic job market. "I don't know where I'll wind up, but I am just so happy to be moving on with my life."

It's tough to say when exactly Nisha moved from action to maintenance, but somewhere along the way, "not being much of a drinker" just became who she was. "I don't know if I am or ever was an alcoholic," she explained. "But if I'd kept drinking the way I was—if I *hadn't* changed my ways—then in five or ten more years I probably would have been an alcoholic. Fortunately, drinking is not a problem now, and I don't think it ever will be. I feel like who I am now—happier, healthier, better me . . . this *is* me."

Nisha's story makes all that sound easy, and in a way it is. In young adulthood, our brains, our lives, and our identities are on the move, and with so much in motion, our habits are on the move, too. So the next time you go reaching for that thing you do that maybe you wish you didn't, remember there is something else that's well within reach if you want it—and that's change.

FIFTEEN

HOW TO DECIDE

A good decision is based on knowledge and not on numbers.

—Plato

Adults make approximately 35,000 decisions a day—or somewhere around 70, depending on whom you ask. Either way, it's a lot.

The 35,000 number comes from research that estimates the largely unconscious choices we make. Should I sit in the chair or on the sofa? Should I click on this website or that one? Should I pass this person on the left or the right? Should I grab the blue pen or the black one? Should I look at my phone again or not? If the figure of 35,000 is anywhere near correct, we are making decisions like these about once every two seconds while we're awake. Only about 70 choices each day are conscious decisions, however, meaning they are ones we put some thought into. What should I have for dinner? What should I post on social media? What should I wear? Which car should I buy? How should I vote? What should I say?

Conscious decision-making can feel especially difficult for twenty-somethings because an estimated 80 percent of life's most consequential decisions are made by around the age of 35. Do I go to graduate school and how do I pay for it? Which job do I take? Where should I live? Whom do I love? How do I love? Should I have kids? Should I move for my job?

Should I move in with my partner? Our twenties are a time when what we decide to do—or not do—can have a significant impact on the years, and even the decades, to come.

In recent years, there has been a lot of talk about choice overload, or how difficult it is to make decisions when there are so many options, but the trouble with being a twentysomething isn't that of choosing among dozens of brands of yogurt or jeans. The real difficulty is making what feel like life's most defining decisions when so much is uncertain or unknown.

In a classic 1992 study on decision-making, researchers presented young adults with a hypothetical scenario in which they had just completed a difficult exam. In three different, randomized conditions of the study, subjects were told that they failed the exam, they were told they passed the exam, or they were left unsure about how they performed. Then, subjects were asked whether they would like to buy a special low-priced vacation package to Hawaii.

Perhaps surprising is that both the majority of those who were told they passed *and* the majority of those who were told they failed opted to purchase the trip, albeit likely for different reasons. Those who passed were probably ready to celebrate, while those who failed likely decided to cheer themselves up. The most notable finding in the study, however— from a decision-making perspective, anyway—is that those who didn't know how they had performed were the least likely to opt for Hawaii. This finding was noteworthy because it is irrational. If we're going to take a trip whether we pass a test or not, then *not knowing* whether we pass or fail shouldn't make a difference.

But it does. What this 1992 study stumbled on is *uncertainty paralysis*, or the brain-scrambling effect that unknowns can have on our ability to decide. I say stumbled on because, in the early 1990s, researchers were only beginning to understand how uncertainty affects our thoughts, feelings, and behaviors, and the notion that ambiguity can leave us unable to think or act was somewhat new. The brain-as-computer metaphor was just starting its meteoric rise, and more than three decades later, as tech dominates the worldwide cultural landscape, scientists and laypeople still like to believe that for everything there is an answer or an algorithm and maybe even a hack.

That brings me to a related, much less discussed finding from that same 1992 study: most of those who were unsure about how they'd performed on the test were willing to pay a fee to find out their results, so as to make their vacation decision easier. Again, this makes little sense. Given that the results would not likely change their choice to go on the trip—the majority planned to go either way, remember?—the information does not mean much. What it does mean, though, is that young adults want input that makes life *seem* more certain—and will even pay for it—whether that input actually adds value or not.

In many cases, that's where astrology, psychics, tea leaves, and online personality tests—and sometimes even therapists—come in. Many people will do anything—and sometimes even pay anything—for the secret, or tip, or trick, or app, or conversation that might remove their doubts or make up their minds for them. They have been led to believe that, with big data or tiny habits, they can game their choices and perfect their lives. They want the future to be quantifiable and predictable. But it's not.

In 1954, famed statistician Jimmie Savage made a distinction between large-world problems and small-world ones. A small-world problem is one in which all choices, probabilities, and consequences can be known. Rolling the dice and calculating your chances of coming up with a four is a small-world problem. So is playing the lottery or betting on a horse, and understanding what exactly you might win or lose. Small-world problems may be risky in that the odds are often against you, but at least you know what the odds are.

Large-world problems aren't risky; they are uncertain. And, in decision-making, there's a difference here. Large-world problems are situated in a world that is, well, large, and thus all choices, consequences, and probabilities cannot be determined. Unplanned events, chance

HOW TO DECIDE ~ 181

encounters, too many variables, and too many unknowables prevent us from modeling either the present or the future with any certainty. The world simply is too large and too much hasn't happened yet.

According to Savage, "A person has only one decision to make in his whole life. He must, namely, decide how to live." That largest of large-world problems is, of course, subdivided into countless other ones—something that Phoebe Waller-Bridge captures so well in her writing for her television show *Fleabag*: "I want someone to tell me what to wear every morning. I want someone to tell me what to eat, what to like, what to hate, what to rage about, what to listen to, what band to like, what to buy tickets for, what to joke about, what not to joke about. I want someone to tell me what to believe in, who to vote for, and who to love, and how to tell them. I just think I want someone to tell me how to live my life."

What makes large-world problems so difficult is that we can never know all our alternatives, whether they be for jobs, or partners, or cities, or all the things that might—or might not—happen if we choose one over another. That's why there are no right answers for whom to marry, how many children to have, or what are the associated probabilities of happiness or success. So it goes for when and where to vacation. For which apartment to rent or home to buy. For what outfit to wear. For what to believe. For what couch to buy. For which hobby to take up. For whether we should be an accountant or a teacher. No formula can give us the answers to our lives.

Where a lot of young adults go wrong is in treating large-world problems like small-world ones—and they're not the only folks who do so. "The point that the calculus of probability can determine the best action under risk but not under uncertainty is not new; it has been made as often by statisticians as it has been forgotten by cognitive scientists," researchers say. Statisticians may know better, but for cognitive scientists and laypeople alike, it's tempting to believe that we could ever have complete and perfect information for what matters in life or that someone, somewhere could offer it up.

Consider the college student who came to my office because he felt paralyzed by decisions when he "couldn't figure out the algorithm": he would often spend as long as five hours on the phone with his parents, deciding whether to drop a class. Or the man in his early twenties who wanted me to tell him how to spend his spare time. Or the woman in her late twenties who didn't know if she wanted to have children and felt she couldn't date until she was certain. Or the man in his early thirties who was unsure if he should move in with his girlfriend; she wanted to, but he didn't, so which of them should get their way?

Or consider the twentysomething who sent me this message: "I wanted to ask you a question about my relationship. I have been dating someone who I met five months ago, and she is everything I have ever wanted in a partner. Even though we haven't been dating that long, we are very serious about our relationship. However, I am concerned because the future is so uncertain in our twenties. For now, we both live in or near New York, but I want to move out of the Northeast as soon as possible. The only thing keeping me here is my girlfriend. Should I stay close to her? Or move somewhere that I actually want to live, but risk the troubles of a long-distance relationship?"

Each of these people reached out to me because they imagined I might know the answers for their lives. They wanted me to reassure them by removing their fears and doubts.

In a large world, reassurance is a coping mechanism so prevalent—and so problematic—that courses have been developed for psychologists who encounter "reassurance junkies." Indeed, I learned a long time ago that reassurance doesn't help anyone, least of all young adults. Like a drug with a short half-life, reassurance is something that if I give it to clients, they quickly—and even more anxiously—return in search of more.

With the rise of smartphones, it has never been easier to reach out for reassurance, and some twentysomethings text their parents, friends, or therapists multiple times a day for a hit. But, like short-acting medications, a dose of reassurance may reduce anxiety in the moment, but it does little to shore up a person over time. In fact, studies show that seeking reassurance excessively only makes someone feel *more* anxious down the line. Every time we reach out for *re*assurance, we undercut our own developing *self*-assurance. It gets in the way of creating confidence in our ability to manage large-world problems and to see ourselves as capable and strong.

"Everyone says it's a good problem to have," Irma summarized with a sigh, "but it still feels like a problem."

Irma was almost 30 now. I'd last worked with her when she was a senior in college, but she'd reached out recently because she had to choose between two jobs. One was a promotion at her current company and the other was the chance to work at a buzzy big company in another state. When she had come to my office years ago, Irma regularly told me her problems and then said, "What should I do?" She was a reassurance junkie of sorts, often jonesing for right answers and hoping that somehow she might get them from me.

"The thing is," Irma explained, "I wasn't really happy at the company where I am now so that's why I started looking for something new. I applied to this other company where I've always wanted to work. I didn't really think about all the other factors, like whether all the trouble and expense of moving to a new place is worth it, or whether my husband would find a job he liked once we got there, because I didn't have to think about those things yet. Then I got an offer, and I was so excited . . . until I told my current boss I was going to leave, and then *he* offered me a promotion to a role I actually would like. If he hadn't done that, this wouldn't be so difficult."

"If he hadn't done that, there wouldn't be much of a decision to make," I pointed out.

"*I know!*" she exclaimed. "That would have been so much better. Then it would be obvious, and I would just know what to do."

Most of the decisions young adults make are between two (or more) apparently attractive options or between two (or more) options, each with its pros and cons. That's what makes a decision a decision. Try as we might to list the pros and cons of people, places, or positions, not all costs and benefits are equally weighted—nor can they even be quantified—making our lists an organizing exercise at best.

Probably the most famous example of this—maybe even the most infamous example, given its rather dated and sexist particulars—is Charles Darwin's list of reasons to marry or not marry. The upsides of having a spouse, according to what Darwin wrote in his journal, were "children, constant companion who will be interested in [me], object to be beloved and played with, better than a dog anyhow, home and someone to take care of house, female chitchat." (Yes, the father of the theory of evolution, one of the greatest scientists of all time, really wrote that.)

On the other side of the argument, and of Darwin's journal page, were the benefits of not marrying, which included "freedom, not forced to visit relatives, the expense and anxiety of children, perhaps quarreling, loss of time, anxiety and responsibility, less money for books, perhaps my wife won't like London." Though his list of reasons against having a spouse was longer than his list for taking one on, Darwin went on to marry and have ten children.

Times have changed, of course. Rather than a young man trying to decide if "female chitchat" was worth marrying over, in my office was a young woman weighing whether to take a new job. Yet, the more things change, the more they stay the same. As smart as they were, both Darwin and Irma thought maybe they could take a large-world problem and treat it like a small-world problem. They hoped that maybe some simple arithmetic might determine how work, and love, and cities might or might not add up. They longed for a way to make the uncertain certain, as certainty would protect them from actually having to decide.

"I know choices feel hard," I said, "but your choices are what make your life *yours*. Owning your choices is how you own your life."

"Ugh," Irma moaned.

"If I remember correctly, when you were in college, you used to look up the menu online before you went out to a restaurant with friends. You would agonize over what to order because you didn't want to make the wrong choice. I'm pretty sure we talked about this back then. That life isn't black and white, and in most situations, there is no right or wrong choice."

"Yeah, I remember that," she said. "The restaurant thing seems pretty stupid now."

"You must have eaten out countless times since then and made far bigger decisions," I pointed out. "You got married! How did you do it?"

"Yes, I did get married," she laughed. "But I wasn't choosing between *two people*. I love my husband, and it was pretty easy to choose being with him over not being with him. That didn't even feel like a decision."

"Okay, fair enough," I said. "But the restaurant thing—it sounds like you moved on from that."

"Well, yes," she said with an embarrassed roll of her eyes. "I mean, I now realize that I am going to get to eat out thousands of times, and the stakes aren't exactly high. But with this job thing, these two jobs will take me and almost everything in my life in two different directions. There are so many implications I can't even handle it. Everybody says that both jobs are good so there's no wrong answer, and I guess that's what *you're* saying," she said, clearly unconvinced, "but I'm just so worried I'll end up regretting my choice."

Regret is the dissatisfaction we experience when we imagine our lives could have been better if only we had made a different choice. It is a comparison-based form of counterfactual thinking in which how what *is*—or the facts—stacks up against what *might have been*. A particularly painful form of self-blame, regret is among the most frequently experienced negative emotions. In one study of both positive and negative feelings, only love was talked about more.

Not surprisingly, then, Irma was regret-averse, and she hoped that somehow, some way she could make a choice without one day feeling bad about it. Yet, as philosopher Søren Kierkegaard put it two centuries ago, "I see it all perfectly; there are two possible situations—one can either do this or that. My honest opinion and my friendly advice is this: do it or do not do it—you will regret both." As we already know, in uncertain situations, the brain is a simulation machine, churning out catastrophic *what-ifs* and counterfactual *if onlys* often more quickly and more automatically than we can keep up with. But that doesn't make those *what-ifs* and *if onlys* true.

What is true is that regret happens when we view a large-world problem like a small-world problem. In a small world, where all choices, consequences, and probabilities are known, we *can* be certain about how much we would have won if only we had picked a different horse in a race or chosen different numbers on the lottery. In a large world, however, we can never truly compare the choices we made with those we didn't make. We can never know what would have happened if we had taken another job, or married another person, or moved to another city because those scenarios don't play out without us. So, when we conjure up regrets about what might have been, we are comparing what we know to what we don't know. What's worse is that, much like the upward social comparisons we make on social media, we torture ourselves with how the realities of our situation stack up against an imagined ideal.

The idea that we could ever know what might have been is the appealing premise of Matt Haig's best-selling novel *The Midnight Library*. In the book, the main character—after a suicide attempt—gets to see all the other ways her life might have gone had she done some things differently. She finds out that none of those counterfactuals were perfect; each alternative path had its flaws. Only then does she decide to keep living. To be honest, I have mixed feelings about the book. On the one hand, it helpfully reminds people that wallowing in fantastical counterfactuals is probably a wrong-headed, despair-inducing waste of one's time. On the other hand, the novel accomplishes this only by giving the protagonist a hefty dose of reassurance and certainty that none of us will ever get in real life.

The scenario is a fiction, of course, because we can never know whether or how our lives might have been better—or worse—had we made different decisions. And that's what makes regret a fiction, too. When we regret something, we're making up a story about what might have been. Maybe there's a moral to the story, in that perhaps our pangs tell us something about a lesson to be learned. But it is still a story. Regret is a fantasy in which we swap uncertainty for certainty when, very counterintuitively, uncertainty is our friend.

In fact, recent research shows that one way to feel less regret—and to feel less distressed in general—is to accept and even appreciate life's unknowns. When we open our eyes to the enormity of the large world we live in, we recognize that its infinite variations and possibilities are beyond our algorithms, and even our comprehension. Even more different than apples are from oranges, life's various scenarios—whether they be ours or other people's—are too complex to be quantified, modeled, or compared.

What all this means, and what I told Irma, is that while not knowing the right answer can make forward movement feel difficult, that same uncertainty can free us from the feeling we have gone the wrong way. When you accept there aren't any right answers, then you realize there aren't any wrong answers—there are only your answers.

And that's what decisions are.

"What should I do then?" Irma, very characteristically, wanted to know. I stared at her blankly, wondering what part of my large-world lecture she didn't understand.

"I get you're saying that there isn't a right answer about which job to take, that I just have to decide," she clarified, probably in response to my stare. "But what should I do about *how to decide*?"

Large-world problems are solved not with statistics but with heuristics. Heuristics are mental shortcuts that allow us to make decisions without considering all the information—something that's useful when all the information is unavailable or just too much to process. Compared to algorithms, heuristics are often seen as inferior, and maybe for small-world problems they are. But for large-world problems, they are all we'll ever have.

When we use heuristics, rather than trying to factor everything in, we use a smaller number of variables to make up our minds. It's as simple as having priorities or values, and letting our decisions be guided by those. Chances are, I told Irma, she'd made important decisions this way before. When she chose a college, for example, there was certainly more available information than she could factor in, from the number of majors to the number of professors in the astronomy department, from the size of the a cappella group to the volleyball team's winning record, from the style of the dorms to the quality of the food in the cafeteria, from the number of students to the number of parking spots, from where her friends were going to where her parents thought she should attend. How did she go about making up her mind?

"That was a while ago," Irma said, looking up to remember, "but I wanted to go to a school that would challenge me academically. . . . I wanted to be within driving distance of home. . . . I wanted to go to a public school that was affordable and diverse. . . . I think that was about it."

"So, you had some personal criteria—some things you knew about what you wanted—and you went with those," I said.

"Yeah," she replied. "But I only got in to one school that fit those criteria. So, kind of like getting married, the decision was pretty obvious."

"Okay," I said. "But what if there had been two or three schools that fit the bill. How would you have felt if, based on your GPA, and SAT, and extracurriculars, and a whole bunch of other stuff, some big data-crunching company assigned you to a school?"

"I would not have liked that at all," she said.

"Why not?"

"Because I want to feel like I get to decide my life," she said. "Like you said, I want to feel like it's mine."

"Well," I said, "this is your chance."

"My husband and I talked," she told me the next time we spoke. "We agreed that we are still in a very expansive phase of life, so we want to prioritize learning new things and trying new places. We envision maybe buying a place or thinking about kids within the next few years, so we want to build up and build out while we can. That means we're going to go for it and move for the new job."

"Great," I said. "If learning and expansion are your metrics, then remember to make those your measures of success. You can't go out there and grade yourself on criteria you weren't prioritizing, like what other people are earning or doing. So, no matter what else is or isn't happening a year from now, if you're learning and expanding, then you're getting what you wanted."

"This has been such an exhausting week," Irma said, clearly having a tough time thinking ahead. "But I feel so much better now that I've decided. My mind feels more ordered and so does my life. Finally, I know *what* I'm doing."

Before she—or I—could enjoy the moment, she went on: "You know, though. Sometimes, I just wish I had a real *why*."

SIXTEEN

HOW TO CHOOSE PURPOSE

Nothing contributes so much to tranquilize the mind as a purpose—a point on which the soul may fix its eye.

—Mary Shelley, author

Sascha was unsettled after attending his cousin's wedding. The ceremony was held in a big, white church with gleaming stained-glass windows and wooden pews that creaked when he shifted in his seat, which was often. Sascha felt moved, both inside and out, first by the vibrations of the organ music and then, to his surprise, by what the minister said during the ceremony.

"It was something about how if you stay focused on God, your mind will be at peace," he recalled. "The reverend kept saying that, like a mantra almost, and it made me realize how much I wanted something to focus on when my mind was going all crazy. But that wasn't the only thing that resonated. As I watched this wise person up there supporting my cousin and his new wife, I just yearned for it. The support and the wisdom they had around them. That couple, you know, they aren't alone. And I realized how alone I felt. And I'm married!"

As I listened, I thought about how feeling alone was what had brought Sascha to my office in the first place, several years ago. Back then, he'd struggled with a sort of existential dread. He was the kind of twentysomething who could look around and see all the bad things in the world and wonder what the point was of doing anything at all.

It had been a while since he'd been to my office, or since I had heard him talk that way. But now, here we were again.

"I thought when I got married," he said now, "I'd never go to another wedding and feel alone. I'm so happy to have a partner, but now I feel like *we* are alone. We're just trying to figure everything out for ourselves. It all just seems so *arbitrary*. I feel like I need some bigger structure or mission. I feel like I need a religion . . . or something. When I was growing up, my parents' attitude was that I could choose my own religion when I was an adult. Well, that's now, and I know more about the Greek myths than I do about the Bible."

I kept listening.

"But it's not just the Bible, you know. My best friend is Muslim, and he prays, like, five times a day. If he's at work or he can't do it, it's fine, but as much as he can, he gets out of bed or stops what he's doing to pray when he's supposed to. He said it creates peace and discipline on the inside, and it connects him with something bigger than himself on the outside. I envy him because I think he worries and stresses a lot less than I do. When things go wrong for him, he's human, and it's hard, but he also says that what helps is knowing it's in God's hands, that God has his back. I look at my cousin and my friend, and I just feel like they have something I don't."

Sascha is part of the rise of nones—those who are unaffiliated with a religion and who now represent more than half the U.S. population. Religion has long been a way for cultures to reduce uncertainty, and as such, it has also proved to be a significant predictor of positive mental health. In recent years, however, young adults have been less drawn to organized religion as a way of organizing themselves and their lives. Increasingly, they're asking themselves—and their therapists—how they can have what religion offers, how they and their lives can be "good without God."

I asked Sascha this question, as well as whether he thought some sort of organized religion was what he needed. "I don't think so," he said. "Despite the envy I feel toward people who have that, I don't really think religion is for me."

"Then what are you thinking?" I asked. "Or, shall I say, what's got you thinking about this now?"

"It was going to that wedding," he began. "And I just started law school. When I was in college, the point was to get As and get myself to law school. I did that. Now, I look around at all these people who are doing these amazing things, like starting companies or making all this money in consulting. Or I look at people who aren't killing themselves in law school and being digital nomads, with these amazing lives."

"Tough comparisons," I said.

"It's confusing because I could theoretically do any of those things," he went on. "I know I should just stay in my lane and not worry about what other people are doing, but I don't know what my lane is. I don't know what's important to me, so I'm constantly setting myself up to be miserable. I think what I really need is some kind of purpose."

Sascha was right.

Purpose is a self-organizing form of personal certainty. Some would say purpose is our reason for being, but even more, it is our reason for *doing*— our own personal *why*. Purpose is why we go to work even when we don't feel like it. It's why we take up a cause even when it's an uphill battle. It's why we care for our kids even when it's difficult. It's why we get out of bed even when we're worn out. It's why we are content to do what we do—or to love whom we love—even when we could be doing something else. As Sascha might put it, your purpose is your lane.

People can have more than one *why* at a time, and whatever it may be right now, that purpose probably should change as we do. Whatever our whys are, purpose is about doing something that matters to the self— and usually even beyond the self. This beyond-the-self orientation is important because it connects us to something outside our own concerns. It enlarges our perspective and helps us look outward and forward. Some say that the cure for being anxious about an uncertain future is to take a deep breath and put your mind on the here and now. However, another more productive—and maybe more courageous—way is to dare to look ahead with a *why*.

Whether you're driving a car, or riding a bike, or running a race, or living a life, looking ahead—rather than in the mirror, or at your feet, or at your phone—is how you stay on track. "You'll feel more settled when life gets more settled," I often tell my clients, and one of the most settling things of all is finding something besides yourself on which to steady your gaze.

Getting beyond the self is, perhaps paradoxically, good for the self. Having a sense of purpose is associated with a host of mental health benefits, including positivity, goal directedness, motivation, perseverance, self-esteem, connectedness, well-being, and life satisfaction. It also helps combat what Sascha was doing: overthinking who he is or who he isn't. When we focus on what's important—to us—we feel less socially anxious and we're less interested in what others are doing. Purpose even disrupts the relationship between social media and self-esteem such that young adults with a purpose are less affected by the likes or feedback they do or don't get online.

"What's wrong with me that I don't have that?" Sascha wanted to know after we talked about purpose for a while. "I just feel so lost or behind."

There was nothing wrong with Sascha, and he wasn't behind.

Developmentally speaking, purpose comes into focus rather slowly. By the age of 30, only about half of young adults say they have one and the other half do not—yet. Settling on a purpose often takes time and experience, although doing so is nothing to be taken for granted: about one-fourth of adults ultimately say they never feel like they have that something bigger than themselves.

Cross-culturally, most adults who do find purpose say it lies in their relationships or in their work, or both. "Love and work, work and love . . . that's all there is," Freud purportedly said. Love and work may not be all there is, but those two aspects of our lives do take up most of our waking hours, so it makes sense for us to want them both to mean something.

"I feel ungrateful because I should be happy. I have a great partner, and I never look around and think I want to be with someone else, so people would say I'm lucky. But I get so hung up on not having work figured out."

"Your brain has solved the love problem, so it has moved on to trying to solve the work problem," I said. "That doesn't make you an ingrate."

Sascha was experiencing what one researcher calls *purpose anxiety*. Purpose anxiety is not a disorder. It's simply a label to describe the normal yet negative feelings that often go along with not yet knowing your own personal reasons for being—and even staying—alive.

In a 2014 study of adults of all ages, more than 90 percent reported having experienced purpose anxiety at some point in their lives. About three-fourths said they experienced it as they searched for their purpose, and two-thirds said they experienced it as they were trying to live out that purpose. Not surprisingly, young adults were the least likely to have found their purpose and were the most likely to feel anxious about not yet having done so. Although it's never too late to make a difference to something or someone, after around age 35, searching for a purpose can feel especially frustrating.

At age 28, Sascha was getting frustrated already: "I guess I need to think more about what is really important to me."

"Yes and no," I said.

Not long ago, I taught a class on purpose. Or, I should say, about sixty twentysomethings and I delved into this topic together. Given that purpose is self-determined, we started by coming up with some questions to foster self-reflection: What is a change you would like to see in the world? How might you use your interests or strengths to make your community or the world a better place? What are your values and beliefs, and what are you doing to put them into practice? What are you good at, and how might those skills be put to good use? What would you like for people to say about you twenty years from now—or when you're gone? Or, simply, who and what do you care about?

Sascha was right that living a meaningful life probably requires that you put some thought into what has meaning for you. But sometimes, when questions feel unanswerable, they can contribute to purpose anxiety in young adults. So, from there, our class moved on to reading psychiatrist Viktor Frankl's classic *Man's Search for Meaning*. Part memoir and part manifesto, the book tells of Frankl's time in Nazi death camps during World War II, as well as his approach to therapy, which centers on helping people look outward, rather than inward, for purpose. "Meaning is to be discovered in the world rather than within man or his own psyche, as though it were a closed system," Frankl wrote.

That's why, I told Sascha, I recommend that twentysomethings look for purpose not in their minds—or in their therapy sessions—but, rather, in the lives they live day to day. "When it comes to work, twentysomethings are my why," I told Sascha. "But I'd never heard of that as a specialty—I don't think it *was* a specialty—when I was in graduate school. I had to see different kinds of clients and find out what felt most meaningful to me. I had to find the kind of work where I felt I could do the most good."

"Now that I think about it," Sascha said, "I only had one job between college and law school. So, I know one thing that isn't the thing, but that's it so far. I guess I need to do more to figure out where I can do the most good. But then I look around, and there are so many problems in the world. I don't know if I can do any good at all."

It's true. Every day, in the news and on social media, twentysomethings are confronted with some of the largest large-world problems ever: climate change, inequality, war, trauma, racism, sexism, disease, poverty, corruption, gun violence. Some might say it's easy to find a reason to give up on life, but maybe it's just as easy to look around and find a reason not to do so. Existential threats present us with some of our most urgent and undeniable *whys*.

If Frankl could forge his purpose in a Nazi death camp—a situation he had no hope of changing and little hope of surviving—then my students and I agreed that we could do it, too. So, one course assignment was to start doing—or to keep doing—something that might help us feel what it's like to have purpose. Then, at the end of the semester, on an essay exam, the students talked about how that went:

> I found my purpose in this class. I want to be a teacher because there is a difference between learning and memorizing, and I feel that growing up, teachers were there to teach students to memorize rather than to learn. If schools taught more about the importance of self-reflection and ways to find your path in life, then I feel that this could tie directly into mental health, decreasing levels of depression, anxiety, and worthlessness. No person can single-handedly change our country's education system or solve mental health issues. However, one person can be an influence on others, which can spread wider and wider until people are talking and demanding change.

> I've been interviewing people of all ages about their relationships. My parents got divorced and the divorce rate really bothers me. But this is something I can change by having a better relationship one day and showing my kids a better way.

> I joined a "Courageous Conversations" club. I find that braving discussions on heavy topics, such as the Israel-Palestine conflict, is very purposeful for me. I try to approach these conversations as civilly as possible, and there are often drastic differences in points of view, but in the end, everyone in the discussion walks away with new information. Not being afraid to talk about problems has made a huge impact in my life and I think it is one of the most effective ways to eventually solve global issues.

Volunteering with political organizations is something I have always done, even before this class. It gives me an ongoing sense of purpose because there are always problems to work on. Having meaningful interests to always keep me going no matter what else is happening is important because you never really know for sure what will happen next.

Climate change is scary, but no one knows what other changes might happen, how people might change or what technologies might come along. I'm a human being, so I'm technically part of the problem. But I'm an engineer and I started interning for a renewable energy company that is trying to be part of the solution.

I'm the Publicity Chair for a Latino organization in my community. As part of a diverse city, I try to expand my learning beyond my own circle, so sometimes I feel frustrated when we have low attendance or when the only people that come to our events are Latinos. But we still try to do our best no matter how many people come to an event.

I used to want to work in criminal justice, but now I want to be a reporter. From working at Legal Aid, I've learned that justice isn't always defined by winning or losing; sometimes justice is simply listening, caring, and helping someone tell their story. I want to help more people tell their stories.

It has always been my dream to come up with a well-equipped school in Kibera—the largest slum in Africa and also where I grew up. I came to realize that it might take me longer than expected to make this dream a reality, so I decided to start a mentorship program for students from high schools there. Through this, so many teens have been able to regain their hope and rediscover their talents. I am totally optimistic that this strategy is going to make a great difference in my community.

Just going to college has purpose for me. I'm the first person in my family to go to college, but I definitely won't be the last.

I'm a sexual abuse survivor. I started looking into going to law school so I can give kids something I once desperately needed: A person who will say, "I believe you, what he did was wrong, and I will fight to bring you closure."

My dead-end temp job actually gave me a lot of purpose. I know I want a job that I feel has a purpose both for myself and for the world. I want to be proud of myself for my accomplishments and for how far I've come throughout my life. Since I want those things but don't know whether they'll happen or not, that keeps me motivated to work toward them every day.

I used to think that everyone has a core purpose that they must fulfill. This led to a lot of pressure to choose exactly the right career path and try to solve the problems that I was "destined" to solve. It's been liberating to realize that maybe there are different purposes for different phases of life.

One thing I learned from my students is that, once they were engaged with the world, not a single person said they shouldn't do anything because they couldn't do everything. Not one said they shouldn't even try because they weren't sure they would succeed. Not one said that their efforts didn't matter or that there was nowhere in the world for them to pitch in. Not one said someone else's purpose seemed better or more important than their own.

Sure, students who sign up for a course like mine are a self-selected group, but in a way, that's the point: They're already *choosing* to put purpose in their lives.

· · ·

"The last of the human freedoms," Frankl argues, is "to choose one's attitude in any given set of circumstances, to choose one's own way." To Frankl, purpose is all around us. So, whether our lives have meaning depends not on whether we find purpose but on whether we *choose* purpose. Indeed, the word *purpose* comes from the French *proposer*, meaning "to suggest." Our purpose is what *we* suggest matters most in life.

"But it all just feels so *arbitrary*," Sascha said, still struggling. "And now my wife and I are talking a lot about big choices, like whether to have kids. I look at the news, and I just don't know how I can plan for the future or bring kids into the world. That's where I feel envious of my cousin, who has all this certainty and community through his religion."

"Religion is a choice, you know. Your cousin, and your friend—maybe they inherited religion from their parents, like you wish you had, but still, they are *choosing* to follow it every day," I said as Sascha cocked his head in thought.

I pressed on.

"Career is a choice. Community is a choice. Partnering is a choice. Parenting is a choice. Purpose is a choice," I began. "But that's the paradox of purpose: Purpose *is* a choice, but once you make a commitment to something or someone outside of yourself, it doesn't feel like a choice anymore. It feels like an imperative, like something you can't just walk away from. You either choose something like that or you don't. But waiting for it to be handed to you or revealed to you is probably not going to work."

"But what if I do all those things, what if I make all those choices, what if I have kids and I find something important, and the world ends in ten years?"

"Then you died trying," I said only partly in jest. "But here's the bigger question: What if the world *doesn't* end in ten years? What would you like your life—and the world—to be like then?"

PART III

WHAT NEXT?

SEVENTEEN

THE TONIC OF HOPE

There is no medicine like hope, no incentive so great, and no tonic so powerful as expectation of something better tomorrow.

—Orison Swett Marden, author

It gets better.

This isn't unrealistic optimism or magical thinking. It is a data-driven view supported by multiple studies in adult development, which have one consistent message: Life gets better as we age—and so does mental health.

It shouldn't be surprising by now, but around the world, young adults ages 18 to 34 are most likely to experience mental health problems such as anxiety and depression and to be more severely affected by their symptoms. After this age, however, these problems tend to decrease, as does the extent to which adults report being debilitated by whatever symptoms they have.

And, likewise, in a 2022 study of adults in the United States, well-being increased across every decade of adulthood from the twenties to the eighties. So did happiness and satisfaction. So did self-reports of mental and physical health. So did meaning and purpose. So did close relationships. So did financial and material stability. According to this study, life got better in every single way that was measured, even though the report itself seemed to highlight the negative. "Our findings support evidence of a mental health crisis that has disproportionally affected young adults," the authors noted, without emphasizing the good news that we can expect our lives to get better over time.

These findings and more show that, although young adulthood is when we're most likely to have a hard time, there are a lot of good things to come. Yet, because so much of what young adults see, especially on social media, is from their peers, this trajectory—this perspective—is one they hear little about. It's not just social media that leaves out this point of view. All too often, even physicians forget to normalize growth, an omission that can harm their patients' mental health.

In a 2014 article titled "Is There a Getting Better from This, or Not?," researchers put forth what they call "a sobering proposition—namely, the duration of and struggles with various mental disorders may be linked, in part, to our ways of framing, perceiving and narrating them." Indeed, many of the patients interviewed for that article clearly recalled the moment they were told their problems were permanent: "All you heard was, 'Lifetime, lifetime, it's a lifetime illness, you're forever going to need meds,'" said one young woman. "There's no hope for recovery."

"I don't know if I need all these," Brianna said somewhat nervously the first time we met, as she pulled from her purse a zippered plastic bag crammed with prescription pill bottles.

"Can you tell me what they are?" I asked, more rhetorically than literally, assuming that she could.

"I kind of can," she answered.

A public school teacher, Brianna had done her homework. "This one is for sleeping and this one is for anxiety," she began as she passed pill bottles to me and read a piece of paper with notes jotted on it. "I'm not completely sure, but Google says these two can be used for depression. And I think this one is maybe for a rash."

"Where did all these come from?" I asked.

"From my doctor back home," Brianna said. "Back when I was in college."

"And how old are you now?"

"I'm twenty-four."

Brianna was from a rural community, she went on to explain. She was the oldest of three children and the most responsible person in the home. Her mother was an alcoholic, and the kids' various fathers were gone.

"I got into my dream school for college," she explained. "But once I got there, it was a nightmare. I went from being the smartest kid at my high school to being one of thousands of smart kids from all over the state. And most of them were way better off than me."

I kept listening.

"I felt so much pressure to succeed, for myself and for my family, I melted down. My doctor prescribed all these meds, and I don't know if they helped or not. I think what I needed to do was to learn how to study and perform at a higher level—which my high school hadn't taught me—but once I did, things got better."

"Then what?"

"I did student teaching at the public high school here, and that went really well," Brianna said with a smile. "And then they offered me a job. Things seem good or like they're headed in the right direction, so like I said, I'm here because I'm hoping that maybe I don't need all this medication anymore."

Although she didn't come out and say it, Brianna wanted me to be hopeful, too—and I was.

As a psychologist, I deal in hope, or at least I try to. Remember that one of the three routes to better mental health is expectations, and hope is a form of positive expectation. While hopelessness is associated with all sorts of physical and mental health problems, having positive expectations is almost universally related to better outcomes all around.

Hope is a tonic with incredible healing power and, fortunately, it is also a resource that many twentysomethings already have. In a 2012 study of more than 3,000 young adults, 48 percent reported that they experienced symptoms of depression, anxiety, social anxiety, eating problems, substance abuse, or work stress. When asked, however, about twice that amount, or 95 percent, said they had hope. So, we need to talk more about *that*.

According to a 2017 review of the research, hope offers five life-changing, even life-saving, benefits for young adults:

1. Hope is the single strongest predictor of well-being and mental health for those in their twenties and beyond. It also helps people feel less anxious and depressed.

2. Twentysomethings who have hope are more likely to set goals, work toward them, and overcome obstacles because they believe their efforts can make a difference. Not surprisingly, they achieve more at work and in love and life.

3. Hope weakens the link between adverse life events—like bad parents or global pandemics—and negative mental health. As for Brianna, even when life is difficult, those who have hope find ways to keep moving ahead.

4. Twentysomethings who are hopeful about their futures are more likely to engage in beneficial behaviors, such as healthy eating and exercise, and they're less likely to abuse substances. They believe their choices and their actions matter.

5. Young adults who feel hopeful about the future are less likely to think about ending their lives. They can imagine solutions to their problems besides, as so many have described it to me, "just being gone."

Hope, then, isn't just kicking back and assuming that we might *feel* better with age; technically speaking, that's optimism. Hope is the belief that we can *do* better, and sometimes that belief begins with recognizing that we already are.

• • •

"I *am* doing a lot better than I was five years ago," Brianna said when I asked, "but I don't know if it's just the medication."

"I don't know either," I said. "What I do know is that twentysome-things tend to feel better as they get older."

"That's encouraging," she said.

"But it's not just getting older," I continued. "From what you've told me, you're not the same person you were five years ago. You have more skills. You're better able to cope."

"My pill bottles feel like daily reminders that I can't cope," she said. "They make me feel like I can't succeed on my own."

"But you did succeed on your own," I clarified. "You got yourself into college. You got yourself through school, right?"

"I don't even know how I did that," she said.

"Let's talk about it, then," I replied. "How did you do it?"

"Gosh," she sighed, like even remembering made her tired. "I studied a lot. I was working tons of hours waiting tables. I had this planner with all my classes and assignments and work shifts on it. I followed that thing religiously because I didn't have a minute to spare. Or to sleep."

"What kept you going?"

"My little sister being stuck at home while my mom was going crazy and my brother was getting into drugs," she replied. "I was trying to be there for her. I had to do well in school and get a job, so I could bring her here to live with me. I'm working on that now. I want her to go to community college."

"So, you've really been there for your sister," I said. "Who's there for you?"

"I have a lot of nice friends," Brianna said with a smile. "I've always had a lot of nice friends."

"So, you're smart and you're organized and determined. You've worked hard and you have good relationships," I summed up. "That's how you did it."

"That's reassuring," she said with a half-hearted smile.

"I'm not trying to reassure you," I said. "I'm going by the evidence. You have a good track record of making good things happen for yourself. You've been doing it for years. I have no reason to believe you can't keep doing it."

"I have done well with school and with my job," she said almost proudly. "But those things are really concrete, so it's kind of easy—even though it was hard work—to tackle them. Plus, I had to, so I could pay my bills and help my sister out. But I haven't really thought much about life after that."

"Maybe it's time to start," I said.

The twentysomething brain is still wiring up, and one skill young adults are still developing is how to look forward to their own future. After moving through life one semester or one year at a time, it is new to try to think several years or even decades down the line. When twentysomethings do think ahead, they tend to think negatively about their uncertain futures. I'll be alone forever! I'll be depressed forever! I'll be broke forever! They spend so much time thinking about all the bad things they are sure will happen that there is little room in their minds for the good things that could.

My favorite definition of hope is from a 1969 book by psychologist Ezra Stotland: "Hope is an expectation greater than zero of achieving a goal." I love what this line says about the human spirit and the power of possibility. That is, to be hopeful, maybe we don't need a 51 percent probability of succeeding or a 99 percent chance of having life go our way. Maybe all we need to be hopeful is that the thing we hope for is possible.

When I think of this perspective on hope, I remember the professor who helped me during my own mental health crisis. I never did call him at home, like he said I could, but I did show up at his office several more times, especially when I wasn't doing so well. One afternoon—I had been confessing my thoughts about stepping in front of a train—I presented him with this stumper:

"Do you think I could ever be happy?" I asked.

"Not if you kill yourself," he said.

In retrospect, this was a brave, maybe even risky, response. Rather than offering up some bullshit guarantee that my life would be better one day, my professor simply pointed out that my life definitely would not improve if I didn't stick around for it. As long as I kept living, he seemed to be saying, I had a greater than zero chance of being happy and healthy. That might not seem like much to go on, but somehow, the way he flipped the logic on me, it upended the way I thought about my life.

As we know by now, negative thoughts and feelings are often more about possibilities than probabilities. Remember that negative feelings like anxiety increase when the odds of something bad happening shift from 0 to 1 percent, but not from 50 to 51 percent. So, maybe the same thing can be said of *positive* feelings like hope. Maybe just knowing there's a possibility greater than zero that life might go well is sometimes all we need—or all we need to be reminded of.

Everybody comes up with negative possibilities—life's catastrophic what-ifs—when faced with uncertainty. We get caught in downward spirals instead of imagining an upward spiral or how life could get better and better over time. That is, when we're depressed and anxious, we not only see more negative possibilities, we also produce fewer *positive* ones. We talk to our therapists—and our friends—about what might go wrong in life when our mental health is actually *more* improved by paying more attention to what might go *right*.

That's why, more and more, in therapy and in the classroom, I help people rethink their catastrophic what-ifs by asking, "What if there is another way to what-if?" That is, what if, instead of imagining the worst in life, you practice imagining the best? What if, when you time-travel into the future, you try to make it a good trip instead of a bad one?

Different strategies work for different people, but the most widely studied way to look ahead with hope, and where most people begin, is by envisioning their future selves—in a good way. Here's an example:

Think about yourself in the future. Imagine everything has gone as well as it possibly could. You've worked hard and succeeded at accomplishing your goals in four areas: personal, professional, social, and health. Think of this as the realization of your hopes and dreams. Now vividly, and in as much detail as possible, describe—to yourself, to another person, or to your journal—all that you see.

"You can't be what you can't see," the saying goes. More than just positive visualization, an exercise like this is useful because the more vivid and specific our musings about our futures, the more likely we are to take concrete steps toward reaching them. In some of my favorite studies about how this works, researchers have used virtual reality to help twentysomethings see how they would look when they are old. Those people were more likely to set aside money toward retirement, stop smoking, or start exercising than people who did *not* see their age-morphed selves.

Of course, you don't need gadgets to turn positive expectations into realities. Here are five more ways to take action toward reaching who you hope to be:

Make a plan for your future self. Choose something specific you're excited about in the years ahead. Identify three steps you can take toward that goal, as well as one obstacle that might get in your way and how you might get around it. Write all this down to make it more real.

"One thing I'm excited about is having my sister come live with me," Brianna said, "so here are the three things I'm doing about it. I'm looking for a two-bedroom apartment. I'm helping her get what she needs to register for community college. And I'm helping her look for a job here in town. Guilt could get in the way—you know, us feeling bad about both of us leaving my mom and my brother behind. But I didn't renew my lease on my studio apartment, so that'll force me to move by the end of the year, one way or the other."

Save money for your future self. There is a fair bit of research on how the more connected we feel to our future selves, the more money we save. Thoughts influence actions, but it is also true that actions influence thoughts. So, with some twentysomethings, I go about things the other way around. I encourage them to save money in order to help their futures feel more real. No matter what you're saving for, the act of investing in your future self is a reminder that there are good things to come—and that you can do something about them.

"I have a retirement plan through my school," Brianna said. "It isn't much and it's still hard to believe I could ever get old enough or save enough to retire. But it does make me feel less anxious, knowing that I am putting at least some money away. Even better is that I am saving up for some fun things I want to do in the near future, like going to Spain. When I was a kid, all I could think about was getting out of my house or my town, so I've only recently let myself think about going to another country."

Remember your future self. In a 2018 study of young adults who have fitness apps, researchers found that only about half of the participants used them regularly. Maybe not surprisingly, those who received daily messages reminding them of their goals were more active than those who did not receive such reminders. Similarly, in a 2017 study, those who were asked to envision their best possible selves via text messages each day were more hopeful about the future and less depressed—until the text messages stopped.

You don't have to use technology, but one way or another, keep reminding yourself of the person you might want to be. For Brianna, that meant buying a keychain from the community college her sister might soon attend, as well as putting a picture of Spain on the lock screen of her phone. Whatever your hopes and dreams, your present self is probably busy and easily distracted, so you'll need cues to keep the future alive in your mind.

Spend time with your future self. Most twentysomethings have moved through life surrounded by people in the same grade or of the same age. So, to be able to think ahead, it helps to be exposed to people of older ages and in later stages of life. Talk to those who are further along with work, or love, or life. Hang out with older relatives, siblings, or friends.

"I am getting to know some of the older teachers at my job," Brianna told me. "And by 'older,' I mean like five or ten years older. It gives me a glimpse into their personal lives, which helps. I see people getting married and having kids. I see how they balance different things they want. I didn't grow up seeing people have happy marriages and happy homes, so seeing it now, up close, makes it seem less abstract and more attainable. I feel closer to it. I start to think maybe I could be one of those people. Like, if they can do it, I can do it."

Exchange letters with your future self. In a 2021 study, Japanese adolescents were asked to write a letter to the person they might be in three years, and to have that person write back to who they are now. Although writing a letter to one's future self resulted in better academic performance, career planning, and decision making than not writing a letter, this was even more true for those who *exchanged* letters with their older selves. Getting outside of one's present self by taking the perspective of that possible future person made the connection even more powerful.

This is what I asked one young woman to do—not Brianna, but a woman who wrote to me during the pandemic, sure that lockdowns had ruined her twenties and, therefore, her whole life. "It gave me a jolt," she reported back about writing the letters. "Talking to my future self made me realize there's no way that person is going to be sitting around in lockdown ten years from now. So I'd better start thinking about who that person is going to be. But what really surprised me was that my future self was really kind, writing back in response, reminding me not to be too hard on myself that I don't have it all figured out yet. Yeah, things haven't gone the way I thought they would, but it's not too late to have a good life. The future is a ways off, and I don't know exactly how it's all going to work out, but good things can still happen."

Yes, they can.

In one eloquent sentence, author Rebecca Solnit sums up how exactly good things happen. She tell us how to hope in three steps: "To be hopeful means to be uncertain about the future, to be tender toward possibilities, to be dedicated to change all the way down to the bottom of your heart."

Hope begins with uncertainties and unknowns.

AN UNCERTAIN EMBRACE

The most precious thing in life is its uncertainty. Leaving something incomplete makes it interesting and gives one the feeling there is room for growth.

—Yoshida Kenkō, Buddhist monk and essayist

In 2019 in the United Kingdom, a first-of-its-kind therapy group gathered under a rather unusual name: Making Friends with Uncertainty. The twenty-four adults in the group had a variety of diagnoses, including general anxiety disorder, panic disorder, social anxiety disorder, obsessive compulsive disorder, and major depressive disorder. None had identified uncertainty as their problem, so while some were open-minded toward the group's approach, others were skeptical. Either way, they were instructed to "tolerate not knowing" whether the group was right for them or would work, and to use it as an opportunity to learn skills.

In the six two-hour sessions that followed, facilitators kept the focus on one thing: how uncertainty affects the way people think, feel, and act. Rather than feeling divided or identified by their different diagnoses, the group members were united by the universality of unknowns. Everyone knows what it feels like to doubt whether they'll ever be safe, or successful, or happy, or loved. Everyone knows what it feels like to be sleepless and scared about what might or might not happen next. "Everyone can relate to uncertainty in life," said one group member.

Even the group experience itself offered a learning opportunity about uncertainty: "The least helpful session was the first, when I was not sure what was going to happen," one member said. Yet, as the group went on and participants shared their reactions to unknowns in and out of sessions, they learned to accept them, rather than to try to control them or avoid them. "I understand this will not immediately stop causing discomfort," noted one person, while another recognized, "If I work on this, it can help, so I don't go down a spiral toward depression and anxiety." Indeed, by the end of the program, 75 percent of people in the group reported improvement or recovery on symptoms of depression or anxiety, and 63 percent saw marked improvement in their ability to tolerate unknowns.

Making friends with uncertainty might seem bold, but if I were running the group, I would take it somewhere even more revolutionary. I would argue for learning not just to tolerate uncertainty but also to embrace it. Uncertainty *can* be your friend, and friends aren't just people we put up with. We have adventures with them. We throw our arms around them. Our lives are better because they're a part of them. The same is true for unknowns.

Uncertainty intensifies our emotions—not just the bad ones but the good ones, too. Studies show that when we go into an experience, or an event, or even a relationship in which there is mystery or suspense, we enjoy it more. It's unwrapping a gift to prolong the anticipation. Not seeing a wedding dress until the big day. Not knowing the sex of your baby before it's born. Receiving a random act of goodwill. Being asked on a date or to lunch by someone new. Starting a book or a movie when you don't know how it will end. Getting a compliment, or a promotion, or a good grade you weren't expecting. We may think we want to banish unknowns, but research shows that, if life goes as planned, it winds up feeling only satisfactory. For life to exceed our expectations, we have to venture into the unexpected.

An earlier chapter presented the kinds of items that scientists use to understand how people think about unknowns. The best we can do, according to the research, is to disagree with statements like these: "When I am uncertain, I cannot go forward"; "I dislike being uncertain about my future"; "I feel anxious or angry when life is not settled." But the data, and experience, tell me that this is not the best life has to offer. Imagine an uncertainty scale in which you'd say yes to items like these:

Unforeseen events make life exciting.
It is often not possible, or even desirable, to have complete information.
Some of the best things in life are uncertain.
I look forward to life's surprises.
It's freeing not to be able to quantify where I stand sometimes.
When I am uncertain, I pay more attention to life.
When I am uncertain, I can think of more than one way ahead.
I don't expect the future to be certain because so much is still up to me.
I don't mind when life is not settled.
I enjoy imagining the future.
I find it liberating when there is not a right answer to things.
When faced with choices, I make a decision and I don't look back.
I embrace uncertain situations.

Look at it this way: If uncertainty acts as a transdiagnostic stressor, then being able to embrace uncertainty can be a transdiagnostic *buffer* that can protect your mental health every day. In the twenty-first century, opening your heart and mind to the inevitabilities and upsides of unknowns may be the most transformative skill of all. And, fortunately, this is something else that becomes more possible with age and experience. As we feel more certain of *ourselves*, we're freed up to enjoy the good surprises to come. We're also more equipped to face the not-so-good ones—and to ask for help when we need it.

More than anything else, uncertainty is what has brought so many twenty-somethings to my office. Yet my purpose, with a client, a student, or a reader, is not to tie up people's futures in neat little packages but, rather, to send them back into the world more knowledgeable, more capable, and more hopeful than before.

Of course, that's what someone did for me so many decades ago.

Before I graduated from college, I went to my professor's office to say goodbye—and to tell him about my new job. Just like I had the first time we spoke, I broke into tears. But this time the tears were different. The first afternoon I cried in his office, I was scared. I was scared of what was wrong with me and of what I might do. On this day, however, I felt emboldened about what was right with me and excited about what I might do.

"You saved my life," I told him.

Then, in the doorway, he again did something I didn't expect—he hugged me. Like the phone number he'd once offered, this gesture made me feel I was okay and that maybe—possibly—my life would be, too. As I turned and walked down the hallway, I picked up my pace, ready to leave my past struggles behind.

"Let me know what happens!" he called out enthusiastically, like he was expecting good things.

As I stepped outside and into the vast openness of my uncertain future, I felt the warmth of the sun and of one thing I was sure: even if things became difficult again, there are people who care.

For twenty-five years, I've said I work with young adults because that's where the action is. But to be more accurate, I should say that's where the action begins. Despite our cultural obsession with how great our twenties are supposed to be, I don't know a single person in their thirties or beyond who would go back to being a twentysomething. I say that not to mean that the twenties are bad, as much as I mean that the twenties are when life starts to get good.

I don't know how any of my clients', students', or readers' lives will turn out, and that's what makes working with twentysomethings so wondrous. I do know that, if life goes well enough, as you age, you will probably become happier and healthier, simply because you're more likely to have—and do—what makes people healthier and happier.

You'll wake up, not to overwhelming unknowns but to whatever it is that you have decided matters most. You'll open your eyes to a chosen partner, or purpose, or profession. You'll get out of bed for the children, or the friends, or the work you love. And you'll walk out your door into the place you've decided to inhabit—or visit—at least for now. As you get older, you'll likely feel more settled because you *are* more settled, not just on the outside but on the inside, too.

If any of those prospects appeal to you, move toward them by taking up the uncertainties ahead. Start by getting the best job you can as soon as you can—and, by best, I mean the one where you'll learn the most. Don't worry so much about whether you're in the right job or the wrong one, because there's no such thing. Remember, the average young adult has nine different jobs by age 35, so you'll get to make the job choice more than once.

The same goes for love. I don't know if you'll have nine different relationships, but you'll probably have more than one, so use them to discover what you want and need from a partner—and what you want and need to do to *be* a good partner. Some of your relationships won't work out, but that doesn't mean there's anything wrong with you or with the other person. It probably just means you aren't right for each other. If your heart gets broken in the process, it's working properly.

When life is difficult, stay strong and keep your body moving in a way you enjoy. Be kind to your mind while it is still wiring up. Your brain is learning whatever your day-to-day life is teaching it, so be careful about reaching for alcohol, drugs, food, porn, or social media for comfort or relief.

Reach for people, instead. They're better for you. And they'll probably like you more than you think, so get out there and let them do that. New people are where new jobs, new lovers, new apartments, and new ideas come from. They are also where new friends come from, and you're going to need some friends.

Friends make the world a friendlier place. They are where safety, empathy, and loyalty come from, both the kind you get and the kind you give. Friendships are where you practice caring about someone besides yourself. They are where you practice being a good partner and a good parent and a good person.

As you go along, remember that the best things in life can't be quantified, so revel in no longer being able to grade or rank yourself. No two lives are the same, so don't try to measure your success by the yardstick of another person's progress. Spend less time looking backwards or sideways at what might have been, and spend more time looking ahead at what might still be.

The next time you start to describe yourself as *anxious* or *depressed*, use the word *uncertain* instead, and notice how this changes how you think about your situation and yourself. Let go of the depressing certainty or the crippling anxiety that life will be dreadful, and open your heart and mind to the possibility that it might be sublime. Dare to envision—and work toward—life going well and then delight in that when life exceeds your expectations.

One way or another, you'll become someone you can't entirely plan for. You'll become someone who doesn't exist yet. You'll find meaning in work that you haven't heard of yet. You'll travel to places you haven't been yet. Your life will be changed by people you don't know yet. You'll fall in love with someone you haven't met yet. You'll have more kids or fewer kids than you thought you would, and they'll blow up your heart in ways you never thought possible. The most difficult moments of your twenties will be forgotten, while your most defining moments will be joys and accomplishments you never foresaw.

And when these things happen, celebrate! Own your successes so you feel more confident about what's still to come. Spread the word when life goes well, and expand the collective notion of what could be. Share your triumphs with the people who love you so others can also enjoy them. Let the people who helped you know how you are and where you are—and maybe let a twentysomething know they can get there, too.

A life of uncertainty is an ongoing revelation and, as it turns out, so is good news.

Acknowledgments

This book, and my life as I know it, would not be possible without twentysomethings. Little did I know when I began graduate school—back when I was in my twenties—that I would spend the next quarter of a century focused on that age. Sometimes people ask if I want to do something bigger or better with my career, but to me, there is nothing bigger or better. So much is happening—or is about to happen—in my clients' twenties that being a part of that has been the pleasure and privilege of a lifetime.

I appreciate the institutions that continue to support my work, especially Semester at Sea and the University of Virginia. A special thanks to my colleagues at UVA's Student Health and Wellness and especially to Dr. Andy Thomson, who has read countless drafts of my chapters over the years and who also happens to be an excellent psychiatrist—one who advocates for skills over pills. Every book I have written has been made possible by the professor whose office I walked into for help back when I was in my twenties. Teachers everywhere are often the unsung mental health providers for young people.

At Simon & Schuster, I am sincerely grateful to Eamon Dolan for being a truly great editor. Like an experienced therapist, Eamon sees how a book can be better, and he cares enough about authors and audiences to find a nice way to say so. Also at Simon & Schuster, I am forever indebted to Jonathan Karp, who, many years ago, took a chance on me and *The Defining Decade*.

Far and away, though, no one has done more for my career than Tina

Bennett. I read in an interview somewhere that Tina is not only one of the best agents in the business but also one of the nicest. The result is a rare form of fierceness and loyalty that I know I am, personally and professionally, fortunate to receive.

Most people find their purpose in work and in love, and I am no exception. To the loves of my life—John and Jay and Hazel—thank you for making these the best years of my life. Jay and Hazel, my soon-to-be twentysomethings, maybe you'll read my books one day and find something helpful when you need it, or at least enjoy a glimpse of what I was doing on my laptop all those hours. As much as I love my clients and students and readers, being your mom is the most heart-exploding job I've ever had.

Because of those named above—and because of the countless twentysomethings I cannot name—my life, so far, has turned out better than I imagined when I was young. Here's to hoping for more of that for us all.

Notes

INTRODUCTION: THE TWENTYSOMETHING TREATMENT

3 *what might be going on is a lot*: "Stress in America: Generation Z," American Psychological Association, press release, 2018, https://www.apa.org/news/press/releases/stress/2018/stress-gen-z.pdf; and "Stress in America," American Psychological Association, press release, 2019, https://www.apa.org/news/press/releases/stress/2019/stress-america-2019.pdf.

3 *"fear of the unknown"*: Howard Phillips Lovecraft, *Supernatural Horror in Literature*, the Palingenesis Project (London: Wermod and Wermod, 2013).

4 *what they are averse to, really, is uncertainty*: Frank Hyneman Knight, *Risk, Uncertainty and Profit*, vol. 31 (Boston: Houghton Mifflin, 1921).

4 *so is pretty much everyone else*: R. Nicholas Carleton, "Fear of the Unknown: One Fear to Rule Them All?," *Journal of Anxiety Disorders* 41 (2016): 5–21.

4 *A 2020 study by the American Psychological Association*: "Stress in America 2020: A National Mental Health Crisis," American Psychological Association, report, October 2020, https://www.apa.org/news/press/releases/stress/2020/report-october.

4 *Seventy-five percent of all mental health disorders*: Ronald C. Kessler, Patricia Berglund, Olga Demler, Robert Jin, Kathleen R. Merikangas, et al., "Lifetime Prevalence and Age-of-Onset Distributions of DSM-IV Disorders in the National Comorbidity Survey Replication," *Archives of General Psychiatry* 62, no. 6 (2005): 593–602.

4 *that's where the action is*: Vikram Patel, Alan J. Flisher, Sarah Hetrick, and Patrick McGorry, "Mental Health of Young People: A Global Public-Health Challenge," *The Lancet* 369, no. 9569 (2007): 1302–13.

4 *pandemic may have finally brought it into the headlines*: Mark E. Czeisler, Rashon I. Lane, Emiko Petrosky, Joshua F. Wiley, Aleta Christensen, et al., "Mental Health, Substance Use, and Suicidal Ideation During the COVID-19 Pandemic—United States, June 24–30, 2020," *Morbidity and Mortality Weekly Report* 69, no. 32 (2020): 1049.

4 *long been more likely*: Ronald C. Kessler, G. Paul Amminger, Sergio Aguilar-Gaxiola, Jordi Alonso, Sing Lee, et al., "Age of Onset of Mental Disorders: A Review of Recent Literature," *Current Opinion in Psychiatry* 20, no. 4 (2007): 359; Darrel A. Regier, M. E. Farmer, D. S. Rae, J. K. Myers, M. R. L. N. Kramer, et al., "One-Month Prevalence of Mental Disorders in the United States and Sociodemographic Characteristics: The Epidemiologic Catchment Area Study," *Acta Psychiatrica Scandinavica* 88, no. 1 (1993): 35–47.

4 *40 percent of twentysomethings report problems*: "Anxiety and Depression: Household Pulse Survey," Centers for Disease Control and Prevention, https://www.cdc.gov/nchs/covid19/pulse/mental-health.htm.

4 *twice as likely to have a mental health diagnosis*: "Addressing the Unprecedented Behavioral-Health Challenges Facing Generation Z," McKinsey & Company, 2022, https://www.mckinsey.com/industries/healthcare-systems-and-services/our-insights/addressing-the-unprecedented-behavioral-health-challenges-facing-generation-z.

4 *less likely to be receiving treatment*: Substance Abuse and Mental Health Services Administration, "Behavioral Health Barometer: United States, 2015," HHS Publication no. SMA–16–Baro–2015 (Rockville, MD: Substance Abuse and Mental Health Services Administration, 2015), https://store.samhsa.gov/sites/default/files/d7/priv/sma16-baro-2015.pdf.

5 *not a single mental health provider*: C. Holly, A. Andrilla, Davis G. Patterson, Lisa A. Garberson, Cynthia Coulthard, and Eric H. Larson, "Geographic Variation in the Supply of Selected Behavioral Health Providers," *American Journal of Preventive Medicine* 54, no. 6 (2018): S199–S207.

5 *they go on social media*: "Addressing the Unprecedented Behavioral-Health Challenges."

7 *because they can*: "Anxiety and Depression: Household Pulse Survey," National Center for Health Statistics, U.S. Census Bureau, report, 2020–23, https://www.cdc.gov/nchs/covid19/pulse/mental-health.htm.

ONE. AN UNCERTAIN AGE

12 *"In this world . . ."*: William MacDonald, , *The Writings of Benjamin Franklin*, vol. 10, ed. Albert Henry Smyth (New York: Macmillan Company, 1907): 68–69.

13 *nine different jobs*: "Number of Jobs Held by Individuals from Age 18 Through Age 34 in 1998–2019 by Educational Attainment, Sex, Race, Hispanic or Latino Ethnicity, and Age," U.S. Bureau of Labor Statistics, https://www.bls.gov/news.release/nlsyth.t01.htm.

13 *financial help from their parents*: Daniel de Vise, "Nearly Half of Parents with Adult Children Still Pay Their Bills," *The Hill*, March 23, 2023, https://

thehill.com/business/personal-finance/3915186-nearly-half-of-parents
-with-adult-children-still-pay-their-bills/.

13 *bills that are unpaid and overdue*: Kassandra Martincheck, Jennifer Andre,
and Miranda Santillo, "What Can Policymakers Do to Help Young Adults
Cope with Debt?," Urban Institute, December 13, 2022, https://www
.urban.org/research/publication/what-can-policymakers-do-help-young
-adults-cope-debt.

13 *move each year*: Zachary Scherer, "Young Adults Most Likely to Change Living Arrangements," U.S. Census Bureau, August 31, 2020, https://www
.census.gov/library/stories/2020/08/young-adults-most-likely-to-change
-living-arrangements.html.

13 *a third of workers*: Daniel de Vise, "Nearly 30 Percent of Work Remains
Remote as Workers Dig In," *The Hill*, February 20, 2023, https://thehill.
com/policy/technology/3862069-nearly-30-percent-of-work-remains-re
mote-as-workers-dig-in.

13 *loneliest years of all*: Jamie Ballard, "Millennials Are the Loneliest Generation," YouGovAmerica, July 30, 2019, https://today.yougov.com/topics
/society/articles-reports/2019/07/30/loneliness-friendship-new-friends
-poll-survey.

13 *twentysomething women are single*: Anna Brown, "A Profile of Single Americans," Pew Research Center, August 20, 2020, https://www.pewresearch.
org/social-trends/2020/08/20/a-profile-of-single-americans/; Risa Gelles-
Watnick, "For Valentine's Day, Five Facts About Single Americans," Pew
Research Center, February 8, 2023, https://www.pewresearch.org/fact
-tank/2023/02/08/for-valentines-day-5-facts-about-single-americans/.

13 *who will eventually marry is on its way down*: Lydia Saad, "Fewer Young
People Say 'I Do' to Any Relationship," Gallup, June 8, 2015, https://news
.gallup.com/poll/183515/fewer-young-people-say-relationship.aspx.

13 *walk down the aisle*: Decennial Censuses, 1890 to 1940, and Current Population Survey, Annual Social and Economic Supplements, 1947 to 2022,
U.S. Census Bureau, https://www.census.gov/content/dam/Census/library
/visualizations/time-series/demo/families-and-households/ms-2.pdf.

13 *have one's first child*: Anne Morse, "Fertility Rates: Declined for Younger
Women, Increased for Older Women," U.S. Census Bureau, April 6, 2022,
https://www.census.gov/library/stories/2022/04/fertility-rates-declined-for
-younger-women-increased-for-older women.html.

13 *careers and salaries are likely not established*: "The Five Career Stages and How
to Succeed in Each," *Indeed*, March 28, 2023, https://www.indeed.com/ca
reer-advice/career-development/career-stages; Michael Cheary, "32: The Age
of Career Contentment," *Reed*, https://www.reed.co.uk/career-advice/32
-the-age-of-career-contentment.

13 *first-time home buyer*: "2022 Profile of Home Buyers and Sellers," National Association of Realtors, report, 2022, https://www.nar.realtor/sites/default /files/documents/2022-highlights-from-the-profile-of-home-buyers-and -sellers-report-11-03-2022_0.pdf.

14 *exposed to gun violence*: School Shootings Database, *Washington Post*, https:// www.washingtonpost.com/education/interactive/school-shootings-data base/.

14 *most common site for mass shootings*: Violence Project Database, https://www .theviolenceproject.org/mass-shooter-database/, accessed May 10, 2023.

14 *may one day say "Me, Too"*: Nikki Graf, "Sexual Harassment at Work in the Era of #MeToo," Pew Research Center, April 4, 2018, https://www.pew research.org/social-trends/2018/04/04/sexual-harassment-at-work-in-the -era-of-metoo/.

15 *interprets uncertainty as danger*: Jos F. Brosschot, Bart Verkuil, and Julian F. Thayer, "The Default Response to Uncertainty and the Importance of Perceived Safety in Anxiety and Stress: An Evolution-Theoretical Perspective," *Journal of Anxiety Disorders* 41 (2016): 22–34.

15 *firing up the amygdala*: Cyril Herry, Dominik R. Bach, Fabrizio Esposito, Francesco di Salle, Walter J. Perrig, et al., "Processing of Temporal Unpredictability in Human and Animal Amygdala," *Journal of Neuroscience* 27, no. 22 (2007): 5958–66.

15 "*. . . do their triggering*": Joseph LeDoux, *The Emotional Brain: The Mysterious Underpinnings of Emotional Life* (New York: Simon & Schuster, 1998), 168–69.

15 *a state of readiness*: Paul J. Whalen, "Fear, Vigilance, and Ambiguity: Initial Neuroimaging Studies of the Human Amygdala," *Current Directions in Psychological Science* 7, no. 6 (1998): 177–88.

15 *a smoke detector*: Randolph M. Nesse, "Natural Selection and the Regulation of Defenses: A Signal Detection Analysis of the Smoke Detector Principle," *Evolution and Human Behavior* 26, no. 1 (2005): 88–105.

15 *smoke alarms that blare both day and night*: Jos F. Brosschot, Bart Verkuil, and Julian F. Thayer, "Generalized Unsafety Theory of Stress: Unsafe Environments and Conditions, and the Default Stress Response," *International Journal of Environmental Research and Public Health* 15, no. 3 (2018): 464.

15 *expecting an electrical shock*: John Oliver Cook and Lehman W. Barnes Jr., "Choice of Delay of Inevitable Shock," *Journal of Abnormal and Social Psychology* 68, no. 6 (1964): 669.

16 "*hating waiting*": Ema Tanovic, Greg Hajcak, and Jutta Joormann, "Hating Waiting: Individual Differences in Willingness to Wait in Uncertainty," *Journal of Experimental Psychopathology* 9, no. 1 (2018): 1–12.

16 *made more mistakes*: Jessica L. Alquist, Roy F. Baumeister, Dianne M. Tice,

and Tammy J. Core, "What You Don't Know Can Hurt You: Uncertainty Impairs Executive Function," *Frontiers in Psychology* 11 (2020): 576001.

16 *trouble living with unknowns*: R. Nicholas Carleton, "Into the Unknown: A Review and Synthesis of Contemporary Models Involving Uncertainty," *Journal of Anxiety Disorders* 39 (2016): 30–43.

16 *uncertainty is a developmental variable*: R. Nicholas Carleton, Gabrielle Desgagné, Rachel Krakauer, and Ryan Y. Hong, "Increasing Intolerance of Uncertainty over Time: The Potential Influence of Increasing Connectivity," *Cognitive Behaviour Therapy* 48, no. 2 (2019): 121–36.

16 *how uncertainty affects our mental health*: Alessandro Massazza, Hanna Kienzler, Suzan Al-Mitwalli, Nancy Tamimi, and Rita Giacaman, "The Association Between Uncertainty and Mental Health: A Scoping Review of the Quantitative Literature," *Journal of Mental Health* 32, no. 2 (2022): 1–12.

16 *called a* transdiagnostic stressor: Dane Jensen, Jonah N. Cohen, Douglas S. Mennin, David M. Fresco, and Richard G. Heimberg, "Clarifying the Unique Associations Among Intolerance of Uncertainty, Anxiety, and Depression," *Cognitive Behaviour Therapy* 45, no. 6 (2016): 431–44; Alison E. J. Mahoney and Peter M. McEvoy, "A Transdiagnostic Examination of Intolerance of Uncertainty Across Anxiety and Depressive Disorders," *Cognitive Behaviour Therapy* 41, no. 3 (2012): 212–22; Peter M. McEvoy and David M. Erceg-Hurn, "The Search for Universal Transdiagnostic and Trans-Therapy Change Processes: Evidence for Intolerance of Uncertainty," *Journal of Anxiety Disorders* 41 (2016): 96–107; Peter M. McEvoy and Alison E. J. Mahoney, "To Be Sure, to Be Sure: Intolerance of Uncertainty Mediates Symptoms of Various Anxiety Disorders and Depression," *Behavior Therapy* 43, no. 3 (2012): 533–45; Sarah Shihata, Peter M. McEvoy, Barbara Ann Mullan, and R. Nicholas Carleton, "Intolerance of Uncertainty in Emotional Disorders: What Uncertainties Remain?," *Journal of Anxiety Disorders* 41 (2016): 115–24.

17 *very definition of* anxiety: Sergio Linsambarth, Rodrigo Moraga-Amaro, Daisy Quintana-Donoso, Sebastian Rojas, and Jimmy Stehberg, "The Amygdala and Anxiety," in *The Amygdale—Where Emotions Shape Perception, Learning and Memories*, ed. Barbara Ferry, 139–71 (Chicago: InTech, 2017).

17 *how we think and feel about those unknowns*: Gioia Bottesi, Igor Marchetti, Claudio Sica, and Marta Ghisi, "What Is the Internal Structure of Intolerance of Uncertainty? A Network Analysis Approach," *Journal of Anxiety Disorders* 75 (2020): 102293; Paul J. Whalen, "The Uncertainty of It All," *Trends in Cognitive Sciences* 11, no. 12 (2007): 499–500.

17 *Think about whether you agree or disagree with the following statements*: R. Nicholas Carleton, M. A. Peter J. Norton, and Gordon J. G. Asmundson,

"Fearing the Unknown: A Short Version of the Intolerance of Uncertainty Scale," *Journal of Anxiety Disorders* 21, no. 1 (2007): 105–17; R. Nicholas Carleton, Patrick Gosselin, and Gordon J. G. Asmundson, "The Intolerance of Uncertainty Index: Replication and Extension with an English Sample," *Psychological Assessment* 22, no. 2 (2010): 396.

18   *the more likely you are to feel anxious*: Ema Tanovic, Dylan G. Gee, and Jutta Joormann, "Intolerance of Uncertainty: Neural and Psychophysiological Correlates of the Perception of Uncertainty as Threatening," *Clinical Psychology Review* 60 (2018): 87–99.

18   *"Young Adults in California . . ."*: Paloma Esquivel, "Young Adults in California Experience Alarming Rates of Anxiety and Depression, Poll Finds," *Los Angeles Times*, September 30, 2022, https://www.latimes.com/world-nation/newsletter/2022-09-30/california-young-adults-anxiety-depression-rates-todays-headlines.

18   *young adults worry* more: Christine E. Gould and Barry A. Edelstein, "Worry, Emotion Control, and Anxiety Control in Older and Young Adults," *Journal of Anxiety Disorders* 24, no. 7 (2010): 759–66.

18   *reasons why this is so*: Lucy Armstrong, Viviana M. Wuthrich, Ashleigh Knight, and Richard Joiner, "Worry and Depression in the Old and Young: Differences and Mediating Factors," *Behaviour Change* 31, no. 4 (2014): 279–89.

TWO. THE NOCEBO EFFECT

21   DSM *became a surprise bestseller*: Arden Dier, "There's a New Bible on the Bestseller List: It's the DSM-5 and That's Not Necessarily Great," Newser, June 14, 2022, https://www.newser.com/story/321729/best-selling-psychiatry-manual-might-not-be-helping-everyone.html; Venay Minon, "The Diagnostic and Statistical Manual of Mental Disorders Is Suddenly a Bestseller on Amazon—This Is Not Good for Anyone's Mental Health," *Toronto Star*, June 14, 2022, https://www.thestar.com/entertainment/opinion/2022/06/14/the-diagnostic-and-statistical-manual-of-mental-disorders-is-suddenly-a-bestseller-on-amazon-this-is-not-good-for-anyones-mental-health.html; Will Pavia, "Psychiatry Manual Tops Bestseller List," *Times*, June 18, 2022, https://www.thetimes.co.uk/article/psychiatry-manual-tops-bestseller-list-0nzzz60lc.

21   Diagnostic and Statistical Manual: American Psychiatric Association, *Diagnostic and Statistical Manual of Mental Disorder*, 5th ed., text revision (Washington, DC: American Psychiatric Association, 2022).

22   *by joining up with various identities*: Michael A. Hogg, "Uncertainty–Identity Theory," *Advances in Experimental Social Psychology* 39 (2007): 69–126.

22   *2022 study of young adults*: Center for Collegiate Mental Health, Center

for Collegiate Mental Health 2022 Annual Report, 2023, https://ccmh.psu.edu/assets/docs/2022%20Annual%20Report.pdf.

24 *"an important lesson . . ."*: Quoted in Donald D. Price, Damien G. Finniss, and Fabrizio Benedetti, "A Comprehensive Review of the Placebo Effect: Recent Advances and Current Thought," *Annual Review of Psychology* 59 (2008): 565–90.

24 *the* nocebo *effect is the power*: Alia J. Crum, Kari A. Leibowitz, and Abraham Verghese, "Making Mindset Matter," *British Medical Journal* 356 (2017): j674.

25 *tracking sleep problems*: Kelly Glazer Baron, Sabra Abbott, Nancy Jao, Natalie Manalo, and Rebecca Mullen, "Orthosomnia: Are Some Patients Taking the Quantified Self Too Far?," *Journal of Clinical Sleep Medicine* 13, no. 2 (2017): 351–54.

25 *conundrum about informed consent*: Dieneke Hubbeling, Manhal Zarroug, and Robert Bertram, "Effects of Patient Mindset Raise a Legal Dilemma," *British Medical Journal* 356 (2017): j1271.

25 *believing anxiety won't improve*: Hans S. Schroder, Courtney P. Callahan, Allison E. Gornik, and Jason S. Moser, "The Fixed Mindset of Anxiety Predicts Future Distress: A Longitudinal Study," *Behavior Therapy* 50, no. 4 (2019): 710–17.

25 *genetic risk for health problems*: Bradley P. Turnwald, J. Parker Goyer, Danielle Z. Boles, Amy Silder, Scott L. Delp, et al., "Learning One's Genetic Risk Changes Physiology Independent of Actual Genetic Risk," *Nature Human Behaviour* 3, no. 1 (2019): 48–56.

26 *cyberchondria*: Gioia Bottesi, Claudia Marino, Alessio Vieno, Marta Ghisi, and Marcantonio M. Spada, "Psychological Distress in the Context of the COVID-19 Pandemic: The Joint Contribution of Intolerance of Uncertainty and Cyberchondria," *Psychology & Health* 37, no. 11 (2022): 1396–413.

26 *associated with the hashtag #mentalhealth*: Corey H. Basch, Lorie Donelle, Joseph Fera, and Christie Jaime, "Deconstructing TikTok Videos on Mental Health: Cross-sectional, Descriptive Content Analysis," *JMIR Formative Research* 6, no. 5 (2022): e38340.

27 *fertile ground for social contagion*: Hannes Rosenbusch, Anthony M. Evans, and Marcel Zeelenberg, "Multilevel Emotion Transfer on YouTube: Disentangling the Effects of Emotional Contagion and Homophily on Video Audiences," *Social Psychological and Personality Science* 10, no. 8 (2019): 1028–35.

27 *"a pandemic within a pandemic"*: Caroline Olvera, Glenn T. Stebbins, Christopher G. Goetz, and Katie Kompoliti, "TikTok Tics: A Pandemic Within a Pandemic," *Movement Disorders Clinical Practice* 8, no. 8 (2021): 1200–05.

27 *tics shown in the videos*: Alonso Zea Vera, Adrienne Bruce, Jordan Garris,

Laura Tochen, Poonam Bhatia, et al., "The Phenomenology of Tics and Tic-Like Behavior in TikTok," *Pediatric Neurology* 130 (2022): 14–20.

27   *A 2021* Wall Street Journal *article*: "Inside TikTok's Algorithm: A WSJ Video Investigation," *Wall Street Journal*, July 21, 2021, https://www.wsj.com/articles/tiktok-algorithm-video-investigation-11626877477.

28   *One Twitter user*: Daniella Emanuel, "23 Tweets About Dating Gen Z'ers That'll Make You Feel Like You Dodged a Bullet If You Were Born Before 1996," Buzzfeed, July 23, 2022, https://www.buzzfeed.com/daniellaemanuel/gen-zers-sharing-date.

30   *moderate social anxiety*: A. C. Miers, A. W. Blöte, M. de Rooij, C. L. Bokhorst, and P. M. Westenberg, "Trajectories of Social Anxiety During Adolescence and Relations with Cognition, Social Competence, and Temperament," *Journal of Abnormal Child Psychology* 41, no. 1 (2013): 97–110.

31   *a situational stressor*: Laura Strom, "Situational Symptoms or Serious Depression: What's the Difference?," National Alliance on Mental Illness, blog, April 3, 2017, https://www.nami.org/Blogs/NAMI-Blog/April-2017/Situational-Symptoms-or-Serious-Depression-What-s.

32   *negative life events*: Scott M. Monroe, Samantha F. Anderson, and Kate L. Harkness, "Life Stress and Major Depression: The Mysteries of Recurrences," *Psychological Review* 126, no. 6 (2019): 791.

32   *half of people who are depressed*: Jonathan Rottenberg, Andrew R. Devendorf, Todd B. Kashdan, and David J. Disabato, "The Curious Neglect of High Functioning After Psychopathology: The Case of Depression," *Perspectives on Psychological Science* 13, no. 5 (2018): 549–66.

THREE. WHY MEDICATION IS NOT ALWAYS THE BEST MEDICINE

36   *taking a prescription psychoactive medication*: "Mental Health Care: Household Pulse Survey," Centers for Disease Control and Prevention, https://www.cdc.gov/nchs/covid19/pulse/mental-health-care.htm.

36   *most commonly used prescription drug of any kind*: Crescent B. Martin, Craig M. Hales, Qiuping Gu, and Cynthia L. Ogden, "Prescription Drug Use in the United States, 2015–2016," Centers for Disease Control and Prevention, report, 2019, https://pubmed.ncbi.nlm.nih.gov/31112126/.

37   *"a media psychocircus of suggestion"*: This quote and other information in this paragraph are found in Allan V. Horwitz and Jerome C. Wakefield, *The Loss of Sadness: How Psychiatry Transformed Normal Sorrow into Depressive Disorder* (New York: Oxford University Press, 2007).

37   *"by joining up with various identities"*: Presidential Proclamation 2158, July 17, 1990, https://www.loc.gov/loc/brain/proclaim.html.

37   *adopted the same medical model*: Brett J. Deacon, "The Biomedical Model

of Mental Disorder: A Critical Analysis of Its Validity, Utility, and Effects on Psychotherapy Research," *Clinical Psychology Review* 33, no. 7 (2013): 846–61.

37 *an estimated 80 percent of people*: Joanna Moncrieff, Ruth E. Cooper, Tom Stockmann, Simone Amendola, Michael P. Hengartner, et al., "The Serotonin Theory of Depression: A Systematic Umbrella Review of the Evidence," *Molecular Psychiatry* (2022): 1–14.

37 *a headline-making study*: Moncrieff et al., "The Serotonin Theory."

38 *been the magic bullet*: James M. Ferguson, "SSRI Antidepressant Medications: Adverse Effects and Tolerability," *Primary Care Companion to the Journal of Clinical Psychiatry* 3, no. 1 (2001): 22.

38 *Consider this 2008 study*: Erick H. Turner, Annette M. Matthews, Eftihia Linardatos, Robert A. Tell, and Robert Rosenthal, "Selective Publication of Antidepressant Trials and Its Influence on Apparent Efficacy," *New England Journal of Medicine* 358, no. 3 (2008): 252–60.

38 *the "file drawer problem"*: Robert Rosenthal, "The File Drawer Problem and Tolerance for Null Results," *Psychological Bulletin* 86, no. 3 (1979): 638.

39 *because of the placebo effect*: Irving Kirsch, Thomas J. Moore, Alan Scoboria, and Sarah S. Nicholls, "The Emperor's New Drugs: An Analysis of Antidepressant Medication Data Submitted to the US Food and Drug Administration," *Prevention & Treatment* 5, no. 1 (2002): 23a; Winfried Rief, Yvonne Nestoriuc, Sarah Weiss, Eva Welzel, Arthur J. Barsky, et al., "Meta-Analysis of the Placebo Response in Antidepressant Trials," *Journal of Affective Disorders* 118, nos. 1–3 (2009): 1–8.

39 *mild or moderate symptoms of depression*: Jay C. Fournier, Robert J. DeRubeis, Steven D. Hollon, Sona Dimidjian, Jay D. Amsterdam, et al., "Antidepressant Drug Effects and Depression Severity: A Patient-Level Meta-Analysis," *JAMA* 303, no. 1 (2010): 47–53.

39 *may not outweigh the downsides*: Janus Christian Jakobsen, Kiran Kumar Katakam, Anne Schou, Signe Gade Hellmuth, Sandra Elkjær Stallknecht, et al., "Selective Serotonin Reuptake Inhibitors versus Placebo in Patients with Major Depressive Disorder: A Systematic Review with Meta-Analysis and Trial Sequential Analysis," *BMC Psychiatry* 17, no. 1 (2017): 1–28.

39 *happen more often online*: David M. B. Christmas, "'Brain Shivers': From Chat Room to Clinic," *Psychiatric Bulletin* 29, no. 6 (2005): 219–21; Adele Framer, "What I Have Learnt from Helping Thousands of People Taper Off Antidepressants and Other Psychotropic Medications," *Therapeutic Advances in Psychopharmacology* 11 (2021): 1–18.

39 *their emotional side effects*: Claire Cartwright, Kerry Gibson, John Read, Ondria Cowan, and Tamsin Dehar, "Long-Term Antidepressant Use: Patient

Perspectives of Benefits and Adverse Effects," *Patient Preference and Adherence* 10 (2016): 1401; John Read, Claire Cartwright, and Kerry Gibson, "Adverse Emotional and Interpersonal Effects Reported by 1829 New Zealanders While Taking Antidepressants," *Psychiatry Research* 216, no. 1 (2014): 67–73; John Read and James Williams, "Adverse Effects of Antidepressants Reported by a Large International Cohort: Emotional Blunting, Suicidality, and Withdrawal Effects," *Current Drug Safety* 13, no. 3 (2018): 176–86.

39 *may trigger manic episodes*: Peter R. Breggin, "Suicidality, Violence and Mania Caused by Selective Serotonin Reuptake Inhibitors (SSRIs): A Review and Analysis," *International Journal of Risk & Safety in Medicine* 16, no. 1 (2004): 31–49; Rashmi Patel, Peter Reiss, Hitesh Shetty, Matthew Broadbent, Robert Stewart, et al., "Do Antidepressants Increase the Risk of Mania and Bipolar Disorder in People with Depression? A Retrospective Electronic Case Register Cohort Study," *British Medical Journal Open* 5, no. 12 (2015): e008341.

40 *a variety of off-label conditions*: Jenna Wong, Aude Motulsky, Michal Abrahamowicz, Tewodros Eguale, David L. Buckeridge, et al., "Off-Label Indications for Antidepressants in Primary Care," *British Medical Journal* 356 (2017): j603.

40 *125,000 medical and pharmacy claims*: Angela S. Czaja and Robert Valuck, "Off-label Antidepressant Use in Children and Adolescents Compared with Young Adults: Extent and Level of Evidence," *Pharmacoepidemiology and Drug Safety* 21, no. 9 (2012): 997–1004.

40 *"rise of all-purpose antidepressants"*: Julia Calderone, "The Rise of All-Purpose Antidepressants," *Scientific American*, November 1, 2014, https://www.scientificamerican.com/article/the-rise-of-all-purpose-antidepressants/.

40 *The use of benzodiazepines*: Sumit D. Agarwal and Bruce E. Landon, "Patterns in Outpatient Benzodiazepine Prescribing in the United States," *JAMA Network Open* 2, no. 1 (2019): e187399.

40 *brains and bodies can become dependent*: Guy Chouinard, "Issues in the Clinical Use of Benzodiazepines: Potency, Withdrawal, and Rebound," *Journal of Clinical Psychiatry* 65 (2004): 7–12.

41 *". . . the gain from benzos . . ."*: Quoted in Harriet Brown, "I Tried to Get Off Ativan and Learned Some Dark Things in the Process," *Vice*, January 12, 2017, https://www.vice.com/en/article/nzn8dq/i-tried-to-get-off-ativan.

41 *second only to opioids*: Greta A. Bushnell, Mark Olfson, and Silvia S. Martins, "Sex Differences in US Emergency Department Non-fatal Visits for Benzodiazepine Poisonings in Adolescents and Young Adults," *Drug and Alcohol Dependence* 221 (2021): 108609.

41 *tripled since 2000*: Brian J. Piper, Christy L. Ogden, Olapeju M. Simoyan,

Daniel Y. Chung, James F. Caggiano, et al., "Trends in Use of Prescription Stimulants in the United States and Territories, 2006 to 2016," *PloSone* 13, no. 11 (2018): e0206100; Daniel J. Safer, "Recent Trends in Stimulant Usage," *Journal of Attention Disorders* 20, no. 6 (2016): 471–77.

41 *skyrocketing during the pandemic*: Melissa L. Danielson, Michele K. Bohm, Kimberly Newsome, Angelika H. Claussen, Jennifer W. Kaminski, Scott D. Grosse, Lila Siwakoti, Aziza Arifkhanova, Rebecca H. Bitsko, and Lara R. Robinson, "Trends in Stimulant Prescription Fills Among Commercially Insured Children and Adults—United States, 2016–2021," Centers for Disease Control and Prevention, *Morbidity and Mortality Weekly Report* 72, no. 13 (2023): 327–32.

41 *A 2023 study found that stimulant use*: Elizabeth Bowman, David Coghill, Carsten Murawski, and Peter Bossaerts, "Not So Smart? 'Smart' Drugs Increase the Level but Decrease the Quality of Cognitive Effort," *Science Advances* 9, no. 24 (2023): eadd4165.

41 *about one in five college students*: Kari Benson, Kate Flory, Kathryn L. Humphreys, and Steve S. Lee, "Misuse of Stimulant Medication Among College Students: A Comprehensive Review and Meta-Analysis," *Clinical Child and Family Psychology Review* 18, no. 1 (2015): 50–76.

41 *often off-label and without a formal evaluation*: Daniel J. Safer, "Recent Trends in Stimulant Usage," *Journal of Attention Disorders* 20, no. 6 (2016): 471–77.

42 *stimulant prescriptions for adults*: Amy R. Board, Gery Guy, Christopher M. Jones, and Brooke Hoots, "Trends in Stimulant Dispensing by Age, Sex, State of Residence, and Prescriber Specialty—United States, 2014–2019," *Drug and Alcohol Dependence* 217 (2020): 108297; Safer, "Recent Trends in Stimulant Usage."

42 *"a prescribing cascade"*: Thomas J. Moore, Phillip W. Wirtz, Jill N. Curran, and G. Caleb Alexander, "Medical Use and Combination Drug Therapy Among US Adult Users of Central Nervous System Stimulants: A Cross-Sectional Analysis," *British Medical Journal Open* 13, no. 4 (2023): e069668.

42 *a wide range of ages and difficulties*: Stephen Crystal, Mark Olfson, Cecilia Huang, Harold Pincus, and Tobias Gerhard, "Broadened Use of Atypical Antipsychotics: Safety, Effectiveness, and Policy Challenges," *Health Affairs* 28, Suppl. 1 (2009): w770–w781; Mark Olfson, Marissa King, and Michael Schoenbaum, "Treatment of Young People with Antipsychotic Medications in the United States," *JAMA Psychiatry* 72, no. 9 (2015): 867–74.

42 *"antipsychotics are becoming antidepressants"*: Urban Groleger, "Off-Label Use of Antipsychotics: Rethinking 'Off-Label,'" *Psychiatria Danubina* 19, no. 4 (2007): 350-53.

42 *hallucinogens . . . show promise*: Danilo De Gregorio, Argel Aguilar-Valles, Katrin H. Preller, Boris Dov Heifets, Meghan Hibicke, et al., "Hallucinogens in Mental Health: Preclinical and Clinical Studies on LSD, Psilocybin, MDMA, and Ketamine," *Journal of Neuroscience* 41, no. 5 (2021): 891–900.

42 *put that promise into practice*: Cassandra Willyard, "Mind-bending Therapies," *Nature*, August 25, 2022, https://media.nature.com/original/magazine -assets/d41586-022-02205-w/d41586-022-02205-w.pdf.

43 *"the psychopharmacology revolution was born"*: Robert Whitaker, *Anatomy of an Epidemic: Magic Bullets, Psychiatric Drugs, and the Astonishing Rise of Mental Illness in America* (New York: Crown, 2011): 47.

43 *A stunning 80 percent of first-time prescriptions*: Whitaker, *Anatomy of an Epidemic*.

43 *According to a 2021 article*: Polly Mosendz and Caleb Melby, "ADHD Drugs Are Convenient to Get Online. Maybe Too Convenient," *Bloomberg*, March 11, 2022, https://www.bloomberg.com/news/features/2022-03-11 /cerebral-app-over-prescribed-adhd-meds-ex-employees-say.

45 *discontinuation syndrome*: Mark Horowitz and Michael Wilcock, "Newer Generation Antidepressants and Withdrawal Effects: Reconsidering the Role of Antidepressants and Helping Patients to Stop," *Drug and Therapeutics Bulletin* 60, no. 1 (2022): 7–12; Mark Abie Horowitz and David Taylor, "Tapering of SSRI Treatment to Mitigate Withdrawal Symptoms," *The Lancet: Psychiatry* 6, no. 6 (2019): 538–46.

45 *the polite term for drug withdrawal*: Horowitz and Taylor, "Tapering of SSRI Treatment."

45 *2019 review of studies of antidepressant withdrawal*: James Davies and John Read, "A Systematic Review into the Incidence, Severity and Duration of Antidepressant Withdrawal Effects: Are Guidelines Evidence-based?," *Addictive Behaviors* 97 (2019): 111–21.

46 *remain on them for more than five years*: John Read, Aimee Gee, Jacob Diggle, and Helen Butler, "Staying on, and Coming off, Antidepressants: The Experiences of 752 UK Adults," *Addictive Behaviors* 88 (2019): 82–85.

46 *they may* worsen *long-term outcomes*: Giovanni A. Fava, "May Antidepressant Drugs Worsen the Conditions They Are Supposed to Treat? The Clinical Foundations of the Oppositional Model of Tolerance," *Therapeutic Advances in Psychopharmacology* 10 (2020): 970325; Giovanni A. Fava and Emanuela Offidani, "The Mechanisms of Tolerance in Antidepressant Action," *Progress in Neuro-Psychopharmacology and Biological Psychiatry* 35, no. 7 (2011): 1593–602; Shannon Hughes and David Cohen, "A Systematic Review of Long-Term Studies of Drug Treated and Non-Drug Treated Depression," *Journal of Affective Disorders* 118, nos. 1–3 (2009): 9–18.

46 *relapse rates are higher*: Steven D. Hollon, Robert J. DeRubeis, Paul W. Andrews, and J. Anderson Thomson, "Cognitive Therapy in the Treatment and Prevention of Depression: A Fifty-Year Retrospective with an Evolutionary Coda," *Cognitive Therapy and Research* 45, no. 3 (2021): 402–17.

46 *quality of life is lower*: Omar A. Almohammed, Abdulaziz A. Alsalem, Abdullah A. Almangour, Lama H. Alotaibi, Majed S. Al Yami, et al., "Antidepressants and Health-Related Quality of Life (HRQoL) for Patients with Depression: Analysis of the Medical Expenditure Panel Survey from the United States," *PloS one* 17, no. 4 (2022): e0265928.

46 *perturbing the still-developing brain*: Paul W. Andrews, Susan G. Kornstein, Lisa J. Halberstadt, Charles O. Gardner, and Michael C. Neale, "Blue Again: Perturbational Effects of Antidepressants Suggest Monoaminergic Homeostasis in Major Depression," *Frontiers in Psychology* 2 (2011): 159.

47 *"do more harm than good"*: Paul William Andrews, J. Anderson Thomson Jr., Ananda Amstadter, and Michael C. Neale, *"Primum Non Nocere*: An Evolutionary Analysis of Whether Antidepressants Do More Harm than Good," *Frontiers in Psychology* 3 (2012): 117.

47 *Jamison wrote in her* An Unquiet Mind, *a best-selling memoir*: Kay Redfield Jamison, *An Unquiet Mind: A Memoir of Moods and Madness*, vol. 4 (London: Pan Macmillan, 2015).

FOUR. WHY THE TIME FOR HOW IS NOW

50 *a J-shaped curve*: Ying Chen, Richard G. Cowden, Jeffery Fulks, John F. Plake, and Tyler J. VanderWeele, "National Data on Age Gradients in Well-Being Among US Adults," *JAMA Psychiatry* 79, no. 10 (2022): 1046–47.

50 *meta-analysis of almost one hundred different studies*: Brent W. Roberts, Kate E. Walton, and Wolfgang Viechtbauer, "Patterns of Mean-Level Change in Personality Traits Across the Life Course: A Meta-analysis of Longitudinal Studies," *Psychological Bulletin* 132, no. 1 (2006): 1.

51 *all the things he didn't know how to do*: Marij A. Hillen, Caitlin M. Gutheil, Tania D. Strout, Ellen M. A. Smets, and Paul K. J. Han, "Tolerance of Uncertainty: Conceptual Analysis, Integrative Model, and Implications for Healthcare," *Social Science & Medicine* 180 (2017): 62–75.

51 *lack confidence in our own abilities*: Kees van den Bos, "Making Sense of Life: The Existential Self Trying to Deal with Personal Uncertainty," *Psychological Inquiry* 20, no. 4 (2009): 197–217.

51 *what brain development looks like*: Richard A. I. Bethlehem, Jakob Seidlitz, Simon R. White, Jacob W. Vogel, Kevin M. Anderson, et al., "Brain Charts for the Human Lifespan," *Nature* 604, no. 7906 (2022): 525–33; Yongbin Wei, Han Zhang, and Yong Liu, "Charting Normative Brain

Variability Across the Human Lifespan," *Neuroscience Bulletin* 39, no. 2 (2023): 362–64.

52 *half the brain's volume*: Irina S. Buyanova and Marie Arsalidou, "Cerebral White Matter Myelination and Relations to Age, Gender, and Cognition: A Selective Review," *Frontiers in Human Neuroscience* 15 (2021): 662031.

52 *white matter* matters: R. Douglas Fields, "White Matter Matters," *Scientific American* 298, no. 3 (2008): 54–61.

52 *from bottom to top*: Helen M. Branson, "Normal Myelination: A Practical Pictorial Review," *Neuroimaging Clinics* 23, no. 2 (2013): 183–95.

52 *right on time*: Daniel J. Miller, Tetyana Duka, Cheryl D. Stimpson, Steven J. Schapiro, Wallace B. Baze, et al., "Prolonged Myelination in Human Neocortical Evolution," *Proceedings of the National Academy of Sciences* 109, no. 41 (2012): 16480–85.

52 *a process called* smart wiring: Marie E. Bechler, Matthew Swire, and Charles Ffrench-Constant, "Intrinsic and Adaptive Myelination—A Sequential Mechanism for Smart Wiring in the Brain," *Developmental Neurobiology* 78, no. 2 (2018): 68–79.

53 *those who speak German*: Xuehu Wei, Helyne Adamson, Matthias Schwendemann, Tomás Goucha, Angela D. Friederici, et al., "Native Language Differences in the Structural Connectome of the Human Brain," *NeuroImage* 270 (2023): 119955.

53 *the experiences you have*: Laurence D. Steinberg, *Age of Opportunity: Lessons from the New Science of Adolescence* (Boston: Houghton Mifflin Harcourt, 2014).

53 *The largest slice of client improvement*: John C. Norcross, *Psychotherapy Relationships that Work: Therapist Contributions and Responsiveness to Patients* (New York: Oxford University Press, 2002).

54 *A 2023 follow-up story revealed*: Azeen Ghorayshi, "How Teens Recovered from the 'TikTok Tics,'" *New York Times*, February 13, 2023, https://www.nytimes.com/2023/02/13/health/tiktok-tics-gender-tourettes.html.

FIVE. HOW TO THINK

59 default-mode network *refers*: M. E. Raichle, "The Brain's Default Mode Network," *Annual Review of Neuroscience* 38 (2015): 433–47.

60 *mental simulations of what might*: Eric C. Anderson, R. Nicholas Carleton, Michael Diefenbach, and Paul K. J. Han, "The Relationship Between Uncertainty and Affect," *Frontiers in Psychology* 10 (2019): 2504.

60 *called* negativity bias: Catherine J. Norris, "The Negativity Bias, Revisited: Evidence from Neuroscience Measures and an Individual Differences Approach," *Social Neuroscience* 16, no. 1 (2021): 68–82.

60 *"Bad is stronger than good"*: Roy F. Baumeister, Ellen Bratslavsky, Catrin

Finkenauer, and Kathleen D. Vohs, "Bad Is Stronger than Good," *Review of General Psychology* 5, no. 4 (2001): 323–70.

60 *younger adults spend more time than older adults*: Cheryl L. Grady, Andrea B. Protzner, Natasa Kovacevic, Stephen C. Strother, Babak Afshin-Pour, et al., "A Multivariate Analysis of Age-Related Differences in Default Mode and Task-Positive Networks Across Multiple Cognitive Domains," *Cerebral Cortex* 20, no. 6 (2010): 1432–47.

60 *have a harder time switching out*: Jessica R. Andrews-Hanna, Jonathan Smallwood, and R. Nathan Spreng, "The Default Network and Self-Generated Thought: Component Processes, Dynamic Control, and Clinical Relevance," *Annals of the New York Academy of Sciences* 1316, no. 1 (2014): 29–52.

61 *catastrophizing is worst-case–scenario thinking*: A. Ellis, *Reason and Emotion in Psychotherapy* (Oxford: Lyle Stuart, 1962); Resham Gellatly and Aaron T. Beck, "Catastrophic Thinking: A Transdiagnostic Process Across Psychiatric Disorders," *Cognitive Therapy and Research* 40, no. 4 (2016): 441–52.

61 *negative shifts from 0 to 1 percent*: Andrew Caplin and John Leahy, "Psychological Expected Utility Theory and Anticipatory Feelings," *Quarterly Journal of Economics* 116, no. 1 (2001): 55–79.

62 *Consider this telling study*: Graham C. L. Davey, "The Catastrophising Interview Procedure," *Worry and Its Psychological Disorders: Theory, Assessment, and Treatment* (2006): 157–78.

64 *a theme of personal inadequacy*: Graham C. L. Davey and Suzannah Levy, "Catastrophic Worrying: Personal Inadequacy and a Perseverative Iterative Style as Features of the Catastrophizing Process," *Journal of Abnormal Psychology* 107, no. 4 (1998): 576.

66 *one-third thought about killing themselves*: Center for Collegiate Mental Health, 2022 Annual Report, Publication no. STA 23-168, January 2023, https://ccmh.psu.edu/assets/docs/2022%20Annual%20Report.pdf.

66 *suicide isn't a symptom*: Rebecca Clay, "How to Assess and Intervene with Patients at Risk of Suicide," *American Psychological Association: Monitor on Psychology* 53, no. 4 (2022), https://www.apa.org/monitor/2022/06/continuing -education-intervene-suicide.

67 *Solving for worst-case scenarios*: Jonathan B. Grayson, "OCD and Intolerance of Uncertainty: Treatment Issues," *Journal of Cognitive Psychotherapy* 24, no. 1 (2010): 3.

69 *first-and-fast ways of thinking*: Norris, "Negativity Bias, Revisited."

69 *asking yourself "What else?"*: Tomoko Sugiura and Yoshinori Sugiura, "Relationships Between Refraining from Catastrophic Thinking, Repetitive Negative Thinking, and Psychological Distress," *Psychological Reports* 119, no. 2 (2016): 374–94.

70 *real cure for catastrophizing*: Graham C. L. Davey, Michael Jubb, and

Catherine Cameron, "Catastrophic Worrying as a Function of Changes in Problem-Solving Confidence," *Cognitive Therapy and Research* 20, no. 4 (1996): 333–44.

SIX. HOW TO FEEL

74 borderline personality disorder *generally refers to*: John G. Gunderson, *Borderline Personality Disorder: A Clinical Guide* (Washington, DC: American Psychiatric Association, 2009); National Library of Medicine, *Borderline Personality Disorder: Treatment and Management* (London: British Psychological Society and Royal College of Psychiatrists, 2009), available through National Institutes of Health, https://www.ncbi.nlm.nih.gov/books/NBK55415/.

74 *less than 1 percent of the population*: National Library of Medicine, *Borderline Personality Disorder: Treatment and Management.*

76 *uncertainty makes our emotions*: Eric C. Anderson, R. Nicholas Carleton, Michael Diefenbach, and Paul K. J. Han, "The Relationship Between Uncertainty and Affect," *Frontiers in Psychology* 10 (2019): 2504.

77 *ranging in age from 18 to 94*: Laura L. Carstensen, Monisha Pasupathi, Ulrich Mayr, and John R. Nesselroade, "Emotional Experience in Everyday Life Across the Adult Life Span," *Journal of Personality and Social Psychology* 79, no. 4 (2000): 644.

77 *Researchers in this and similar studies*: James J. Gross, Laura L. Carstensen, Monisha Pasupathi, Jeanne Tsai, Carina Götestam Skorpen, et al., "Emotion and Aging: Experience, Expression, and Control," *Psychology and Aging* 12, no. 4 (1997): 590.

78 *our personalities change more in our twenties*: Grant W. Edmonds, Joshua J. Jackson, Jennifer V. Fayard, and Brent W. Roberts, "Is Character Fate, or Is There Hope to Change My Personality Yet?," *Social and Personality Psychology Compass* 2, no. 1 (2008): 399–413.

79 *within about five years' time*: National Library of Medicine, "Borderline Personality Disorder"; Mary C. Zanarini, Frances R. Frankenburg, John Hennen, and Kenneth R. Silk, "The Longitudinal Course of Borderline Psychopathology: 6-Year Prospective Follow-Up of the Phenomenology of Borderline Personality Disorder," *American Journal of Psychiatry* 160, no. 2 (2003): 274–83.

79 *focus on the skills they may be lacking*: Amelia Aldao, Dylan G. Gee, Andres de los Reyes, and Ilana Seager, "Emotion Regulation as a Transdiagnostic Factor in the Development of Internalizing and Externalizing Psychopathology: Current and Future Directions," *Development and Psychopathology* 28 (2016): 927–46; Teresa M. Leyro, Michael J. Zvolensky, and Amit Bernstein, "Distress Tolerance and Psychopathological Symptoms and Disorders: A Review of the Empirical Literature Among Adults," *Psychological Bulletin*

136, no. 4 (2010): 576; Sophie Mattingley, George J. Youssef, Victoria Manning, Liam Graeme, and Kate Hall, "Distress Tolerance Across Substance Use, Eating, and Borderline Personality Disorders: A Meta-Analysis," *Journal of Affective Disorders* 300 (2022): 492–504; Thomas L. Webb, Eleanor Miles, and Paschal Sheeran, "Dealing with Feeling: A Meta-Analysis of the Effectiveness of Strategies Derived from the Process Model of Emotion Regulation," *Psychological Bulletin* 138, no. 4 (2012): 775.

79 *the ability to live with uncertainty*: Gioia Bottesi, Veronica Tesini, Silvia Cerea, and Marta Ghisi, "Are Difficulties in Emotion Regulation and Intolerance of Uncertainty Related to Negative Affect in Borderline Personality Disorder?," *Clinical Psychologist* 22, no. 2 (2018): 137–47.

79 *Mindfulness interventions don't bring*: Joseph Wielgosz, Simon B. Goldberg, Tammi R. A. Kral, John D. Dunne, and Richard J. Davidson, "Mindfulness Meditation and Psychopathology," *Annual Review of Clinical Psychology* 15 (2019): 285–316.

80 *there can be a kind of urgency*: Gioia Bottesi, Eleonora Carraro, Anna Martignon, Silvia Cerea, and Marta Ghisi, "'I'm Uncertain: What Should I Do?': An Investigation of Behavioral Responses to Everyday Life Uncertain Situations," *International Journal of Cognitive Therapy* 12, no. 1 (2019): 55–72; Sophie A. Palitz, Lara S. Rifkin, Lesley A. Norris, Mark Knepley, Nicole J. Fleischer, et al., "But What Will the Results Be?: Learning to Tolerate Uncertainty Is Associated with Treatment-Produced Gains," *Journal of Anxiety Disorders* 68 (2019): 102146.

80 *less confidence in their ability to problem-solve*: Fredda Blanchard-Fields, "Everyday Problem Solving and Emotion: An Adult Developmental Perspective," *Current Directions in Psychological Science* 16, no. 1 (2007): 26–31; Matthew K. Nock and Wendy Berry Mendes, "Physiological Arousal, Distress Tolerance, and Social Problem-Solving Deficits Among Adolescent Self-Injurers," *Journal of Consulting and Clinical Psychology* 76, no. 1 (2008): 28.

81 *as long as we expect them to last*: Timothy D. Wilson and Daniel T. Gilbert, "Affective Forecasting: Knowing What to Want," *Current Directions in Psychological Science* 14, no. 3 (2005): 131–34.

81 *They use meditation as a pain reliever*: Anne Harrington and John D. Dunne, "When Mindfulness Is Therapy: Ethical Qualms, Historical Perspectives," *American Psychologist* 70, no. 7 (2015): 621.

82 *it is about accepting discomfort*: Emily K. Lindsay and John David Creswell, "Mindfulness, Acceptance, and Emotion Regulation: Perspectives from Monitor and Acceptance Theory (MAT)," *Current Opinion in Psychology* 28 (2019): 120–25.

82 *less activity in the amygdala*: Allison S. Troy, Amanda J. Shallcross, Anna

Brunner, Rachel Friedman, and Markera C. Jones, "Cognitive Reappraisal and Acceptance: Effects on Emotion, Physiology, and Perceived Cognitive Costs," *Emotion* 18, no. 1 (2018): 58.

82 *We experience less fear, less pain, and less avoidance*: Hedy Kober, Jason Buhle, Jochen Weber, Kevin N. Ochsner, and Tor D. Wager, "Let It Be: Mindful Acceptance Down-Regulates Pain and Negative Emotion," *Social Cognitive and Affective Neuroscience* 14, no. 11 (2019): 1147–58; Martin Wolgast, Lars-Gunnar Lundh, and Gardar Viborg, "Cognitive Reappraisal and Acceptance: An Experimental Comparison of Two Emotion Regulation Strategies," *Behaviour Research and Therapy* 49, no. 12 (2011): 858–66.

82 *our heart rate lowers*: Carissa A. Low, Annette L. Stanton, and Julienne E. Bower, "Effects of Acceptance-Oriented versus Evaluative Emotional Processing on Heart Rate Recovery and Habituation," *Emotion* 8, no. 3 (2008): 419.

82 *Normalizing is simply recognizing*: Blake E. Ashforth and Glen E. Kreiner, "Normalizing Emotion in Organizations: Making the Extraordinary Seem Ordinary," *Human Resource Management Review* 12, no. 2 (2002): 215–35; Ruth A. Baer, Gregory T. Smith, Jaclyn Hopkins, Jennifer Krietemeyer, and Leslie Toney, "Using Self-Report Assessment Methods to Explore Facets of Mindfulness," *Assessment* 13, no. 1 (2006): 27–45.

82 *In a 2018 study with a diverse group*: Brett Q. Ford, Phoebe Lam, Oliver P. John, and Iris B. Mauss, "The Psychological Health Benefits of Accepting Negative Emotions and Thoughts: Laboratory, Diary, and Longitudinal Evidence," *Journal of Personality and Social Psychology* 115, no. 6 (2018): 1075.

83 *enhanced problem-solving*: Danielle N. Forjan, Michelle R. Tuckey, and Yiqiong Li, "Problem Solving and Affect as Mechanisms Linking Daily Mindfulness to Task Performance and Job Satisfaction," *Stress and Health* 36, no. 3 (2020): 338–49; E. Halland, M. De Vibe, I. Solhaug, O. Friborg, J. H. Rosenvinge, et al., "Mindfulness Training Improves Problem-Focused Coping in Psychology and Medical Students: Results from a Randomized Controlled Trial," *College Student Journal* 49, no. 3 (2015): 387–98.

83 *In another 2018 study*: Michael de Vibe, Ida Solhaug, Jan H. Rosenvinge, Reidar Tyssen, Adam Hanley, et al., "Six-Year Positive Effects of a Mindfulness-Based Intervention on Mindfulness, Coping and Well-Being in Medical and Psychology Students: Results from a Randomized Controlled Trial." *PloS One* 13, no. 4 (2018): e0196053.

83 "*. . . from a pending house foreclosure . . .*": Randolph M. Nesse and Phoebe C. Ellsworth, "Evolution, Emotions, and Emotional Disorders," *American Psychologist* 64, no. 2 (2009): 129.

83 *one of the best ways to calm down*: Amelia Aldao, Susan Nolen-Hoeksema, and Susanne Schweizer, "Emotion-Regulation Strategies Across Psycho-

pathology: A Meta-Analytic Review," *Clinical Psychology Review* 30, no. 2 (2010): 217–37; Aseel Sahib, Junwen Chen, Diana Cárdenas, and Alison L. Calear, "Intolerance of Uncertainty and Emotion Regulation: A Meta-Analytic and Systematic Review," *Clinical Psychology Review* 101 (2023): 102270.

SEVEN. HOW TO WORK

85   *single biggest driver of positive personality change*: Jaap J. A. Denissen, Maike Luhmann, Joanne M. Chung, and Wiebke Bleidorn, "Transactions Between Life Events and Personality Traits Across the Adult Lifespan," *Journal of Personality and Social Psychology* 116, no. 4 (2019): 612; Nathan W. Hudson, Brent W. Roberts, and Jennifer Lodi-Smith, "Personality Trait Development and Social Investment in Work," *Journal of Research in Personality* 46, no. 3 (2012): 334–44; Brent W. Roberts, Kate Walton, Tim Bogg, and Avshalom Caspi, "De-investment in Work and Non-Normative Personality Trait Change in Young Adulthood," *European Journal of Personality* 20, no. 6 (2006): 461–74.

85   *more emotionally stable as we age*: Wiebke Bleidorn, "What Accounts for Personality Maturation in Early Adulthood?," *Current Directions in Psychological Science* 24, no. 3 (2015): 245–52; Brent W. Roberts, Kate E. Walton, and Wolfgang Viechtbauer, "Patterns of Mean-Level Change in Personality Traits Across the Life Course: A Meta-Analysis of Longitudinal Studies," *Psychological Bulletin* 132, no. 1 (2006): 1.

85   *a 2013 study of nearly 900,000*: Wiebke Bleidorn, Theo A. Klimstra, Jaap J. A. Denissen, Peter J. Rentfrow, Jeff Potter, et al., "Personality Maturation Around the World: A Cross-Cultural Examination of Social-Investment Theory," *Psychological Science* 24, no. 12 (2013): 2530–40.

87   *something called* identity capital: James E. Côté, "The Role of Identity Capital in the Transition to Adulthood: The Individualization Thesis Examined," *Journal of Youth Studies* 5, no. 2 (2002): 117–34.

88   *According to economists at the U.S. Federal Reserve*: Danielle Paquette, "Your Lifetime Earnings Are Probably Determined in Your 20s," *Wall Street Journal*, February 10, 2015, https://www.washingtonpost.com/news/wonk/wp/2015/02/10/your-lifetime-earnings-are-probably-determined-in-your-twenties/; Fatih Guvenen, Fatih Karahan, Serdar Ozkan, and Jae Song, "What Do Data on Millions of U.S. Workers Reveal About Life-Cycle Earning Dynamics?," Federal Reserve Bank of New York, Staff Report no. 710, September 2019, https://www.newyorkfed.org/medialibrary/media/research/staff_reports/sr710.pdf

88   *a 2022 study of 3,000 employees*: "Upskilling Study," *Workplace Intelligence*, October 27, 2022, http://workplaceintelligence.com/upskilling-study.

88   *According to the chaos theory of careers*: Robert G. L. Pryor and Jim Bright, "Chaos in Practice: Techniques for Career Counsellors," *Australian Journal of Career Development* 14, no. 1 (2005): 18–28.

88   *changing, unpredictable, and boundaryless*: Yanjun Guan, Michael B. Arthur, Svetlana N. Khapova, Rosalie J. Hall, and Robert G. Lord, "Career Boundarylessness and Career Success: A Review, Integration and Guide to Future Research," *Journal of Vocational Behavior* 110 (2019): 390–402.

88   *about nine jobs by the age of 35*: "Number of Jobs Held by Individuals from Age 18 Through Age 34 in 1998–2019 by Educational Attainment, Sex, Race, Hispanic or Latino Ethnicity, and Age," U.S. Bureau of Labor Statistics, news release, last modified March 29, 2022, https://www.bls.gov/news.release/nlsyth.t01.htm.

88   *Personal, professional, and financial—and even emotional—stability*: Yunkyoung Loh Garrison, Ki-Hak Lee, and Saba Rasheed Ali, "Career Identity and Life Satisfaction: The Mediating Role of Tolerance for Uncertainty and Positive/Negative Affect," *Journal of Career Development* 44, no. 6 (2017): 516–29.

89   *the leading cause of stress in adulthood*: "Stress in America: Generation Z," American Psychological Association, press release, October 2018, https://www.apa.org/news/press/releases/stress/2018/stress-gen-z.pdf.

89   *Imposter syndrome isn't a real disorder*: "Imposter Syndrome," *Psychology Today*, https://www.psychologytoday.com/us/basics/imposter-syndrome, accessed April 26, 2023.

91   *What researchers call the* power of proximity: Natalia Emanuel, Emma Harrington, and Amanda Pallais, "Power of Proximity." Working paper, September 19, 2022, https://nataliaemanuel.github.io/ne_website/EHP_Power_of_Proximity.pdf.

91   *nearly two-thirds of on-the-job learning*: Kyle Herkenhoff, Jeremy Lise, Guido Menzio, and Gordon M Phillips, "Production and Learning in Teams," National Bureau of Economic Research, technical report, 2018, https://www.nber.org/system/files/working_papers/w25179/w25179.pdf.

91   *such as inventors, teachers, and salespeople*: Literature reviewed in Emanuel et al., "Power of Proximity."

EIGHT. HOW TO BE SOCIAL

97   *single, fastest-rising concern among*: "Trends in Social Anxiety Symptoms and Isolation in Students Seeking College Counseling Services," Center for Collegiate Mental Health, report, April 5, 2023, https://ccmh.psu.edu/index.php?option=com_dailyplanetblog&view=entry&year=2023&month=04&day=04&id=42:trends-in-social-anxiety-symptoms-and-isolation-in-student-seeking-college-counseling-services.

97   *Indicators of social anxiety disorder*: Murray B. Stein and Dan J. Stein, "Social Anxiety Disorder," *The Lancet* 371, no. 9618 (2008): 1115–25.

97   *fastest-rising mental health problem*: Center for Collegiate Mental Health, 2022 annual report, https://ccmh.psu.edu/assets/docs/2022%20Annual%20 Report.pdf.

97   *common and normal experience of social uncertainty*: Roderick M. Kramer and Jane Wei, "Social Uncertainty and the Problem of Trust in Social Groups: The Social Self in Doubt," in *The Psychology of the Social Self*, eds. Tom R. Tyler, Roderick M. Kramer, and Oliver P. John, pp. 153–76 (Mahwah, NJ: Erlbaum, 1999).

98   *moderate social anxiety that will . . . get better with age*: A. C. Miers, A. W. Blöte, M. De Rooij, C. L. Bokhorst, and P. M. Westenberg, "Trajectories of Social Anxiety During Adolescence and Relations with Cognition, Social Competence, and Temperament," *Journal of Abnormal Child Psychology* 41, no. 1 (2013): 97–110.

98   *still the third most common mental health diagnosis*: Eric P. Morris, Sherry H. Stewart, and Lindsay S. Ham, "The Relationship Between Social Anxiety Disorder and Alcohol Use Disorders: A Critical Review," *Clinical Psychology Review* 25, no. 6 (2005): 734–60.

98   *more likely to have problems with alcohol*: Kathleen Ries Merikangas, Shelli Avenevoli, Suddhasatta Acharyya, Heping Zhang, and Jules Angst, "The Spectrum of Social Phobia in the Zurich Cohort Study of Young Adults," *Biological Psychiatry* 51, no. 1 (2002): 81–91; Morris et al., "Relationship Between Social Anxiety Disorder and Alcohol Use."

98   *men are more likely to seek treatment*: Maya Asher, Anu Asnaani, and Idan M. Aderka, "Gender Differences in Social Anxiety Disorder: A Review," *Clinical Psychology Review* 56 (2017): 1–12.

100 *In a 2005 television interview*: "Bambi Francisco Interviews Mark Zuckerberg in 2005," posted May 13, 2015, YouTube, 6:13, https://www.youtube .com/watch?v=A4erAm-cJbg.

100 *An evolutionary trap is when a modern*: Christopher Kemp, "Trapped!," *New Scientist* 221, no. 2960 (2014): 43–45.

101 *social media hijacks is our need to be liked*: Joseph Firth, John Torous, Brendon Stubbs, Josh A. Firth, Genevieve Z. Steiner, et al., "The 'Online Brain': How the Internet May Be Changing Our Cognition," *World Psychiatry* 18, no. 2 (2019): 119–29.

101 *2022 study showed on MRI brain scans*: Daniel A. Abrams, Percy K. Mistry, Amanda E. Baker, Aarthi Padmanabhan, and Vinod Menon, "A Neurodevelopmental Shift in Reward Circuitry from Mother's to Non-familial Voices in Adolescence," *Journal of Neuroscience* 42, no. 20 (2022): 4164–73.

101 *those around us of our same age*: P. Michiel Westenberg, Eleonora Gullone, Caroline L. Bokhorst, David A. Heyne, and Neville J. King, "Social Evaluation Fear in Childhood and Adolescence: Normative Developmental Course and Continuity of Individual Differences," *British Journal of Developmental Psychology* 25, no. 3 (2007): 471–83.

101 *tracking the hearts and minds of friends*: Simone P. W. Haller, Kathrin Cohen Kadosh, Gaia Scerif, and Jennifer Y. F. Lau, "Social Anxiety Disorder in Adolescence: How Developmental Cognitive Neuroscience Findings May Shape Understanding and Interventions for Psychopathology," *Developmental Cognitive Neuroscience* 13 (2015): 11–20.

101 *In 1956, researchers asked*: Henry Angelino, Joseph Dollins, and Edmund V. Mech, "Trends in the 'Fears and Worries' of School Children as Related to Socio-Economic Status and Age," *Journal of Genetic Psychology* 89, no. 2 (1956): 263–76.

102 *grand-scale sociometer*: Mark R. Leary, Ellen S. Tambor, Sonja K. Terdal, and Deborah L. Downs, "Self-Esteem as an Interpersonal Monitor: The Sociometer Hypothesis," *Journal of Personality and Social Psychology* 68, no. 3 (1995): 518.

102 *a safer, more quantifiable alternative*: Nicholas Hutchins, Andrew Allen, Michelle Curran, and Lee Kannis-Dymand, "Social Anxiety and Online Social Interaction," *Australian Psychologist* 56, no. 2 (2021): 142–53; Shiri Prizant-Passal, Tomer Shechner, and Idan M. Aderka, "Social Anxiety and Internet Use–A Meta-Analysis: What Do We Know? What Are We Missing?," *Computers in Human Behavior* 62 (2016): 221–29.

102 *avoidance and impression management*: Rachel Evans, Kenny Chiu, David M. Clark, Polly Waite, and Eleanor Leigh, "Safety Behaviours in Social Anxiety: An Examination Across Adolescence," *Behaviour Research and Therapy* 144 (2021): 103931.

102 *a 2019 study of Facebook users*: Sophie E. Carruthers, Emma L. Warnock-Parkes, and David M. Clark, "Accessing Social Media: Help or Hindrance for People with Social Anxiety?," *Journal of Experimental Psychopathology* 10, no. 2 (2019): 1–11.

103 *a 2022 study of Instagram users*: Ly-Anne Toh, Prudence Millear, Andrew Allen, and Lee Kannis-Dymand, "Putting on Your Best Face: Investigating Social Anxiety in Instagram Users," *Australian Psychologist* 57, no. 3 (2022): 197–208.

103 *the more unsure we feel about ourselves*: Bethany Butzer and Nicholas A. Kuiper, "Relationships Between the Frequency of Social Comparisons and Self-Concept Clarity, Intolerance of Uncertainty, Anxiety, and Depression," *Personality and Individual Differences* 41, no. 1 (2006): 167–76; Erin A. Vogel, Jason P. Rose, Bradley M. Okdie, Katheryn Eckles, and Brittany

Franz, "Who Compares and Despairs? The Effect of Social Comparison Orientation on Social Media Use and Its Outcomes," *Personality and Individual Differences* 86 (2015): 249–56.

103 *"Instagram-contingent self-worth"*: Richard B. Lopez and Isabel Polletta, "Regulating Self-Image on Instagram: Links Between Social Anxiety, Instagram Contingent Self-Worth, and Content Control Behaviors," *Frontiers in Psychology* 12 (2021): 3700.

103 *engaging in* upward *social comparisons*: Abraham P. Buunk and Frederick X. Gibbons, "Social Comparison: The End of a Theory and the Emergence of a Field," *Organizational Behavior and Human Decision Processes* 102, no. 1 (2007): 3–21.

103 *"Look up and feel down!"*: Desirée Schmuck, Kathrin Karsay, Jörg Matthes, and Anja Stevic, "'Looking Up and Feeling Down': The Influence of Mobile Social Networking Site Use on Upward Social Comparison, Self-Esteem, and Well-Being of Adult Smartphone Users," *Telematics and Informatics* 42 (2019): 101240.

103 *"Compare and despair"*: Vogel et al., "Who Compares and Despairs?"

103 *". . . no faster way to crash a population . . ."*: Kemp, "Trapped!."

103 *rare health advisory about social media use*: "Health Advisory on Social Media Use in Adolescence," American Psychological Association, 2023, https://www.apa.org/topics/social-media-internet/health-advisory-adolescent-social-media-use.

103 *using social media actively to connect*: Philippe Verduyn, Oscar Ybarra, Maxime Résibois, John Jonides, and Ethan Kross, "Do Social Network Sites Enhance or Undermine Subjective Well-Being? A Critical Review," *Social Issues and Policy Review* 11, no. 1 (2017): 274–302.

104 *groups are more effective for social anxiety*: Diana E. Damer, Kelsey M. Latimer, and Sarah H. Porter, "'Build Your Social Confidence': A Social Anxiety Group for College Students," *Journal for Specialists in Group Work* 35, no. 1 (2010): 7–22; James D. Herbert, Brandon A. Gaudiano, Alyssa A. Rheingold, Valerie H. Myers, Kristy Dalrymple, et al., "Social Skills Training Augments the Effectiveness of Cognitive Behavioral Group Therapy for Social Anxiety Disorder," *Behavior Therapy* 36, no. 2 (2005): 125–38.

104 *". . . usually go better than we think . . ."*: Gillian M. Sandstrom and Erica J. Boothby, "Why Do People Avoid Talking to Strangers? A Mini Meta-Analysis of Predicted Fears and Actual Experiences Talking to a Stranger," *Self and Identity* 20, no. 1 (2021): 47–71.

105 *The liking gap is the now well-documented*: Erica J. Boothby, Gus Cooney, Gillian M. Sandstrom, and Margaret S. Clark, "The Liking Gap in Conversations: Do People Like Us More than We Think?," *Psychological Science* 29, no. 11 (2018): 1742–56.

107 *2018 study of college suite-mates*: Boothby et al., "The Liking Gap in Conversations."

NINE. HOW TO BEFRIEND

110 *loneliest people in the United States*: "New Cigna Study Reveals Loneliness at Epidemic Levels in America," Cigna newsletter, May 1, 2018, https://www.multivu.com/players/English/8294451-cigna-us-loneliness-survey/ and https://www.cigna.com/static/www-cigna-com/docs/about-us/news room/studies-and-reports/combatting-loneliness/cigna-2020-loneliness -factsheet.pdf; Jamie Ballard, "Millennials Are the Loneliest Generation," YouGovAmerica, July 30, 2019, https://today.yougov.com/topics/society /articles-reports/2019/07/30/loneliness-friendship-new-friends-poll-survey; "Loneliness in America: How the Pandemic Has Deepened an Epidemic of Loneliness and What We Can Do About It," Making Caring Common project, February 2021, Harvard Graduate School of Education, https://mcc.gse.harvard.edu/reports/loneliness-in-america.

111 *the strange situation*: Lenny Van Rosmalen, René Van der Veer, and Frank Van der Horst, "Ainsworth's Strange Situation Procedure: The Origin of an Instrument," *Journal of the History of the Behavioral Sciences* 51, no. 3 (2015): 261–84.

111 *recently have researchers become interested*: Ashleigh I. Aviles and Debra M. Zeifman, "Casting a Wider Net: Parents, Pair Bonds, and Other Attachment Partners in Adulthood," in *Attachment: The Fundamental Questions*, eds. Ross A. Thompson, Jeffry A. Simpson, and Lisa J. Berlin, pp. 53–59 (New York: Guilford, 2021); R. Chris Fraley, "Attachment in Adulthood: Recent Developments, Emerging Debates, and Future Directions," *Annual Review of Psychology* 70 (2019): 401–22.

111 *don't have a steady partner*: L. Bonos and E. Guskin, "It's Not Just You: New Data Shows More than Half of Young People in America Don't Have a Romantic Partner," *Washington Post*, March 21, 2019, https://www.washingtonpost.com/lifestyle/2019/03/21/its-not-just-you-new-data-shows-more -than-half-young-people-america-dont-have-romantic-partner; Risa Gelles-Watnick, "For Valentine's Day, Five Facts About Single Americans," Pew Research Center, fact sheet, February 8, 2023, https://www.pewresearch.org /fact-tank/2023/02/08/for-valentines-day-5-facts-about-single-americans.

112 *that's where friends come in*: Peter Huxley, Tapas Mishra, Bazoumana Ouattara, and Mamata Parhi, "Understanding Determinants of Happiness under Uncertainty," working paper 02-13, Association Française de Cliométrie, 2013.

113 *the tend-and-befriend model*: Shelley E. Taylor, "Tend and Befriend: Biobehavioral Bases of Affiliation Under Stress," *Current Directions in Psychological Science* 15, no. 6 (2006): 273–77.

113 *foster healthy risk-taking and growth*: David S. Lee, Oscar Ybarra, Richard Gonzalez, and Phoebe Ellsworth, "I-Through-We: How Supportive Social Relationships Facilitate Personal Growth," *Personality and Social Psychology Bulletin* 44, no. 1 (2018): 37–48.

113 *on an emotional level*: Patricia M. Sias and Heidi Bartoo, "Friendship, Social Support, and Health," in *Low-Cost Approaches to Promote Physical and Mental Health*, ed. Luciano L'Abate, pp. 455–72 (New York: Springer, 2007).

113 *lower levels of depression, anxiety, and anger*: Chong Man Chow, Holly Ruhl, and Duane Buhrmester, "Romantic Relationships and Psychological Distress Among Adolescents: Moderating Role of Friendship Closeness," *International Journal of Social Psychiatry* 61, no. 7 (2015): 711–20; Alan R. King, Tiffany D. Russell, and Amy C. Veith, "Friendship and Mental Health Functioning," in *The Psychology of Friendship*, eds. Mahzujd Hojjat and Anne Moyer, p. 249 (New York: Oxford University Press, 2016).

113 *quality matters more than quantity*: Melikşah Demir, Haley Orthel-Clark, Metin Özdemir, and Sevgi Bayram Özdemir, "Friendship and Happiness Among Young Adults," in *Friendship and Happiness: Across the Life-Span and Cultures*, pp. 117–35 (Dordrecht: Springer, 2015).

113 *doubling the number of face-to-face friends*: John F. Helliwell and Haifang Huang, "Comparing the Happiness Effects of Real and On-Line Friends," *PloS one* 8, no. 9 (2013): e72754.

114 *those who are seen as "popular"*: Rachel K. Narr, Joseph P. Allen, Joseph S. Tan, and Emily L. Loeb, "Close Friendship Strength and Broader Peer Group Desirability as Differential Predictors of Adult Mental Health," *Child Development* 90, no. 1 (2019): 298–313.

114 *we move from parents to partners*: Joseph P. Allen, Rachel K. Narr, Jessica Kansky, and David E. Szwedo, "Adolescent Peer Relationship Qualities as Predictors of Long-Term Romantic Life Satisfaction," *Child Development* 91, no. 1 (2020): 327–40.

114 *better predictors of healthy romantic relationships*: Joseph P. Allen, Meghan A. Costello, Amanda F. Hellwig, Corey Pettit, Jessica A. Stern, et al., "Adolescent Caregiving Success as a Predictor of Social Functioning from Ages 13 to 33," *Child Development* 00 (2023): 1–15; Joseph P. Allen, Meghan Costello, Jessica Kansky, and Emily L. Loeb, "When Friendships Surpass Parental Relationships as Predictors of Long-Term Outcomes: Adolescent Relationship Qualities and Adult Psychosocial Functioning," *Child Development* 93, no. 3 (2022): 760–77.

114 *better predictors than our early experiences with dating and sex*: Joseph P. Allen, Rachel K. Narr, Jessica Kansky, and David E. Szwedo, "Adolescent Peer Relationship Qualities as Predictors of Long-Term Romantic Life Satisfaction," *Child Development* 91, no. 1 (2020): 327–40.

114 *"voluntary interdependence"*: Paul H. Wright, "A Model and a Technique for Studies of Friendship," *Journal of Experimental Social Psychology* 5, no. 3 (1969): 295–309.

114 *what's called* social prescribing: Helen J. Chatterjee, Paul M. Camic, Bridget Lockyer, and Linda J. M. Thomson, "Non-Clinical Community Interventions: A Systematised Review of Social Prescribing Schemes," *Arts & Health* 10, no. 2 (2018): 97–123.

116 *published an article about*: Julie Jargon, "How to Find and Keep Friends: A Guide for Middle Age," *Wall Street Journal*, January 29, 2022, https://www.wsj.com/articles/being-a-parent-is-lonelyheres-how-to-find-and-keep-friends-in-2022-11643465968; Catherine Pearson, "How to Make and Keep Friends as an Adult," *New York Times*, October 1, 2022, https://www.nytimes.com/2022/10/01/well/live/how-to-make-friends-adult.html; Julie Beck, "The Six Forces that Fuel Friendship," *The Atlantic*, June 10, 2022, https://www.theatlantic.com/family/archive/2022/06/six-ways-make-maintain-friends/661232.

116 *Remember the 2019 study*: Ballard, "Millennials Are the Loneliest."

117 *amount of time we spend together* by choice: Jeffrey A. Hall, "How Many Hours Does It Take to Make a Friend?," *Journal of Social and Personal Relationships* 36, no. 4 (2019): 1278–96.

118 *spend only about 30 minutes per day socializing*: "American Time Use Survey," U.S. Bureau of Labor Statistics, June 23, 2022, https://www.bls.gov/news.release/atus.nr0.htm.

118 *more time socializing online*: "2023 Digital Media Trends: Immersed and Connected," Deloitte, April 2023, https://www2.deloitte.com/us/en/insights/industry/technology/media-industry-trends-2023.html.

119 *shyness was the leading reason*: Ballard, "Millennials Are the Loneliest."

119 *once they make connections*: Thomas L. Rodebaugh, Michelle H. Lim, Erik A. Shumaker, Cheri A. Levinson, and Tess Thompson, "Social Anxiety and Friendship Quality over Time," *Cognitive Behaviour Therapy* 44, no. 6 (2015): 502–11.

TEN. HOW TO LOVE

122 *half the cases of first-time depression*: Scott M. Monroe, Paul Rohde, John R. Seeley, and Peter M. Lewinsohn, "Life Events and Depression in Adolescence: Relationship Loss as a Prospective Risk Factor for First Onset of Major Depressive Disorder," *Journal of Abnormal Psychology* 108, no. 4 (1999): 606.

122 *a lot to say about a lost love*: Anne M. Verhallen, Remco J. Renken, Jan-Bernard C. Marsman, and Gert J. Ter Horst, "Romantic Relationship

Breakup: An Experimental Model to Study Effects of Stress on Depression (-like) Symptoms," *PLoS One* 14, no. 5 (2019): e0217320.

123 *"Love is one of the most powerful sensations"*: Helen Fisher, "The Brain in Love," TED talk, 2008, https://www.ted.com/talks/helen_fisher_the_brain_in _love/transcript.

123 *Love is a drive*: Helen Fisher, "The Drive to Love: The Neural Mechanism for Mate Selection," in *The New Psychology of Love*, eds. Robert J. Sternberg and Karin Sternberg, pp. 87–115 (New Haven: Yale University Press, 1990).

123 *romantic uncertainty*: Leanne K. Knobloch and Kristen L. Satterlee, "Relational Uncertainty: Theory and Application," in *Uncertainty, Information Management, and Disclosure Decisions: Theories and Applications*, eds. D. Afifi and W. A. Afifi, pp. 106–27 (London: Routledge/Taylor & Francis Group, 2009).

123 *maddening and destabilizing*: Fisher, "The Drive to Love."

123 *"one is very crazy"*: Ernest Jones, *The Life and Work of Sigmund Freud* (Lexington: MA: Plunkett Lake Press, 2019): 87.

123 *"never so defenseless"*: Sigmund Freud, *Civilization and Its Discontents* (London: Norton, 2005): 62.

124 *estimated 95 percent of young adults have rejected*: Roy F. Baumeister, Sara R. Wotman, and Arlene M. Stillwell, "Unrequited Love: On Heartbreak, Anger, Guilt, Scriptlessness, and Humiliation," *Journal of Personality and Social Psychology* 64, no. 3 (1993): 377.

124 *"The pain of grief . . ."*: Colin Murray Parkes and Holly G. Prigerson, *Bereavement: Studies of Grief in Adult Life* (London: Routledge, 2013).

126 *with depression remit spontaneously*: Harvey A. Whiteford, M. G. Harris, G. McKeon, A. Baxter, C. Pennell, et al., "Estimating Remission from Untreated Major Depression: A Systematic Review and Meta-Analysis," *Psychological Medicine* 43, no. 8 (2013): 1569–85.

127 *our brain is desperately trying to solve*: Paul W. Andrews and J. Anderson Thomson Jr., "The Bright Side of Being Blue: Depression as an Adaptation for Analyzing Complex Problems," *Psychological Review* 116, no. 3 (2009): 620.

127 *might fare better next time*: Paul W. Andrews, Marta M. Maslej, J. Anderson Thomson Jr., and Steven D. Hollon, "Disordered Doctors or Rational Rats? Testing Adaptationist and Disorder Hypotheses for Melancholic Depression and Their Relevance for Clinical Psychology," *Clinical Psychology Review* 82 (2020): 101927.

127 *a breakup can lead to growth*: T. Y. Tashiro and Patricia Frazier, "'I'll Never Be in a Relationship like that Again': Personal Growth Following Romantic Relationship Breakups," *Personal Relationships* 10, no. 1 (2003): 113–28.

127 *making sense of a breakup*: Jessica Kansky and Joseph P. Allen, "Making Sense and Moving on: The Potential for Individual and Interpersonal Growth Following Emerging Adult Breakups," *Emerging Adulthood* 6, no. 3 (2018): 172–90.

127 *work to understand their breakups*: Evgenia Milman, Robert A. Neimeyer, Marilyn Fitzpatrick, Christopher J. MacKinnon, Krista R. Muis, et al., "Rumination Moderates the Role of Meaning in the Development of Prolonged Grief Symptomatology," *Journal of Clinical Psychology* 75, no. 6 (2019): 1047–65.

127 *make catastrophic (mis)interpretations*: Paul A. Boelen and Albert Reijntjes, "Negative Cognitions in Emotional Problems Following Romantic Relationship Break-ups," *Stress and Health: Journal of the International Society for the Investigation of Stress* 25, no. 1 (2009): 11–19.

ELEVEN. HOW TO HAVE SEX

132 *the three A's*: Al Cooper, "Sexuality and the Internet: Surfing into the New Millennium," *Cyberpsychology & Behavior* 1, no. 2 (1998): 187–93.

132 *most-visited websites*: Joel Khalili, "These Are the Most Popular Websites Right Now—and They Might Just Surprise You," *Tech Radar*, July 13, 2021, https://www.techradar.com/news/porn-sites-attract-more-visitors-than-netflix-and-amazon-youll-never-guess-how-many.

132 *an estimated 90 percent of young men*: Matthew B. Ezzell, L. Coleman, and J. M. Hald, "Pornography Makes the Man: The Impact of Pornography as a Component of Gender and Sexual Socialization," in *The Philosophy of Pornography: Contemporary Perspectives*, eds. Lindsay Coleman and Jacob M. Held, pp. 17–34 (London: Rowman & Littlefield, 2014).

132 *primary form of sex education in America*: Ezzell et al., "Pornography Makes the Man."

132 *porn consumers are female*: Dan J. Miller, "The Contents and Consumption of Porn: Who Is Watching What Exactly?," in *Sex Education Research: A Look Between the Sheets*, ed. William J. Taverner, pp. 107–117 (New York: Routledge, 2023).

132 *first glimpse of pornography*: Ezzell et al., "Pornography Makes the Man."

133 *porn's unofficial fourth A*: For information on pornography addiction, see https://pornaddiction.com and https://www.yourbrainonporn.com.

135 *"massive human experiment . . ."*: Gary Wilson, "Eliminate Chronic Internet Pornography Use to Reveal Its Effects," *Addicta: Turkish Journal on Addictions* 3, no. 2 (2016): 209–21.

135 *more likely to experience anxiety*: Wilson, "Eliminate Chronic Internet Pornography."

135 *2016 review of studies*: Brian Y. Park, Gary Wilson, Jonathan Berger,

Matthew Christman, Bryn Reina, et al., "Is Internet Pornography Causing Sexual Dysfunctions? A Review with Clinical Reports," *Behavioral Sciences* 6, no. 3 (2016): 17.

135   *training their brains and their bodies*: Simone Kühn and Jürgen Gallinat, "Brain Structure and Functional Connectivity Associated with Pornography Consumption: The Brain on Porn," *JAMA Psychiatry* 71, no. 7 (2014): 827–34.

136   *singer Billie Eilish said*: "Billie Eilish Opens up About Surviving Covid and Hosting SNL," Howard Stern website, December 13, 2021, https://www .howardstern.com/news/2021/12/13/billie-eilish-performs-2-songs-live-in -studio-and-opens-up-about-surviving-covid-and-hosting-snl.

137   *decreased confidence in one's ability*: Rosalijn Both, "A Matter of Sexual Confidence: Young Men's Non-Prescription Use of Viagra in Addis Ababa, Ethiopia," *Culture, Health & Sexuality* 18, no. 5 (2016): 495–508; Christopher B. Harte and Cindy M. Meston, "Recreational Use of Erectile Dysfunction Medications and Its Adverse Effects on Erectile Function in Young Healthy Men: The Mediating Role of Confidence in Erectile Ability," *Journal of Sexual Medicine* 9, no. 7 (2012): 1852–59.

137   *"The Viagra Epidemic Among . . ."*: "High Society: The Viagra Epidemic Among Young Men and Its Dangers," Vice News, posted January 29, 2020, YouTube, 22:31, https://www.youtube.com/watch?v=Y0IdDh7iqBQ.

138   *Sexual scripts*: Scott R. Braithwaite, Gwen Coulson, Krista Keddington, and Frank D. Fincham, "The Influence of Pornography on Sexual Scripts and Hooking up Among Emerging Adults in College," *Archives of Sexual Behavior* 44, no. 1 (2015): 111–23; Ana J. Bridges, Chyng F. Sun, Matthew B. Ezzell, and Jennifer Johnson, "Sexual Scripts and the Sexual Behavior of Men and Women Who Use Pornography," *Sexualization, Media, & Society* 2, no. 4 (2016): 1–14.

138   *roles portrayed in pornography*: Braithwaite et al., "The Influence of Pornography"; Chyng Sun, Ana Bridges, Jennifer A. Johnson, and Matthew B. Ezzell, "Pornography and the Male Sexual Script: An Analysis of Consumption and Sexual Relations," *Archives of Sexual Behavior* 45, no. 4 (2016): 983–94.

138   *sometimes callous*: Matthew B. Ezzell, Jennifer A. Johnson, Ana J. Bridges, and Chyng F. Sun, "I (dis) Like It Like That: Gender, Pornography, and Liking Sex," *Journal of Sex & Marital Therapy* 46, no. 5 (2020): 460–73.

139   *have less sex*: Lei Lei and Scott J. South, "Explaining the Decline in Young Adult Sexual Activity in the United States," *Journal of Marriage and Family* 83, no. 1 (2021): 280–295; Scott J. South and Lei Lei, "Why Are Fewer Young Adults Having Casual Sex?," *Socius* 7 (2021): 1–12.

139   *2020 study of nearly 10,000 adults*: Peter Ueda, Catherine H. Mercer, Cyrus Ghaznavi, and Debby Herbenick, "Trends in Frequency of Sexual Activity

and Number of Sexual Partners Among Adults Aged 18 to 44 Years in the US, 2000–2018," *JAMA Network Open* 3, no. 6 (2020): e203833.

141 *habitual users cut back on porn*: Wilson, "Eliminate Chronic Internet Pornography."

TWELVE. HOW TO MOVE

147 *people who are physically active feel better*: "Physical Activity," World Health Organization, fact sheet, October 5, 2022, https://www.who.int/news-room/fact-sheets/detail/physical-activity.

147 *About 30 minutes of moderate-to-vigorous activity*: "Physical Activity," World Health Organization.

147 *the message that "anything counts"*: James Gallagher, "Inside Health: The Lazy Guide to Exercise," *BBC News*, May 8, 2023, https://www.bbc.co.uk/sounds/play/w3ct4nn9.

147 *Any increase in your activity level*: Matthew Pearce, Leandro Garcia, Ali Abbas, Tessa Strain, Felipe Barreto Schuch, et al., "Association Between Physical Activity and Risk of Depression: A Systematic Review and Meta-Analysis," *JAMA Psychiatry* 79, no. 6 (2022): 550–59.

147 *80 percent of youth*: "Physical Activity," World Health Organization.

148 *a 2023 review looked at*: Ben Singh, Timothy Olds, Rachel Curtis, Dorothea Dumuid, Rosa Virgara, et al., "Effectiveness of Physical Activity Interventions for Improving Depression, Anxiety and Distress: An Overview of Systematic Reviews," *British Journal of Sports Medicine* 0 (2023): 1–10.

148 *a clearly viable alternative or adjunct*: Shawn M. Arent, Alan J. Walker, and Michelle A. Arent, "The Effects of Exercise on Anxiety and Depression," in *Handbook of Sport Psychology*, ed. Gershon Tenenbaum and Robert C. Eklund, pp. 872–90 (Hoboken, NJ: John Wiley, 2020); Elizabeth Aylett, Nicola Small, and Peter Bower, "Exercise in the Treatment of Clinical Anxiety in General Practice: A Systematic Review and Meta-Analysis," *BMC Health Services Research* 18 (2018): 1–18; Michael Babyak, James A. Blumenthal, Steve Herman, Parinda Khatri, Murali Doraiswamy, et al., "Exercise Treatment for Major Depression: Maintenance of Therapeutic Benefit at 10 Months," *Psychosomatic Medicine* 62, no. 5 (2000): 633–38; Stuart Biddle, "Physical Activity and Mental Health: Evidence Is Growing," *World Psychiatry* 15, no. 2 (2016): 176; Siri Kvam, Catrine Lykkedrang Kleppe, Inger Hilde Nordhus, and Anders Hovland, "Exercise as a Treatment for Depression: A Meta-Analysis," *Journal of Affective Disorders* 202 (2016): 67–86.

148 *2016 meta-analysis*: Joseph Firth, Marco Solmi, Robyn E. Wootton, Davy Vancampfort, Felipe B. Schuch, et al., "A Meta-Review of 'Lifestyle Psychiatry': The Role of Exercise, Smoking, Diet, and Sleep in the Prevention and

Treatment of Mental Disorders," *World Psychiatry* 19, no. 3 (2020): 360–80; Michaela Pascoe, Alan P. Bailey, Melinda Craike, Tim Carter, Rhiannon Patten, et al., "Physical Activity and Exercise in Youth Mental Health Promotion: A Scoping Review," *British Medical Journal Open Sport & Exercise Medicine* 6, no. 1 (2020): 1–11.

148   *also helps us sleep better*: Christopher E. Kline, "The Bidirectional Relationship Between Exercise and Sleep: Implications for Exercise Adherence and Sleep Improvement," *American Journal of Lifestyle Medicine* 8, no. 6 (2014): 375–79.

148   *2019 meta-analysis of more than 1,200*: Nils Opel, Stella Martin, Susanne Meinert, Ronny Redlich, Verena Enneking, et al., "White Matter Microstructure Mediates the Association Between Physical Fitness and Cognition in Healthy, Young Adults," *Scientific Reports* 9, no. 1 (2019): 1–9.

149   *group movement can be especially beneficial*: Jennifer Heisz, *Move the Body, Heal the Mind: Overcome Anxiety, Depression, and Dementia and Improve Focus, Creativity, and Sleep* (New York: HarperCollins, 2022).

149   *TEDx talk on the topic*: Justin Waddell, "Home Is Where the Heart Is," TED talk, May 15, 2020, https://www.ted.com/talks/justin_waddell_home_is_where_the_heart_is.

149   *Centers for Disease Control does not even mention exercise*: "Mental Health Awareness," Centers for Disease Control and Prevention, January 20, 2011, https://www.cdc.gov/genomics/resources/diseases/mental.htm.

150   *2005 report from the Mental Health Foundation*: "Up and Running?: Exercise Therapy and the Treatment of Mild or Moderate Depression in Primary Care," Mental Health Foundation, report, 2005, https://lx.iriss.org.uk/sites/default/files/resources/up_and_running_full%20report.pdf.

150   *a 2018 study in New Zealand*: Kirsten Way, Lee Kannis-Dymand, Michele Lastella, and Geoff P. Lovell, "Mental Health Practitioners' Reported Barriers to Prescription of Exercise for Mental Health Consumers," *Mental Health and Physical Activity* 14 (2018): 52–60.

152   *annual World Happiness Report*: John F. Helliwell, Richard Layard, Jeffrey D. Sachs, and Jan-Emmanuel de Neve, World Happiness Report 2021, Sustainable Development Solutions Network, annual report, 2021, https://worldhappiness.report.

152   *looked for ways to feel better*: Sandra Amatriain-Fernández, Eric Simón Murillo-Rodríguez, Thomas Gronwald, Sergio Machado, and Henning Budde, "Benefits of Physical Activity and Physical Exercise in the Time of Pandemic," *Psychological Trauma: Theory, Research, Practice, and Policy* 12, no. S1 (2020): S264–S266.

152   *data from more than 13,000 respondents in eighteen countries*: Ralf Brand, Sinika Timme, and Sanaz Nosrat, "When Pandemic Hits: Exercise Frequency

and Subjective Well-Being During COVID-19 Pandemic," *Frontiers in Psychology* 11 (2020): 2391.

153 *moderate exercise is best*: Heisz, *Move the Body*.

154 *memes predictably swept the globe*: "Tiny Bulldozer Helping Massive Cargo Ship Stuck at Suez Canal Makes Way for Hilarious Memes," *News18*, March 26, 2021, https://www.news18.com/news/buzz/tiny-bulldozer-excavator-helping-massive-cargo-ship-stuck-at-suez-canal-makes-way-for-hilarious-memes-3575768.html.

154 *although it did not do the job by itself*: "Suez Canal: How Did They Move the Ever Given?," *BBC News*, March 29, 2021, https://www.bbc.com/news/56523659.

THIRTEEN. HOW TO COOK

156 *a 2018 survey by the American Psychological Association*: "Stress in America: Generation Z," American Psychological Association, press release, October 2018, https://www.apa.org/news/press/releases/stress/2018/stress-gen-z.pdf.

156 *called emotional eating*: Mallory Frayn and Bärbel Knäuper, "Emotional Eating and Weight in Adults: A Review," *Current Psychology* 37, no. 4 (2018): 924–33.

156 *only about 1 percent*: "Eating Disorders," National Institute of Mental Health, fact sheet, https://www.nimh.nih.gov/health/statistics/eating-disorders, accessed April 30, 2023; James I. Hudson, Eva Hiripi, Harrison G. Pope Jr., and Ronald C. Kessler, "The Prevalence and Correlates of Eating Disorders in the National Comorbidity Survey Replication," *Biological Psychiatry* 61, no. 3 (2007): 348–58.

156 *negative feelings that often spark it*: Vidhya Renjan, Peter M. McEvoy, Alicia K. Handley, and Anthea Fursland, "Stomaching Uncertainty: Relationships Among Intolerance of Uncertainty, Eating Disorder Pathology, and Comorbid Emotional Symptoms," *Journal of Anxiety Disorders* 41 (2016): 88–95.

156 *"feed our feelings"*: Catharine, F. Evers, Marijn Stok, and Denise T. D. de Ridder, "Feeding Your Feelings: Emotion Regulation Strategies and Emotional Eating," *Personality and Social Psychology Bulletin* 36, no. 6 (2010): 792–804.

156 *not just any food will do*: Yvonne H. C. Yau and Marc N. Potenza, "Stress and Eating Behaviors," *Minerva Endocrinologica* 38, no. 3 (2013): 255.

157 *stimulate cravings for high-sugar*: Frayn and Knäuper, "Emotional Eating and Weight in Adults."

157 *a defining characteristic of those in their twenties*: Mehta, Clare M., Jeffrey Jensen Arnett, Carlie G. Palmer, and Larry J. Nelson, "Established Adulthood: A New Conception of Ages 30 to 45," *American Psychologist* 75, no. 4 (2020): 431.

157   *a 2021 story in the* New York Times: Anahad O'Connor, "How Food May Improve Your Mood," *New York Times,* May 6, 2021, https://www.nytimes .com/2021/05/06/well/eat/mental-health-food.html.

157   *70 percent of whom are over 30*: Maria Pengue, "25 Insightful New York Times Readership Statistics," *WorkUp* (blog), March 14, 2021, https://letter .ly/new-york-times-readership-statistics.

157   *unhealthy diet is a risk factor for mental health problems*: J. Douglas Bremmer, Kasra Moazzami, Matthew T. Wittbrodt, Jonathon A. Nye, Bruno B. Lima, et al., "Diet, Stress and Mental Health," *Nutrients* 12, no. 8 (2020): 2428.

157   *diets higher in plant-sourced foods*: Felice N. Jacka, Adrienne O'Neil, Rachelle Opie, Catherine Itsiopoulos, Sue Cotton, et al., "A Randomised Controlled Trial of Dietary Improvement for Adults with Major Depression (the SMILES trial)," *BMC Medicine* 15, no. 1 (2017): 1–13.

157   *a 2022 study of more than 10,000 adults*: Eric M. Hecht, Anna Rabil, Euridice Martinez Steele, Gary A. Abrams, Deanna Ware, et al., "Cross-Sectional Examination of Ultra-Processed Food Consumption and Adverse Mental Health Symptoms," *Public Health Nutrition* 25, no. 11 (2022): 3225–34.

157   *so-called second brain*: Bremner et al., "Diet, Stress and Mental Health."

158   *transferring the microbiome of a depressed person*: Thomaz F. S. Bastiaanssen, Sofia Cussotto, Marcus J. Claesson, Gerard Clarke, Timothy G. Dinan, et al., "Gutted! Unraveling the Role of the Microbiome in Major Depressive Disorder," *Harvard Review of Psychiatry* 28, no. 1 (2020): 26.

158   *a 2016 study of more than 12,000 Australian adults*: Redzo Mujcic and Andrew J. Oswald, "Evolution of Well-Being and Happiness After Increases in Consumption of Fruit and Vegetables," *American Journal of Public Health* 106, no. 8 (2016): 1504–10.

158   *2017 experiment, also in Australia*: Felice N. Jacka, Adrienne O'Neil, Rachelle Opie, Catherine Itsiopoulos, Sue Cotton, Mohammedreza Mohebbi, David Castle, et al., "A Randomised Controlled Tial of Dietary Improvement for Adults with Major Depression (the 'SMILES' Trial)," *BMC Medicine* 15, no. 1 (2017): 1–13.

158   *almost 2,000 college students in Appalachia*: Rachel A. Wattick, Rebecca L. Hagedorn, and Melissa D. Olfert, "Relationship Between Diet and Mental Health in a Young Adult Appalachian College Population," *Nutrients* 10, no. 8 (2018): 957.

160   *"cooking confidence"*: Ada L. Garcia, Rebecca Reardon, Matthew McDonald, and Elisa J. Vargas-Garcia, "Community Interventions to Improve Cooking Skills and Their Effects on Confidence and Eating Behaviour," *Current Nutrition Reports* 5, no. 4 (2016): 315–22.

161   *In the 1920s*: Jesse Rhodes, "Marvelous Macaroni and Cheese," *Smithsonian*

Magazine, March 22, 2011, https://www.smithsonianmag.com/arts-culture/marvelous-macaroni-and-cheese-30954740/.

161 *Adults who have cooking skills*: Matthew Chak Leung Lam and Jean Adams, "Association Between Home Food Preparation Skills and Behaviour, and Consumption of Ultra-Processed Foods: Cross-Sectional Analysis of the UK National Diet and Nutrition survey (2008–2009)," *International Journal of Behavioral Nutrition and Physical Activity* 14 (2017): 1–7.

161 *even good for our social lives*: Nicole Farmer, Katherine Touchton-Leonard, and Alyson Ross, "Psychosocial Benefits of Cooking Interventions: A Systematic Review," *Health Education & Behavior* 45, no. 2 (2018): 167–80.

161 *2022 study of almost 700 Australian adults*: Joanna Rees, Shih Ching Fu, Johnny Lo, Ros Sambell, Joshua R. Lewis, et al., "How a 7-Week Food Literacy Cooking Program Affects Cooking Confidence and Mental Health: Findings of a Quasi-Experimental Controlled Intervention Trial," *Frontiers in Nutrition* 9 (2022): 360.

162 *according to psychologist Albert Bandura*: Albert Bandura, "Exercise of Personal and Collective Efficacy in Changing Societies," in *Self-Efficacy in Changing Societies*, ed. Albert Bandura, pp. 1–45 (Cambridge, UK: Cambridge University Press, 1995).

162 *The belief we can accomplish*: Amy B. Trubek, Maria Carabello, Caitlin Morgan, and Jacob Lahne, "Empowered to Cook: The Crucial Role of 'Food Agency' in Making Meals," *Appetite* 116 (2017): 297–305; Julia A. Wolfson, Jacob Lahne, Minakshi Raj, Noura Insolera, Fiona Lavelle, et al., "Food Agency in the United States: Associations with Cooking Behavior and Dietary Intake," *Nutrients* 12, no. 3 (2020): 877.

FOURTEEN. HOW TO CHANGE

166 *most likely to use nonprescription psychoactive drugs*: James G. Murphy and Ashley A. Dennhardt, "The Behavioral Economics of Young Adult Substance Abuse," *Preventive Medicine* 92 (2016): 24–30.

167 *as powerful and benign*: Smita Das, "The CBD Dialectic in Mental Health: Benign and Powerful?," *Psychiatric Services* 71, no. 1 (2020): 2–3.

167 *the younger we are when we start using drugs*: Timmen Cermak, *A Psychiatrist's View of Marijuana* (Cambridge, UK: Cambridge University Press, 2020).

168 *nearly twenty-year study*: Kevin Chen and Denise B. Kandel, "The Natural History of Drug Use from Adolescence to the Mid-Thirties in a General Population Sample," *American Journal of Public Health* 85, no. 1 (1995): 41–47.

170 *the Stages of Change*: John C. Norcross, Paul M. Krebs, and James O. Prochaska, "Stages of Change," *Journal of Clinical Psychology* 67, no. 2 (2011): 143–54.

173 *Various forms of consumption*: LinChiat Chang and Robert M. Arkin, "Materialism as an Attempt to Cope with Uncertainty," *Psychology & Marketing* 19, no. 5 (2002): 389–406; Kimberly Rios Morrison and Camille S. Johnson, "When What You Have Is Who You Are: Self-Uncertainty Leads Individualists to See Themselves in Their Possessions," *Personality and Social Psychology Bulletin* 37, no. 5 (2011): 639–51.

FIFTEEN. HOW TO DECIDE

178 *35,000 decisions a day*: Joel Hoomans, "35,000 Decisions: Great Choices of Strategic Leaders," *The Leading Edge*, March 20, 2015, Roberts Wesleyan College, https://go.roberts.edu/leadingedge/the-great-choices-of-strategic-leaders.

178 *somewhere around 70*: Nick Tasler, "What Is Your Momentum Factor?" *Psychology Today*, August 30, 2012, https://www.psychologytoday.com/us/blog/strategic-thinking/201208/what-is-your-momentum-factor.

178 *life's most consequential decisions*: William R. Mackavey, Janet E. Malley, and Abigail J. Stewart, "Remembering Autobiographically Consequential Experiences: Content Analysis of Psychologists' Accounts of Their Lives," *Psychology and Aging* 6, no. 1 (1991): 50.

179 *choice overload*: Barry Schwartz and Andrew Ward, "Doing Better but Feeling Worse: The Paradox of Choice," in *Positive Psychology in Practice*, eds. P. Alex Linley and Stephen Joseph, pp. 86–104 (New York: John Wiley, 2004).

179 *classic 1992 study on decision-making*: Amos Tversky and Eldar Shafir, "The Disjunction Effect in Choice Under Uncertainty," *Psychological Science* 3, no. 5 (1992): 305–10; Ignazio Ziano, Man Fai Kong, Hong Joo Kim, Chit Yu Liu, Sze Chai Wong, et al., "Replication: Revisiting Tversky and Shafir's Disjunction Effect with an Extension Comparing Between and Within Subject Designs," *Journal of Economic Psychology* 83 (2021): 102350.

180 *famed statistician Jimmie Savage*: Leonard J. Savage, *The Foundations of Statistics*, 2nd ed. (New York: Dover, 1972).

180 *there's a difference here*: Frank Hyneman Knight, *Risk, Uncertainty and Profit*, vol. 31 (Boston: Houghton Mifflin, 1921).

181 *"only one decision to make"*: Savage, *The Foundations*, 83.

181 *her television show* Fleabag: *Fleabag*, season 2, episode 5, directed by Harry Bradbeer, written by Phoebe Waller-Bridge, aired April 1, 2019.

181 *"The point that the calculus . . ."*: Kirsten G. Volz and Gerd Gigerenzer, "Cognitive Processes in Decisions under Risk Are Not the Same as in Decisions under Uncertainty," *Frontiers in Neuroscience* 6 (2012): 105, https://doi.org/10.3389/fnins.2012.00105.

182 *"reassurance junkies"*: Martin Self and Sally Winston, "When Reassurance Seeking Becomes Compulsive," *Psychology Today*, December 23, 2019,

https://www.psychologytoday.com/us/blog/living-sticky-mind/201912 /when-reassurance-seeking-becomes-compulsive; Sally Winston and Martin Self, "Treating the Ressaurance Junkie," *PESI*, March 22, 2019, https://cata log.pesi.com/item/treating-reassurance-junkie-63371.

182 *With the rise of smartphones*: Jon D. Elhai, Robert D. Dvorak, Jason C. Levine, and Brian J. Hall, "Problematic Smartphone Use: A Conceptual Overview and Systematic Review of Relations with Anxiety and Depression Psychopathology," *Journal of Affective Disorders* 207 (2017): 251–59.

183 *seeking reassurance excessively*: Jesse R. Cougle, Kristin E. Fitch, Frank D. Fincham, Christina J. Riccardi, Meghan E. Keough, et al., "Excessive Reassurance Seeking and Anxiety Pathology: Tests of Incremental Associations and Directionality," *Journal of Anxiety Disorders* 26, no. 1 (2012): 117–25.

183 *"What should I do?"*: Gioia Bottesi, Eleonora Carraro, Anna Martignon, Silvia Cerea, and Marta Ghisi, "'I'm Uncertain: What Should I Do?': An Investigation of Behavioral Responses to Everyday Life Uncertain Situations," *International Journal of Cognitive Therapy* 12, no. 1 (2019): 55–72.

184 *Charles Darwin's list of reasons*: C. R. Darwin, "This Is the Question Marry Not Marry" [Memorandum on Marriage, 1838], CUL-DAR210.8.2, *Darwin Online*, ed. John van Wyhe, http:/Darwin-online.org.uk/.

185 *Regret is the dissatisfaction*: Marcel Zeelenberg and Rik Pieters, "A Theory of Regret Regulation 1.0," *Journal of Consumer Psychology* 17, no. 1 (2007): 3–18.

185 *form of counterfactual thinking*: Eric van Dijk and Marcel Zeelenberg, "On the Psychology of 'If Only': Regret and the Comparison Between Factual and Counterfactual Outcomes," *Organizational Behavior and Human Decision Processes* 97, no. 2 (2005): 152–60.

185 *only love was talked about more*: Susan B. Shimanoff, "Commonly Named Emotions in Everyday Conversations," *Perceptual and Motor Skills* 2 (1984): 514.

185 *philosopher Søren Kierkegaard put it*: Quoted in Zeelenberg and Pieters, "Theory of Regret Regulation."

186 *a simulation machine*: Eric C. Anderson, R. Nicholas Carleton, Michael Diefenbach, and Paul K. J. Han, "The Relationship Between Uncertainty and Affect," *Frontiers in Psychology* 10 (2019): 2504.

186 *novel* The Midnight Library: Matt Haig, *The Midnight Library* (New York: Viking, 2020).

186 *probably a wrong-headed*: Kai Epstude, Florian Fessel, Amy Summerville, Rachel Smallman, Adam D. Galinsky, et al., "Repetitive Regret, Depression, and Anxiety: Findings from a Nationally Representative Survey," *Journal of Social and Clinical Psychology* 28, no. 6 (2009): 671–88.

187 *one way to feel less regret*: Van Dijk and Zeelenberg, "On the Psychology of 'If Only.'"

187 *but with heuristics*: Gerd Gigerenzer and Wolfgang Gaissmaier, "Heuristic Decision Making," *Annual Review of Psychology* 62, no. 1 (2011): 451–82; Elkhonon Goldberg and Kenneth Podell, "Adaptive versus Veridical Decision Making and the Frontal Lobes," *Consciousness and Cognition* 8, no. 3 (1999): 364–77; Kirsten G. Volz and Gerd Gigerenzer, "Cognitive Processes in Decisions Under Risk Are Not the Same as in Decisions Under Uncertainty," *Frontiers in Neuroscience* 6 (2012): 105.

SIXTEEN. HOW TO CHOOSE PURPOSE

191 *the rise of the nones*: Michael Lipka, "A Closer Look at America's Rapidly Growing Religious 'Nones,'" Pew Research Center, fact sheet, May 5, 2015, https://www.pewresearch.org/fact-tank/2015/05/13/a-closer-look-at-americas-rapidly-growing-religious-nones/; Benjamin Wormald, "America's Changing Religious Landscape," Pew Research Center, fact sheet, May 5, 2015, https://www.pewresearch.org/religion/2015/05/12/americas-changing-religious-landscape.

191 *be "good without God"*: Greg Epstein, "Good Without God," *The Humanist* 69, no. 6 (2009): 16.

192 *self-organizing form of personal certainty*: Frank Martela and Michael F. Steger, "The Three Meanings of Meaning in Life: Distinguishing Coherence, Purpose, and Significance," *Journal of Positive Psychology* 11, no. 5 (2016): 531–45.

192 *beyond-the-self orientation*: William Damon and Heather Malin, "The Development of Purpose," in *The Oxford Handbook of Moral Development: An Interdisciplinary Perspective*, ed. Lene Arnett Jensen, p. 110 (New York: Oxford University Press, 2020).

193 *host of mental health benefits*: Matthew J. Bundick, "The Benefits of Reflecting on and Discussing Purpose in Life in Emerging Adulthood," *New Directions for Youth Development* 132 (2011): 89–103; Patrick L. Hill, Anthony L. Burrow, and Kendall Cotton Bronk, "Persevering with Positivity and Purpose: An Examination of Purpose Commitment and Positive Affect as Predictors of Grit," *Journal of Happiness Studies* 17, no. 1 (2016): 257–69.

193 *feel less socially anxious*: Todd B. Kashdan and Patrick E. McKnight, "Commitment to a Purpose in Life: An Antidote to the Suffering by Individuals with Social Anxiety Disorder," *Emotion* 13, no. 6 (2013): 1150.

193 *disrupts the relationship between social media and self-esteem*: Anthony L. Burrow and Nicolette Rainone, "How Many Likes Did I Get?: Purpose Moderates Links Between Positive Social Media Feedback and Self-Esteem," *Journal of Experimental Social Psychology* 69 (2017): 232–36.

193 *age of 30, only about half of young adults*: Michael F. Steger, Shigehiro Oishi, and Todd B. Kashdan, "Meaning in Life Across the Life Span: Levels and Correlates of Meaning in Life from Emerging Adulthood to Older Adulthood," *Journal of Positive Psychology* 4, no. 1 (2009): 43–52.

194 *researcher calls* purpose anxiety: Larissa Rainey, "The Search for Purpose in Life: An Exploration of Purpose, the Search Process, and Purpose Anxiety," Master's thesis, University of Pennsylvania, 2014. https://repository.upenn .edu/mapp_capstone/60.

194 *a 2014 study of adults of all ages*: Rainey, "Search for Purpose in Life."

194 *after around age 35*: Kendall Cotton Bronk, Patrick L. Hill, Daniel K. Lapsley, Tasneem L. Talib, and Holmes Finch, "Purpose, Hope, and Life Satisfaction in Three Age Groups," *Journal of Positive Psychology* 4, no. 6 (2009): 500–10.

195 *Frankl's classic* Man's Search for Meaning: Viktor E. Frankl, *Man's Search for Meaning* (New York: Simon and Schuster, 1985).

SEVENTEEN. THE TONIC OF HOPE

203 *Life gets better as we age*: Kristin Gustavson, Ann Kristin Knudsen, Ragnar Nesvåg, Gun Peggy Knudsen, Stein Emil Vollset, et al., "Prevalence and Stability of Mental Disorders Among Young Adults: Findings from a Longitudinal Study," *BMC Psychiatry* 18, no. 1 (2018): 1–15; A. S. Henderson, A. F. Jorm, A. E. Korten, P. Jacomb, H. Christensen, et al., "Symptoms of Depression and Anxiety During Adult Life: Evidence for a Decline in Prevalence with Age," *Psychological Medicine* 28, no. 6 (1998): 1321–28; Ronald C. Kessler, Howard G. Birnbaum, Victoria Shahly, Evelyn Bromet, Irving Hwang, et al., "Age Differences in the Prevalence and Co-morbidity of DSM-IV Major Depressive Episodes: Results from the WHO World Mental Health Survey Initiative," *Depression and Anxiety* 27, no. 4 (2010): 351–64; Darrel A. Regier, M. E. Farmer, D. S. Rae, J. K. Myers, M. R. L. N. Kramer, et al., "One-Month Prevalence of Mental Disorders in the United States and Sociodemographic Characteristics: The Epidemiologic Catchment Area Study," *Acta Psychiatrica Scandinavica* 88, no. 1 (1993): 35–47.

203 *well-being increased across every decade of adulthood*: Ying Chen, Richard G. Cowden, Jeffery Fulks, John F. Plake, and Tyler J. VanderWeele, "National Data on Age Gradients in Well-Being Among US Adults," *JAMA Psychiatry* 79, no. 10 (2022): 1046–47.

204 *a 2014 article titled "Is There . . ."*: Jacob Z. Hess, Jeffrey R. Lacasse, Jordan Harmon, Daniel Williams, and Nathan Vierling-Claassen, "'Is There a Getting Better From This, or Not?' Examining the Meaning and Possibility of Recovery From Mental Disorder," *Child & Youth Services* 35, no. 2 (2014): 116–36.

205   *one of the three routes to better mental health*: Charles R. Snyder, Scott T. Michael, and Jennifer S. Cheavens, "Hope as a Psychotherapeutic Foundation of Common Factors, Placebos, and Expectancies," in *The Heart and Soul of Change: What Works in Therapy*, eds. Mark A. Hubble, Barry L. Duncan, and Scott D. Miller (Washington, DC: American Psychological Association, 1999): 179–200.

205   *having positive expectations is almost universally related*: Jennifer S. Cheavens, Scott T. Michael, and Charles R. Snyder, "The Correlates of Hope: Psychological and Physiological Benefits," in *Interdisciplinary Perspectives on Hope*, ed. Jaklin A. Elliott, pp. 119–32 (Hauppauge, NY: Nova Science, 2005).

205   *a tonic with incredible healing power*: Randolph C. Arnau, David H. Rosen, John F. Finch, Jamie L. Rhudy, and Vincent J. Fortunato, "Longitudinal Effects of Hope on Depression and Anxiety: A Latent Variable Analysis," *Journal of Personality* 75, no. 1 (2007): 43–64; Kerosta Bain, Sarvdeep Kohli, and Anjali Malik, "Self-Efficacy and Hope as Predictors of Mental Health," *Indian Journal of Positive Psychology* 8, no. 4 (2017): 631–35; Song Wang, Xin Xu, Ming Zhou, Taolin Chen, Xun Yang, et al., "Hope and the Brain: Trait Hope Mediates the Protective Role of Medial Orbitofrontal Cortex Spontaneous Activity Against Anxiety," *NeuroImage* 157 (2017): 439–47.

206   *a 2012 study of more than 3,000 young adults*: "College Student Mental Health Survey: Phase IV," University of Michigan Counseling and Psychological Services, 2012, https://www.calameo.com/read/004482878001792c12f32.

206   *a 2017 review of the research*: Stephanie Griggs, "Hope and Mental Health in Young Adult College Students: An Integrative Review," *Journal of Psychosocial Nursing and Mental Health Services* 55, no. 2 (2017): 28–35.

206   *predictor of well-being and mental health*: Anthony Venning, Lisa Kettler, Ian Zajac, Anne Wilson, and Jaklin Eliott, "Is Hope or Mental Illness a Stronger Predictor of Mental Health?," *International Journal of Mental Health Promotion* 13, no. 2 (2011): 32–39.

206   *less likely to think about ending their lives*: Edward C. Chang, Xinying Jiang, Weiyi Tian, Shangwen Yi, Jiting Liu, et al., "Hope as a Process in Understanding Positive Mood and Suicide Protection," *Crisis* 43, no. 2 (2021): 90–97.

206   *technically speaking, that's optimism*: David B. Feldman and Maximilian Kubota, "Hope, Self-Efficacy, Optimism, and Academic Achievement: Distinguishing Constructs and Levels of Specificity in Predicting College Grade-Point Average," *Learning and Individual Differences* 37 (2015): 210–16; Matthew W. Gallagher and Shane J. Lopez, "Positive Expectancies and Mental Health: Identifying the Unique Contributions of Hope and Optimism," *Journal of Positive Psychology* 4, no. 6 (2009): 548–56.

206 *the belief that we can* do *better*: Paul Kwon, Maira Birrueta, Emily Faust, and Emilia R. Brown, "The Role of Hope in Preventive Interventions," *Social and Personality Psychology Compass* 9, no. 12 (2015): 696–704.

208 *think negatively about their uncertain futures*: Susan Cross and Hazel Markus, "Possible Selves Across the Life Span," *Human Development* 34, no. 4 (1991): 230–55.

208 *a 1969 book by psychologist Ezra Stotland*: Ezra Stotland. *The Psychology of Hope* (San Francisco: Josey-Bass, 1969): 2.

209 *an upward spiral*: Eric L. Garland, Barbara Fredrickson, Ann M. Kring, David P. Johnson, Piper S. Meyer, et al., "Upward Spirals of Positive Emotions Counter Downward Spirals of Negativity: Insights from the Broaden-and-Build Theory and Affective Neuroscience on the Treatment of Emotion Dysfunctions and Deficits in Psychopathology," *Clinical Psychology Review* 30, no. 7 (2010): 849–64; Barbara L. Fredrickson and Thomas Joiner, "Positive Emotions Trigger Upward Spirals Toward Emotional Well-Being," *Psychological Science* 13, no. 2 (2002): 172–75; Barbara L. Fredrickson and Thomas Joiner, "Reflections on Positive Emotions and Upward Spirals," *Perspectives on Psychological Science* 13, no. 2 (2018): 194–99.

209 *we also produce fewer* positive *ones*: Nexhmedin Morina, Catherine Deeprose, Christina Pusowski, Marina Schmid, and Emily A. Holmes, "Prospective Mental Imagery in Patients with Major Depressive Disorder or Anxiety Disorders," *Journal of Anxiety Disorders* 25, no. 8 (2011): 1032–37; Jennice S. Vilhauer, Sabrina Young, Chanel Kealoha, Josefine Borrmann, Waguih W. IsHak, et al., "Treating Major Depression by Creating Positive Expectations for the Future: A Pilot Study for the Effectiveness of Future-Directed Therapy (FDT) on Symptom Severity and Quality of Life," *CNS Neuroscience & Therapeutics* 18, no. 2 (2012): 102–9.

209 *mental health is actually* more *improved*: Jennice S. Vilhauer, Julissa Cortes, Nazanin Moali, Sally Chung, James Mirocha, et al., "Improving Quality of Life for Patients with Major Depressive Disorder by Increasing Hope and Positive Expectations with Future Directed Therapy (FDT)," *Innovations in Clinical Neuroscience* 10, no. 3 (2013): 12; Vilhauer et al., "Treating Major Depression."

209 *"another way to what-if"*: Daniel T. Gilbert and Timothy D. Wilson, "Prospection: Experiencing the Future," *Science* 317, no. 5843 (2007): 1351–54.

209 *envisioning their future selves—in a good way*: Waclaw Bak, "Possible Selves: Implications for Psychotherapy," *International Journal of Mental Health and Addiction* 13, no. 5 (2015): 650–58; Paula M. Loveday, Geoff P. Lovell, and Christian M. Jones, "The Best Possible Selves Intervention: A Review of the Literature to Evaluate Efficacy and Guide Future Research," *Journal of Happiness Studies* 19, no. 2 (2018): 607–28.

210 *Think about yourself in the future*: Laura A. King, "The Health Benefits of Writing About Life Goals," *Personality and Social Psychology Bulletin* 27, no. 7 (2001): 798–807.

210 *take concrete steps toward reaching them*: Cécile Nurra and Daphna Oyserman, "From Future Self to Current Action: An Identity-Based Motivation Perspective," *Self and Identity* 17, no. 3 (2018): 343–64.

210 *set aside money for retirement*: Hal E. Hershfield, Daniel G. Goldstein, William F. Sharpe, Jesse Fox, Leo Yeykelis, et al., "Increasing Saving Behavior Through Age-Progressed Renderings of the Future Self," *Journal of Marketing Research* 48 (2011): S23–S37.

210 *stop smoking*: Hayeon Song, Jihyun Kim, Remi J. Kwon, and Younbo Jung, "Anti-Smoking Educational Game Using Avatars as Visualized Possible Selves," *Computers in Human Behavior* 29, no. 5 (2013): 2029–36.

210 *start exercising*: Diane E. Whaley, "Future-Oriented Self-Perceptions and Exercise Behavior in Middle-Aged Women," *Journal of Aging and Physical Activity* 11, no. 1 (2003): 1–17.

211 *the more money we save*: Pam Scholder Ellen, Joshua L. Wiener, and M. Paula Fitzgerald, "Encouraging People to Save for Their Future: Augmenting Current Efforts with Positive Visions of the Future," *Journal of Public Policy & Marketing* 31, no. 1 (2012): 58–72.

211 *a 2018 study of young adults who have fitness apps*: Shuang Liu and Jessica F. Willoughby, "Do Fitness Apps Need Text Reminders? An Experiment Testing Goal-Setting Text Message Reminders to Promote Self-Monitoring," *Journal of Health Communication* 23, no. 4 (2018): 379–86.

211 *in a 2017 study*: Angel Enrique, Juana Bretón-López, Guadalupe Molinari, Rosa M. Baños, and Cristina Botella, "Efficacy of an Adaptation of the Best Possible Self Intervention Implemented Through Positive Technology: A Randomized Control Trial," *Applied Research in Quality of Life* 13 (2018): 671–89.

212 *a 2021 study, Japanese adolescents*: Yuta Chishima and Anne E. Wilson, "Conversation with a Future Self: A Letter-Exchange Exercise Enhances Student Self-Continuity, Career Planning, and Academic Thinking," *Self and Identity* 20, no. 5 (2021): 646–71.

213 *To be hopeful means*: Rebecca Solnit, "We Could Be Heroes: An Election Year Letter," *The Guardian*, October 15, 2012, https://www.theguardian.com/commentisfree/2012/oct/15/letter-dismal-allies-us-left.

EPILOGUE: AN UNCERTAIN EMBRACE

215 *In 2019 in the United Kingdom*: Layla Mofrad, Ashley Tiplady, Danielle Payne, and Mark Freeston, "Making Friends with Uncertainty: Experiences of Developing a Transdiagnostic Group Intervention Targeting Intolerance

of Uncertainty in IAPT: Feasibility, Acceptability and Implications," *Cognitive Behaviour Therapist* 13 (2020): e49.

216 *Uncertainty intensifies our emotions*: Yoav Bar-Anan, Timothy D. Wilson, and Daniel T. Gilbert, "The Feeling of Uncertainty Intensifies Affective Reactions," *Emotion* 9, no. 1 (2009): 123.

216 *an experience, or an event, or even a relationship*: Bar-Anan et al., "The Feeling of Uncertainty"; Erin R. Whitchurch, Timothy D. Wilson, and Daniel T. Gilbert, "'He Loves Me, He Loves Me Not . . .': Uncertainty Can Increase Romantic Attraction," *Psychological Science* 22, no. 2 (2011): 172–75; Timothy D. Wilson, David B. Centerbar, Deborah A. Kermer, and Daniel T. Gilbert, "The Pleasures of Uncertainty: Prolonging Positive Moods in Ways People Do Not Anticipate," *Journal of Personality and Social Psychology* 88, no. 1 (2005): 5.

216 *it winds up feeling only satisfactory*: Jangwook Kwon and Hoon Lee, "Why Travel Prolongs Happiness: Longitudinal Analysis Using a Latent Growth Model," *Tourism Management* 76 (2020): 103944.

220 *so others can also enjoy them*: Shelly L. Gable, Harry T. Reis, Emily A. Impett, and Evan R. Asher, "What Do You Do When Things Go Right? The Intrapersonal and Interpersonal Benefits of Sharing Positive Events," *Journal of Personality and Social Psychology* 87, no. 2 (2004): 228; Brett J. Peters, Harry T. Reis, and Shelly L. Gable, "Making the Good Even Better: A Review and Theoretical Model of Interpersonal Capitalization," *Social and Personality Psychology Compass* 12, no. 7 (2018): e12407.

Index